D0122585

Voices
of
Combat

**Recent Titles in
Contributions to the Study of Music and Dance**

Music and Musket: Bands and Bandsmen of the American Civil War
Kenneth E. Olson

Edmund Thornton Jenkins: The Life and Times of an American Black Composer,
1894–1926
Jeffrey P. Green

Born to Play: The Life and Career of Hazel Harrison
Jean E. Cazort and Constance Tibbs Hobson

Titta Ruffo: An Anthology
Andrew Farkas, editor

Nellie Melba: A Contemporary Review
William R. Moran, compiler

Armseelchen: The Life and Music of Eric Zeisl
Malcolm S. Cole and Barbara Barclay

Busoni and the Piano: The Works, the Writings, and the Recordings
Larry Sitsky

Music as Propaganda: Art to Persuade, Art to Control
Arnold Perris

A Most Wondrous Babble: American Art Composers, Their Music, and the
American Scene, 1950–1985
Nicholas E. Tawa

Voices of Combat

A CENTURY OF LIBERTY AND WAR SONGS, 1765–1865

KENT A. BOWMAN

Contributions to the Study of Music and Dance, Number 10

GREENWOOD PRESS
New York • Westport, Connecticut • London

Library of Congress Cataloging-in-Publication Data

Bowman, Kent A. (Kent Adam), 1947-
 Voices of combat.

 (Contributions to the study of music and dance, ISSN
0193-9041 ; no. 10)
 Bibliography: p.
 Includes index.
 1. Music, Popular (Songs, etc.)—United States—
History and criticism. 2. Patriotic music—United
States—History and criticism. 3. National songs—United
States—History and criticism. 4. War-songs—United
States—History and criticism. I. Title. II. Series.
ML3477.B68 1987   784.7'1973   86-25724
ISBN 0-313-25408-7 (lib. bdg. : alk. paper)

Library of Congress Catalog Card Number: 86-25724
ISBN: 0-313-25408-7
ISSN: 0193-9041

First published in 1987

Greenwood Press, Inc.
88 Post Road West, Westport, Connecticut 06881

Printed in the United States of America

The paper used in this book complies with the
Permanent Paper Standard issued by the National
Information Standards Organization (Z39.48-1984).

10 9 8 7 6 5 4 3 2 1

Contents

Preface

Liberty and war songs offer an interesting subject for study in American history. Some studies of liberty and martial music have been made, but all too often they consist of sketchy surveys of songs as curious and disjointed footnotes to American history. Most works on liberty and war songs are songbooks put together by song collectors; consequently, no effort has been made to relate the songs to each other or to the larger historical context. A detailed and comprehensive study of liberty and martial songs from 1765 to 1865, with attention devoted almost exclusively to lyrics, yields a clear picture of an aspect of evolving American culture in this hundred year period and also reveals the thoughts and feelings of Americans during periods of crisis.

American liberty and war songs written before the Civil War consist almost entirely of contemporary poems set to older European or American melodies. By the outset of the Civil War, both lyrics and music were contemporary, but the process of setting a poem to music not originally composed for it was still the prevalent form. The outstanding contemporary example is "Dixie"; numbers of patriotic pieces sprang from the original song, which was written for a minstrel show. For the first time in the history of American music, Civil War composers like George F. Root and Henry Clay Work began to write many original liberty and war songs. With these two composers American liberty and war music came of age. The emergence of an original American liberty and war music coincided with a similar development in American literature.

Until the Civil War American songwriters primarily expanded their themes and experimented with techniques. This study is therefore organized thematically except for chapter eight, which focuses on the most important Civil War composers. I have concentrated on developments in liberty and war songs, especially those written before and during the Revolution, the War of 1812, the Mexican War, and the Civil War, with an emphasis on the similarities and differences in song themes, techniques, and styles. This work deals with American songs; European music is considered only where it offers insight into the development of American songs.

Melodies, which are often absent from copies of liberty and war songs written before the Civil War, will be discussed only when they have a significant impact on the history of liberty and war music. For example, the melody "Yankee Doodle" is used in a number of ways and in a wide variety of circumstances between the Revolution and the Civil War; it is discussed in detail in chapter three and mentioned from time to time throughout the remainder of this work.

Much liberty and war music, especially before the Civil War, was published in newspapers and broadsides; very little was printed in sheet music form. Since broadsides were particularly perishable, it is not possible to determine accurately how much liberty and war music has been lost. Having looked at approximately ten thousand songs from sources throughout the United States, I would estimate that several thousand liberty and war songs written between 1765 and 1865 have survived. Furthermore, it is often difficult to tell which songs were widely performed before the Civil War. Generally songs like "Yankee Doodle," which was evidently popular, will be given more attention than songs printed only once or twice in newspapers or broadsides.

The appendix and bibliography should prove especially interesting and helpful to students of American music and American history. The appendix contains the lyrics of twelve songs that were chosen because they represent the best examples of the variety of styles and topics of the American war song. A thorough reading of these songs will give the reader a feeling for the types of liberty and war music written between the years 1765 and 1865. The bibliography is classified according to types of primary and secondary materials. Featured among the primary sources is a significant group of newspapers; this is important because newspapers are invaluable sources of liberty and war songs. Some war songs are found nowhere else.

I would like to thank especially my father, John K. Bowman, who inspired me to complete this work, and my mother, Elizabeth, who has always supported my scholarly efforts. I am also grateful to Burnelle Brooks for her unwavering confidence. Gus Seligmann, Richard Lowe, Jim Lee, William Painter, and Anne Abney, through their reading of this work, have made invaluable suggestions. I also appreciate the help of many others too numerous to mention; without this wonderful network I could not have completed this book.

Introduction

The first American music was born from British and European tunes, primarily in the religious and folk traditions.[1] Although the classical song retained an important place in musical performance in America, it had almost no impact on the development of American liberty and war songs; the first signs of an American popular music appeared in the form of the liberty and war songs of colonial protest and rebellion. Much of the first martial and liberty music came to the contentious colonies directly from the British Isles.[2]

The first significant music to reach American shores was not the music of human war; rather, the cosmic battle for the salvation of the soul was the inspiration for most of the songs composed in the newly established colonies. Yet soon after the formation of the colonies, the rich British ballad tradition began to flourish. In the northern colonies this tradition followed the strong religious impulse; in the southern colonies a secular tradition was born, although they, too, fostered much religious music. It is certain that well within the first hundred years of English colonial life secular music was widely distributed throughout the colonies.

Since the northern colonies dominated American music in the early years of colonial development, most surviving songs are those that were sung in New England churches. Much of what is known about the first American song is associated with the worship of a Calvinistic god. In the often hostile wilderness of an unexplored land, the first songs that broke the silence of the virgin forests were the solemn hymns of the Pilgrims and the Puritans. As might be expected, the songs of these early Americans mirrored the monumental concerns of men and women who, for religious reasons, had chosen to isolate themselves from their English brethren, many of whom shared their biblical views and would later follow them to the New World.

Because of the strictly disciplined lives of these early American immigrants, historians like Vernon Parrington and James Truslow Adams have argued that the first New Englanders were disdainful of many pleasures, perhaps including those of secular music.[3] While it is true that the Pilgrims and Puritans had little use for frivolous entertainment, they did employ and enjoy songs in praise of and respect for God. John Tasker Howard and George Kent Bellows note both groups enthusiastically used song in their religious services.

The first religious music heard in American churches owes much to the musical philosophy of Martin Luther, who contributed the basis for Protestant hymnody in Europe.[4] Unlike Luther, although sharing in his utilitarian impulse toward music, the early New Englanders chose to use only music that fit the words of the Bible as they interpreted them.[5] Both Pilgrims and Puritans favored the Psalms when selecting lyrics. Each group used separate songbooks, and in 1640 the Puritans created their own song collection, *The Bay Psalm Book*, which went through several editions,[6] including the important 1698 version, the first to print both lyrics and music.

In the southern colonies a different but significant contribution to American popular song was made by singing slaves. From the almost unknown continent of Africa came a distinctive strain of music that was to influence both religious and folk music traditions. A large part of the musical legacy of slavery was the invention of the banjo, an instrument used in many types of songs that slaves performed. Imported Africans also introduced to American song, at first probably in religious tunes, a series of high pitched sounds used to express sadness in a peculiar but distinctive fashion. The first black music performed in English was most likely the spiritual sung on rest day at the plantation. Spirituals left their mark on martial, entertainment, and art music, while providing a precedent for both black and white songs of protest. The exact contribution of African and European music to black American music remains uncertain, but the important aspect of this blend is the development of two purely American musical forms—jazz and the blues.[7]

An important type of song popular in late colonial America, which would later become the model for much of the liberty and patriotic music of all American wars, was the ballad. The ballad is often conceived as a formal composition, which may or may not be written when originally authored. Many liberty and war songs before 1865, like the folksong, were composed anonymously. Ballad lyrics were nearly always accompanied by an unvarying melody.[8] Some modern ballad specialists, such as Phillips Barry and Tristram Coffin, are quick to point out the ballad's close kinship to folklore, especially in its important quality of lyrical variation. The medium of print is especially important because it serves to preserve the songs in a number of variations,[9] all of which may be considered separate pieces. These songs, generally termed "folk ballads," may thus originate in the tradition of informal composition as they circulate, take on a new but clearly defined text, and then pass again into oral tradition. This process may be repeated any number of times; it is common in the history of liberty and war songs.[9] Two excellent examples are the many versions of "Yankee Doodle" and "Dixie." Because ballads treat material that is characterized by several dramatic elements, such as victory, death, and sorrow, they are especially suited to emotionally charged historical events like wars.[10]

In colonial society, popular ballads were not always held in high esteem. In 1720 the Reverend Thomas Symmes noted that many devout Christians believed that singing ballads distracted young people from their education and turned them toward the broad path of unrighteousness.[11] Perhaps the diversion of popular song appeared sinful because indelicate songs were so often performed in village taverns. Such suggestive pieces as "Bonny Lass Under a Blanket" and "Sweetest When She's Naked" did little to improve the image of the ballad with those hearts and minds ostensibly turned toward more saintly subjects.[12] Folk ballads also suffered from the belief among the upper classes, primarily in New England, that ballad singing was the pastime of common folk like servants and artisans; it is possible that this association with the common man was one of the reasons that American popular music became as distinct from formal music as it did.[13] However, not all of those who were enamored of folk music belonged to the faceless crowd. Notable figures like Benjamin Franklin composed and enjoyed popular songs, as well as other types of music.[14]

The American Revolution likely initiated the beginnings of an American patriotic music because, as historians like Charles M. Andrews and Lawrence Henry Gipson have noted, it severed a dependent culture from its parent. Not only did the Revolution bring into existence a small, struggling country, but it separated a group of colonies from the most powerful nation in the world.[15] This important event inspired the first significant American composers, William Billings and Francis Hopkinson. Although neither was a major influence on world song, both contributed to the origins of an American music. A more important result of the period between 1765 and 1783 was the music of the inspired composers, anonymous and unknown, whose songs helped foster American patriotism. Their compositions, published in newspapers and broadsides, gave voice to the first American liberty and war songs.

NOTES

1. Liberty songs are songs expressing the desire for freedom or condemning oppression. War songs are songs that treat one or more aspects of war such as battles, civilian and military leadership, and prisoner-of-war problems.

2. The word "tune," which might mean either "song" or "melody," is used here to mean song. The word has been avoided when its use might cause confusion in the reader's mind.

3. James Truslow Adams and Vernon L. Parrington are early-twentieth-century historians. Generally speaking, Adams and Parrington, like many historians of their time, found much to criticize in Pilgrim and Puritan cultures.

4. John Tasker Howard and George Kent Bellows, *A Short History of Music in America* (New York: Thomas Y. Crowell, 1957), pp. 11–18.

5. John Anthony Scott, ed., *The Ballad of America: The History of the United States in Story and in Song* (New York: Bantam Books, 1966), p. 28. For the best collection of American hymns, see Albert Christ-Janer, Charles W. Hughes, and Carlton Sprague, *American Hymns Old and New* (New York: Columbia University Press, 1980). This collection covers the time period from the seventeenth century to the present; each section has a short but useful introduction.

6. Gilbert Chase, *America's Music: From the Pilgrims to the Present* (New York: McGraw-Hill, 1955), pp. 16–20.

7. Ronald L. Davis, *A History of Music in American Life*, vol. 1, *The Formative Years 1620–1865* (Malabar, Fla.: Robert Krieger, 1982), pp. 53–56.

8. Tristram Potter Coffin, *The British Traditional Ballad in North America* (Austin: University of Texas Press, 1977), p. 164. Coffin's book is an analysis of the ballad form, not a collection of songs. The most notable American ballad collectors were Francis James Childs of Harvard and John A. Lomax. Both men published several volumes of ballads illustrating the numerous variations of many of the songs.

9. Ibid., 2–3.

10. Ibid., 165.

11. Chase, 15.

12. Davis, 17. For examples of the types of music performed in early New England, see Barbara Lambert, ed., *Music in Colonial Massachusetts, 1630–1820*, vol. 1, *Music in Public Places*, (Charlottesville: University Press of Virginia, 1980).

13. Ibid., 51.

14. Ibid., 36.

15. Charles M. Andrews and Lawrence Henry Gipson are noted historians of the Imperial School, which attempted to describe American colonial history from the British viewpoint.

Voices
of
Combat

1

Fair Liberty's Call

Before 1765 Americans had become concerned that they might lose the rights they believed they possessed as citizens of the British Empire. As early as 1761 James Otis had resolutely maintained that American rights and consequently American liberty were threatened by the writs of assistance. According to Otis, the writs violated colonial rights because they were blanket search warrants. In 1763 Americans again saw a danger to their freedom in the Proclamation of 1763, which forbade the colonists to cross the Appalachians. This measure was followed by the Revenue Act of 1764, designed to produce income for Britain by lowering the tax on molasses and thus discouraging New England shipping merchants from smuggling foreign molasses into the American colonies; formerly the illegal entry of molasses into America had hurt the British treasury. The English government hoped the measure would recoup some of the lost revenue. While the colonists did not approve of the measure, it did not meet with the harsh response evoked by the Stamp Act in 1765. This law elicited the first musical protest against what was, in American eyes, an attempt to deprive Americans of their property and liberty. The protests against a hated law infused American liberty music with an unmistakable vigor.

The text of the Stamp Act was simple and direct. It required that a tax stamp be placed on public papers transmitted to English colonists from both government and private institutions. Covered by the statute were such items as legal instruments, marriage licenses, and newspapers. The colonial response was unusually clamorous and sometimes violent. The ostensible purpose of the law was to support England's defense of her colonies and to help balance the English budget. Many colonists believed that Britain intended to tax the colonies to support a standing army in America, which could be used to deprive Americans of their rights and stifle dissent from the unrepresented colonists.[1]

The Stamp Act was repealed in 1766, but it was followed by the Declaratory Act, which asserted Britain's right to tax her colonies as she saw fit. In 1767 Parliament did so by levying the Townshend Taxes on tea, paint, glass, lead, and paper. Parliament eventually rescinded this act, except for the levy on tea, which was a clear signal to the colonies that Britain retained the authority to tax them. In 1773 Parliament passed the Tea Act, reducing the duty on tea, and giving the troubled East India Company a virtual monopoly on the tea trade between the mother country and her colonies; this measure alarmed American merchants. The final legal step in the confrontation between Britain and her American colonies was a series of punitive measures known in America as the Intolerable Acts, a British retaliation against the Boston Tea Party, which were designed to force the restive colonies, especially Massachusetts, into submission to Parliament's will.

Colonial response to British legislation varied from vocal and newspaper protests to organization. The first colonial organizations took the shapes of the Stamp Act Congress and the radical Sons of Liberty. As American opposition coalesced, committees of correspondence were formed in the colonies, culminating in the First Continental Congress in 1774. When peaceful means of solving British-American conflicts no longer seemed possible, America armed for war. Song in America reflected the colonial position.

The tunes written between 1765 and 1775 were especially important because they were the first numerous American protest songs. American songs were, for the most part, public documents affirming Americans' rights and a desire for fair treatment from England. In those cases where Britain is accused of abusing colonial freedom, specific English figures are often named as villains. In the pre-Revolutionary War songs extant, no American hero clearly emerges. If any figure can be considered a colonial champion in the songs of American origin in the years between 1765 and 1774, it is the Great Commoner, William Pitt, the last prime minister saluted in American music.

American songs of the period between the Stamp Act and the first battle of the war take two forms. They are sometimes enthusiastic and strongly assertive of the rights of free men and sometimes religious and almost plaintive. A powerful note of indignation against many British leaders exists in most of the songs surveyed. Many of the songs ask for a redress of grievances, offering an assurance that Americans will remain loyal to Britain if they are treated fairly. Although some songs declare that Americans will make any sacrifice for liberty, it is not until late 1774 that the tone and content of American protest songs changes to obvious belligerence.

Colonial protest songs were generally circulated in one of two forms. Most songs were published in newspapers and broadsides, the most certain way to reach a large audience. A few pieces, however, like religious composer William Billings' "Chester" and "Lamentation Over Boston," were printed in collections of the author's works. Many songs were published without identifiable melodies, while others were identified with specific tunes but without musical notation. Most were set to popular melodies of the time.

Significant newspapers, like the *Virginia Gazette*, the *Boston Gazette*, and the *Pennsylvania Packet*, published selected songs and poems. A few colonial papers printed Loyalist songs as well as tunes featured in London papers, though most Loyalist work in America was printed in *Rivington's Gazette*, a New York paper, between 1773 and 1783.[2]

As colonial protests against parliamentary regulation became more heated, political songs came to replace in newspapers the usual didactic reflections on love, death, drink, and life's vicissitudes. More often after 1765 American songs began to dispute Britain's right to legislate for the colonies without their support. Although many songs deal with a number of topics, the majority mention Britain's oppression of America.

American songs between 1765 and 1774 differ little from British songs of that period. The language of American protest songs and the music accompanying the lyrics are traditionally British. American songs during this period are American only in theme; several major themes are evident in American pre-war songs. The first and most important of these is the desire for freedom from oppressive legislation. To illustrate the British heritage of liberty shared by Americans, many American writers resorted to historical example, musically citing several cases in support of their views. Before late 1774 American composers continued to assert American loyalty to Britain, affirming their devotion to king and country with songs about the mother-daughter relationship shared by the two lands. American fears of British interference with American's right to worship are mentioned in a few songs. After the Boston Tea Party many poems and a few songs about tea and its symbolic relationship to British injustice were composed.

Liberty songs were generally written to protest British interference in colonial affairs. Two important patriots wrote lyrics for two of the finest American protest songs of the period. John Dickinson's "Liberty Song" was the first highly popular liberty piece written by an American; "The New Massachusetts Liberty Song" by Joseph Warren used historical example to prove Americans' right to freedom from unfair British treatment. Warren was the first important American songwriter to foresee future American greatness.

The first protest song about the violation of American rights published in America is an anonymous, untitled piece printed in Boston in 1765; it generally villifies British legislators and American tax collectors who would steal American liberty for a profit. The song is poetic, drawing on the metaphorical language of the time as shown in its use of the terms "pelf,"[3] for wealth, with the connotation of to pilfer, to make a profit,[4] and "welkin," a versifier's word for sky, with the implication of a wide space in which "liberty's praise" is sounded. The author continues to use metaphor in his declaration that the "puffs" and "vapors" of greedy tyrants will fade into the high blue skies that signify freedom.[5] While historians have speculated on colonial views on taxation, the tune leaves no doubt that Americans will reject internal taxes. The author declares that the colonists will affirm the faith of their forefathers through a repudiation of all restrictions on American freedom. Colonial loyalty to the king is granted, but the stamp paper must be consigned to the flames.

A second major liberty or protest song is from an undated broadside, probably published in late 1766, and is titled, as were so many colonial liberty songs, "A New Song," and subtitled "On the Repeal of the Stamp Act." This song is the first of many to equate British officials with the underworld. The three major devils of this song are John Huske, an American who migrated to Britain, became a member of Parliament, and was credited in America with the promotion of the Stamp Act; Lord Bute, George Grenville's predecessor; and Grenville himself, the first minister of England at the time of the song's composition.[6] The last two were probably connected, in American minds, with the idea of creating a tax to support British forces in America. Since Grenville took office in 1763 and suggested the measure, he is assigned the role of right-hand man to Satan. He is contrasted with Pitt, a "politick messiah,"[7] comparable with King David or Jesus, whose eloquent "tongue like the serpents" (in a strangely contradictory metaphor) might well reverse the three evil influences on Parliament. This work is the first of many American liberty songs with religious overtones.

The liberty tree and the Boston Sons of Liberty, the latter a radical New England patriot group led by Samuel Adams, figure prominently in the songs of the time, especially those published in the *Boston Gazette*. "A Song, Occasioned by a threat to cut down a tree of Liberty" is based on the premise that a tree is sacred because its growth is symbolic of all life and because it grows according to nature's laws. The tree does not harbor a seditious mob but a group of free men who must assert their natural rights as the tree provides protection from the oppressive midday heat of tyranny. If the tree is cut down, men must face the heat of day without relief; that is, they must "kiss the iron rod"[8] of oppression. Yet a time will come, the song offers, when free men will guard the protective tree and thus enjoy the shade of secured liberty.

"We dare to be free"[9] is the slogan of the Sons of Liberty as expressed in "A Song. Addressed to the Sons of Liberty." The author declares that the justice of their cause will be recognized by "posterity" while "slavish knaves," those who abridge American freedom, will "sink into perdition." In support of their cause, the Sons of Liberty cite the "Magna Carta," an example of the vindication of those "Natural Rights," as John Locke so clearly defined them, that belong to all men. In an appeal to ordinary men, the song calls on the New England "farmers" to sustain the "glorious ninety-two" members of the Massachusetts legislature, who have defied Lord Hillsborough, the secretary of colonial affairs. The request for Hillsborough's dismissal was sent to Governor Thomas Hutchinson when Massachusetts lawmakers circulated a letter to the other colonies asking for colonial solidarity in repudiating the odious Townshend Acts.[10] The refusal of the Massachusetts legislators to yield to Hillsborough's official pressure fixed in many colonial minds the numbers ninety-two for freedom (those who voted against Hillsborough) and seventeen for slavery, as the song declares (those who voted with the British ministry).[11] The seventeen are for the radicals no better than beasts of burden, derogatorily "Mules or Asses."

In 1768 the most famous of all pre-war songs was authored by the notable Pennsylvania patriot John Dickinson. The well-known author of "Letters from a Farmer in Pennsylvania," Dickinson was also a lawyer who was a leading exponent of American privilege. According to historian Lawrence H. Gipson, Dickinson's letters were so important in their time that they "became the political Bible of Americans until early in 1776."[12] Those ideas that made the letters a powerful force in early American thought for eight years are contained in capsule form in a song commonly known as the "Liberty Song" (see appendix). Dickinson confirms his belief that Americans will accept no tax for the purpose of revenue to be used at Britain's discretion: "How sweet are the labors/that freemen endure, That they shall enjoy all the profit secure."[13] He further writes, "Not as slaves, but as freemen our money we'll give." This statement implies that Americans will contribute to the British treasury if they are given a voice in determining colonial policy. In stanza six Dickinson states, "Swarms of placemen and pensioners soon will appear"; perhaps he is thinking of the recent customs officials who have been sent to America to drain colonial earnings through a rigid application of the navigation acts in the vice-admiralty courts. The reference also appears in a footnote to this stanza reading "the ministry have already begun to give away in pensions the money they lately took out of our pockets, *without our leave* [emphasis added]."[14]

The "Liberty Song" initiated many of the references standard in the liberty songs of the period. Its author refers to generations past as "worthy forefathers" who faced trying times with unusual courage. These unnamed ancestors not only "bequeath'd . . . their freedom and fame" to the patriots but left them the liberty tree as well. Through the common kinship of freedom, "brave Americans" are urged to unite and "join hand in hand" to insure colonial rights. In a biblical allusion later repeated by Lincoln, Dickinson warns Americans, "By uniting we stand, by dividing we fall." Though Americans must not fall into servitude to England, the author affirms in a positive note that Americans are still proud to be a part of "Britannia's glory and wealth." Britain will be blessed with continued fame and riches if she will simply treat her colonies fairly. It was only three days after Governor Francis Bernard followed Hillsborough's injunction to dismiss the Massachusetts lawmakers that Dickinson wrote his inspiring text. He recognized that music might catalyze patriotic spirit, modestly claiming "indifferent songs are powerful on certain occasions."[15]

In July of 1768 Dickinson had written James Otis a letter, enclosing a copy of the tune; he followed it with a second version a few days later. Dickinson found the first version of the song too adventurous and consequently modified the piece to his satisfaction. The melody that accompanies the lyrics is William Boyce's widely circulated "Hearts of Oak," a standard British patriotic air. The song became popular throughout the colonies in a number of versions in a period of scarcely more than thirty days. The Sons and Daughters of Liberty used the song in a commemoration of the first Stamp Act protests, which had taken place three years before. On 14 August 1769 at Dorchester, Massachusetts, a band of 359 Sons of Liberty heartily sang the song at their yearly meeting. Perhaps, as cultural historian Kenneth Silverman notes, the song's power arose from its widely used performance in chorus and its inspiring harmony, so similar to that taught in New England schools. The song offered a timely dramatic blend of rousing melody and popular political sentiments.[16]

The greatest tribute to the song was the number of parodies and imitations that it spawned. Within two months a Tory lampoon appeared, a song that may well be called the first Loyalist reply to a liberty tune. The parody appeared, peculiarly enough, in the *Boston Gazette*, a paper known to be sympathetic to the radical Sons of Liberty and their cause. "The Parody of a Well Known Liberty Song" was composed at Castle William, a British fortress near Boston, where Tories on occasion retreated from the uprisings of local libertarians.[17] The parody characterizes the radicals as little better than thieves and mobsters. Patriots' brains are called "dull noodles,"[18] and conservatives see the radicals as "monkies" [*sic*] who are "stupidly steady." In religious terms the Tory element believes itself blessed while the patriots are minions of "Old Satan." The liberty trees in America will be put to good use when they are used to hang the unrepentant rascals who must "by no means be spar'd." If American trees are not to be used, then "Tyburn," the famous site of many English executions, will serve nicely.[19] The author of this song may well have been referring to the rumor in America that Samuel Adams and John Hancock would be transported to England and hanged under an old and little-used law (35 Henry VIII), which contained definitions of treason.[20] The American radicals are villified as "mad sots" whose wives are "bunters," women of questionable virtue.[21]

The Loyalists were probably most concerned, as their invective shows, with the threats to their property and safety that came about because of the Stamp Act riots and other disturbances that followed each new British measure. The anonymous author of the piece cries,

> Such Villians [*sic*], such rascals all dangers despise,
> And stick not at mobbing when mischiefs the prize.

They burst thro' all barriers, and piously keep
Such chattels as the vile rascals can sweep.

It is likely that the memory of the looting of and damage to the house of Massachusetts Lieutenant Governor Thomas Hutchinson on 26 August 1765 was foremost in the mind of the writer. As in the case of several protests, notably the Boston Tea Party and the *Gaspeé* (which involved the grounding and burning of a revenue cutter), no arrests followed the vandalism.[22] Recognizing the failure of arrests to halt the mobs, the composer states, in a Loyalist reversal of Dickinson's sentiments, "For short is your harvest, nor long shall you know/The Pleasure of Reaping what other men Sow." The author threatens, "when Red Coats appear,/You'll melt like the locust when Winter is near." In a righteous but erroneous prediction, the composer declares that "All Ages shall speak with Contempt and Amaze,/Of the vilest Banditti that swarmed in these Days." The song closes with the hope that all the radicals will be hanged and peace will reign again.

The patriots did not allow the Tories the last word in this tuneful dispute and replied to "The Parody" with "The Massachusetts Liberty Song." The song was written by Benjamin Church, a Loyalist who posed as a patriot until 1775, when his true sentiments as well as his activities as a British spy were uncovered.[23] The tune answers Tory charges made in "The Parody" and reaffirms the American quest for liberty. As this song clearly indicated, Americans did not yet blame King George for their troubles but were "still firmly persuaded our rights he'll restore."[24] The patriots will not "submit to their [British] chains for a day"; in a forboding note they asked Englishmen to "prevent the fierce conflict which threatens." The song closes with a declaration that Americans "scorn to survive" if they are not allowed to enjoy the freedom that their forefathers so highly valued.

In 1774 Dickinson's tune inspired a memorable warning to Britain that Virginians would support the Boston radicals. The warning took the form of a song titled "The Glorious Seventy-Four." As in the Stamp Act songs of nearly a decade before, the villains of the piece are former Prime Minister Lord Bute and the then current prime minister, Lord North. The song decries British tyranny and claims that American liberty is "Heaven's decree."[25] The most notable change in this liberty song from those of past years is American determination "to fight for . . . freedom with swords and with guns."

Americans included historical evidence in support of their position in many of their compositions. Liberty songs and poems contain many references to historical periods when freedom was won by men secure in their beliefs in the face of absolute authority and overwhelming force. The most significant of these songs were published in early 1775. One of the more popular of these pieces was a lively song titled "The Roast Beef of Old England." This work is the only one that recalls in detail the glorious days of the reign of Queen Elizabeth. Its basic metaphor is the contrast between the solid nutrition of roast beef and the watery weakness of "Coffee and Tea and such Slip-Slops."[26] Roast beef represents all that was strong and virtuous in England in the days before the wealth of empire corrupted Englishmen. The queen and her bishops were devoted to the country, shunning doctrines that smacked of Catholicism. The first five stanzas describe a golden age that existed only in the minds of the composer and a few of his readers. The hardy ancestors of the current generation have given way, in conduct as well as diet, to "sons who whore and game." Corrupt youth manages to "live upon Tea,/And cringe to a venal majority." But nature, the author asserts, will turn things around in America, as the metaphor of the seasons implies. With a warning to the Tories about the changing times, Americans look toward "the new Eighty-Eight." This reference is to the Glorious Revolution of 1688, when an honest Protestant government replaced the supposedly corrupt Catholic regime of James II. Americans view the approaching season as heralding a similar reemergence, when a just American government will replace unjust British rule.

A second prominent song, "The New Massachusetts Liberty Song," uses historical example to warn Americans to guard their liberty and future greatness, since such greatness will rest on the tradition of freedom. The tune offers a confident vision of America's future power. According to music historian Vera Lawrence, Joseph Warren, an important Boston patriot and physician, wrote the song in or near the year 1770. She notes that the song was first delivered in concert 13 February 1770 and was published in Edes and Gill's *North American Almanac and Massachusetts for the Year 1770*.[27] This song exists in several versions with minor variations. The first stanza alludes to the glories of Greece and Rome, implying that the failure of those states to protect the people's rights precipitated their decline. England, poetically called "Proud Albion,"[28] has forgotten that she was once conquered by "Caesar," as well as "Picts," "Danes," and "Normans." After finally ridding herself of these oppressors, Britain established a tradition of freedom that was transferred to America. The colonists now find themselves oppressed by the nation that gave them the heritage of liberty. Americans, however, will preserve the ideal of liberty and nurture it in a new world. Warren believed that America had become as powerful as many of the European nations and even foresaw a time when Americans would challenge Britains as "the Masters of the Main"; France and Spain, too, will ultimately recognize the undeniable power of Americans in world affairs.

The last two pre-war liberty songs were published in broadsides and newspapers in late 1774 and early 1775. In the first, "An American Parody on the Old Song of Rule, Britannia," the famous line "Britons never will be slaves"[29] is interpreted to mean that Americans are the intended slaves of the Britons. This interpretation has serious implications, for in spite of the tension caused by the harsh British actions of 1774, Americans still ultimately considered themselves British citizens. Although "guardian Angels" led Englishmen to carry out "Heaven's Command" to populate the American wilderness, England's greatness, due in part to her colonies' wealth, has caused her to become "swelled with *Luxury* and *Pride*." As many of England's foremost libertarians, such as Algernon Sidney, pointed out, luxury and its concommitant corruption lead to foolish and unjustifiable pride.[30] The song declares that simple, and therefore presumably upright, Americans would gladly support Britain if only London would "with *Justice* and with *Wisdom* reign"; American "youth" and "vigor" could prove an invaluable aid to an aging and weakened motherland. If America were allowed to do so freely, she would joyfully support England's measures.

"American Liberty, A New Song" is one of several compositions to caution against the influences of "papists"[31] and to offer in song an olive branch to "any loyal king." The song denounces Lord North and former Massachusetts governors Hutchinson and Bernard. It recognizes the power of the "navies," undoubtedly the British fleet harbored in and around Boston in early 1775, yet insists that Americans are pledged to defend their freedom and their land. The piece praises the Sons of Liberty and restates Dickinson's earlier call for unity in the lines "divided we shall surely fall,/United we shall stand." In a direct reference to John Locke, the song declares that "liberty and property" are the privileges of all men. "American Liberty" mirrors the tension around Boston in 1775, indicating that American patience with British oppression had grown thin.

Not all American songs depicted a complete conflict of interest between Britain and her American colonies. The first of two important ballads treating a mother-child relationship is a tune titled "The Old Woman Taught Wisdom," probably written about 1767. In this partial allegory, the woman Britain is old and consequently decaying; the metaphor of Britain as an old woman and America as a strong, healthy one is commonplace in some American poems and songs. The aged Britain wants the grown daughter America to earn her own keep. At this request the daughter "was sulky"[32] and refused to recognize "her duty, the laws." The quarrel obviously concerns the Stamp Act and consequent support of British forces in America. "Goody Bull," the good woman England, is counseled by Pitt, appropriately called "the absolute farmer," to make peace with her daughter. The mother's heart has become more callous than that of "Jew or than Turk," eighteenth-century (and earlier) terms synonymous with cruelty and lack of compassion. Although the mother rejects the daughter as a "huzzy" in an unkind reference to the colonies, she ultimately agrees to be guided by Pitt's wisdom. The song ends on an unsettling note; while it is purportedly written by "a peacemaker to Great Britain and her colonies" (as the appended note tells), the last two lines are openly antagonistic toward Britain: "No thanks to you, mother; the daughter replied:/But thanks to my friend here, I've humbled your pride." Surely these sentiments irritated British lawmakers, already sensitive that they had yielded when they did not believe they should have done so.

The second song is a brief one, found in Benjamin Franklin's handwriting but not positively identified as his composition, entitled "The Mother Country." Here England is compared with a "peevish"[33] parent whose reason has been corrupted with age. Americans are compared with servants who are sometimes beaten with the "rattan" when they behave improperly. The rattan was a cane made from the same material, probably brought from Malaya.[34] As might be expected of a song composed in 1771, "bad Neighbors," likely France and Spain, are warned not to tamper with the British or the "sons" will rapidly come to the aid of their parent. Furthermore, the author declares that Englishmen who seek to pervert American liberties will be challenged through the proper legal channels.

Like political liberty, religion was a constant concern, and while religious liberty songs were few, those that found their way into print were strongly critical of the British religious establishment, the Church of England and its perceived Catholic leanings. For the most part, Catholicism and its influences on Protestant services were condemned in America, especially in Puritan New England. This disdain had been passed from generation to generation along with the fear that distracting and unnecessary rituals might creep into the purified ceremonies of the Congregational churches. Of greater concern to the colonists was the possibility that an Anglican archbishop would be appointed for America, which could lead to English interference in American religious matters and thus further restrict colonial freedom. Since many dissenters considered the Anglican church (like the Catholic church) corrupt, they feared that this sort of intrusion would result in religious pollution.[35]

It is to the issue of New England dissent versus English corruption that the first important religious song is addressed. The author charges that the "Vestry,"[36] the local church governing board, has conspired to pull down the "meeting"; the meeting is either the town gathering where freemen's ideas were expressed or the Congregational meetings held on the Sabbath. The song sarcastically states that "dissenters [are] worse than the devil" and so must be stopped from gathering together. The vestry has vowed to save the souls of those gone astray, even if it must "force 'em to heaven." Much of the remainder of the song deals with the efforts of the conspirators to entice a "parson," perhaps George III, through worldly gain, to lead his flock down the so-called true path. The parson has likely joined in a conspiracy with the vestry, usually wealthy men and often Tories, to lead his congregation to unthinkingly support the English government. At first the conscientious parson tells his tempters that "to forsake 'em would surely be wrong." Then "conscience creeps in, that fair light from above," and the pastor realizes in the next line that he had taken the right course in siding with the vestry. His new conscience had advised him to "go where you're best paid." The song ends with the scornful admonition to the new priest to "become bishop'd" so that he may further serve God and his new flock. If this conversion does not suit him, he is advised to make his next mistress "Babylon's Whore," the Calvinist epithet for the Roman Catholic church. This song seems to serve as a general condemnation of the Episcopal church, as no particular individuals are mentioned.

Among the staunch New England Protestants mentioned earlier was the noted composer William Billings, who sometimes employed rapidly paced musical variations in his songs. He was the first notable American composer to write both lyrics and music for an American liberty song. He wrote two tunes with particularly moving religious and patriotic motifs. His first song, "Chester" (see appendix), appeared in 1770 in a collection of his tunes titled *The New-England Psalm-Singer*. Billings later revised the song and included it in his 1778 publication, *The Singing Master's Assistant*. The revised version retained its religious tone and was rendered more patriotic by the addition of four new stanzas. The first version contained only four lines that expressed the determination and faith of the independent New Englanders.[37] They read,

> Let tyrants shake their iron rod,
> And slav'ry clank her galling chains,
> We fear them not, we trust in God,
> New-England's God forever reigns.[38]

Billings' second collection also contains his plaintive "Lamentation Over Boston," probably written in 1774. In this imitation of the 137th Psalm, Billings mourns the fate of his beloved Boston after the Coercive Acts were imposed on the port city in 1774.[39] He also expresses fear of impending conflict. In strong but simple terms he prays, "Forbid it, Lord God."[40] His patriotic feelings center on Boston, and his mind, he prays, will always be with her in her hour of suffering.

British actions in 1774 inspired other songwriters besides Billings. From the London newspaper *The St. James Chronicle* came a song critical of the Quebec Act, a British measure giving English privileges to Canadian Catholics. This new law outraged New England Protestants. In a short introduction "A New Song" is described as a "lullaby"[41] sung by Lord North to his child, the Quebec Act. The child, an orphan, is called a "bantling"; the term is of sixteenth-century origin, likely from the French and closely related to the word "bastard."[42] In the first of four verses the child is compared to "its dad" and is said to closely resemble its "puppet" father. In the second verse the child has been freed of its Protestant tormentor "Lord Chatham," William Pitt. The second verse also refers to "lawn sleeves," the fine fabric used for English church garments; the term was sometimes used, as it is in the song, to represent the Anglican clergy. Here the meaning of the word is also synonymous with excess.[43] The next two verses call for the abolition of the "fam'd reformation"; meant ironically, of course, is the reverence for "penance and pardons," "faggots and fires," the tools of the Inquisition, and "rareeshew relics," here meant to lampoon false relics of Jesus and the saints. The chorus implies that English policies like the Quebec Act "go backwards and forwards" as they become expedient "for the good of the Crown-e." The intent of the song was to describe how the king and the unscrupulous British ministry used religious faith as a means to achieve their political ambitions.

Like the subject of England's interference in American religion, tea was a sensitive topic with the colonists. Despite their celebration of hostile American actions such as the destruction of British tea, American tea songs do not directly threaten rebellion. Nevertheless, it was the Tea Act that provoked the conflicts that led to the first battles of the Revolution. Tea, as might be expected, figured prominently in many songs and poems composed after the staging of the Boston Tea Party in 1773. It is the main subject of two particularly fine songs. The first, "Tea destroyed by Indians," is a broadside, probably published in late 1773 or early 1774, but certainly not before that time, since the song mentions the "Indians"[44] of the December 1773 party. The song is essentially a liberty song, using the subject of tea to introduce its key points. The once beloved beverage has become for many Americans that "accursed tea." An interesting pun is made on the name of the *Dartmouth*, the most famous of the three tea-bearing English ships involved in the Boston Tea Party. The line implies death to tyrants; freedom fighters will "Dart the man that dare oppress the Earth."

The second work is titled, predictably enough, "A New Song." It describes in a general way the visit of the disguised Bostonians to the "Three ill-fated Tea-ships."[45] In this song, as in the previous one (and in nearly every poem or song about tea after 1770), tea leaves are condemned as the "cursed weed of China's coast." In this song, unlike "Tea destroyed by Indians," the colonists regard their actions as protecting "British rights"; colonial and British rights are still synonymous at this time.

Like the tea songs, the first American protest songs were inspired by the passage of measures the colonists considered unfair. The first liberty songs were primarily condemnations of British villains and protests against violations of the rights of British citizens, including American colonists. John Dickinson's "Liberty Song" was the first significant song to emphasize the heritage of colonial freedom. It affirms the colonists' loyalty to the English crown as did other songs requesting a consideration of American rights by appealing to the mother-daughter relationship between the colonies and Britain. The "Liberty Song" also inspired other American liberty songs. Joseph Warren, among others, used history to support Americans' right to freedom from British oppression.

The Boston Tea Party inspired American writers to expand their themes to include protests against the tea tax as a measure specifically directed against Americans. The Intolerable Acts, following the Boston Tea Party, induced American songwriters to compose more belligerent protests, including a strong denunciation of English religious interference in North America.

America's great religious composer, William Billings, added his pen to colonial protests. Americans began to see themselves as the keepers of the flame of liberty.

Though colonial liberty songs treat a variety of subjects, two conclusions about the extant body of these songs may be made. First, an unusual pattern is apparent in the publication of protest songs written between 1765 and 1775. Few songs radical in sentiment were published between 1765 and 1768; however, 1768 proved to be an exceptional year for protest music, possibly because of the passage of the Townshend Acts in 1767 combined with the inspirational writings of John Dickinson in 1768. Between 1769 and 1773 few protest songs were written in spite of noteworthy events such as the Boston Massacre and the *Gaspeé* incident. (This is especially true of the publication of rousing liberty songs.) One song was written about the Boston Massacre, and a few others made reference to it, but the affair did not, for some reason, inspire prolific musical protest. Perhaps American composers realized that the Boston Massacre was not a strong ideological issue. The *Gaspeé* affair produced one song, an undistinguished ballad that graphically describes that event in Rhode Island history. Americans were more likely disturbed by the passage of harmful legislation than by scattered incidents, regardless of their effect. Second, as British suppression of American liberties became more severe in late 1774, American protest songs appeared more frequently and took a more aggressive stance. The heyday of the protest song was reached in 1775, when liberty songs, before and after Lexington and Concord, poured from American presses.[46] While American music did not break away from traditional English song, it did help create a consciousness of the distinction between Americans and their British cousins. American composers had begun to express their ideas in song. Armed conflict brought with it a new type of American music, commemorating battles and inspiring future victories through the recounting of American triumphs. The birth of the American war song was at hand.

NOTES

1. This paragraph and the following two contain points made by Lawrence Henry Gipson in *The Coming of the Revolution, 1763–1775* (New York: Harper and Row, 1962), p. 19.

2. The conclusions about newspaper verse and songs in chapter two are based on research in colonial newspapers cited in this chapter.

3. Untitled song, reprinted in Vera Brodsky Lawrence, *Music for Patriots, Politicians, and Presidents: Harmonies and Discords of the First Hundred Years* (New York: Macmillan, 1975), p. 19.

4. *Oxford English Dictionary* (hereafter cited as *OED*), s.v. "pelf."

5. Ibid., s.v. "welkin."

6. Gipson, 19, 56, 103.

7. "A New Song. On the Repeal of the Stamp Act," reprinted in Lawrence, 21.

Many songs printed during the American Revolution and the War of 1812 are simply titled "A New Song." In the rare instances that two or more songs with this unrevealing title are discussed consecutively, or the same song is cited in two places, a portion of the first line will be quoted. A few of these songs, like the one cited in this note, have printed subtitles.

8. "A Song occasioned by a threat to cut down a Tree of Liberty," *Boston Gazette*, 17 March 1766.

9. "A Song Addressed to the Sons of Liberty," *Boston Gazette*, 15 August 1768.

10. Kenneth Silverman, *A Cultural History of the American Revolution* (New York: Thomas Y. Crowell, 1976), pp. 111–112.

11. Lawrence, 19.

12. Gipson, 184.

13. "Liberty Song. A Song now much in Vogue in North America," reprinted in Frank Moore, *Songs and Ballads of the American Revolution* (Port Washington, N.Y.: Kennikat Press, 1964; originally published in 1855), pp. 37–39. Moore was one of the first important collectors of war songs; he compiled collections of songs from both the American Revolution and the Civil War.

14. Note appended to a song reprinted in Moore, 40. Moore identifies the note as Dickinson's.

15. Reprinted in Silverman, 112.

16. Silverman, 112–113. Silverman states that the original copy of the first version of the "Liberty Song" has been lost.

17. Gipson, 95.

18. "The Parody upon the Well Known Liberty Song," reprinted in Lawrence, 30. This song is one of the few Tory pieces that will be examined in this work because Tory songs are products of British culture. Most, like "The Parody," roundly condemn the American "upstarts."

19. *Oxford Companion to English Literature*, 3d ed., s. v. "Tyburn."

20. Gipson, 192–193.

21. *OED*, s. v. "bunter."

22. Gipson, 93–94.

23. Lawrence, 31.

24. "The Parody Parodis'd or the Massachusetts Liberty Song," reprinted in Moore, 44–47.

25. "The Glorious Seventy-Four," *Virginia Gazette*, 6 October 1774.

26. "The Roast Beef of Old England," *Connecticut or New London Gazette*, 6 January 1775. Jack P. Greene's "Political Mimesis: A Consideration of the Historical and Cultural Roots of Legislative Behavior in the Colonies in the Eighteenth Century," *American Historical Review* 75 (December 1969): 337–361, is a lengthy discussion of the cyclical view in American politics. Greene's thesis is that Parliament's opposition to many Stuart policies until the late 1680s provided the American colonies during their impressionable formative period with a model for opposition to the English government's policies after 1765.

27. Lawrence, 36.

28. "The New Massachusetts Liberty Song," *Connecticut or New London Gazette*, 24 February 1775.

29. "American Parody on the Old Song of Rule Britannia," *Virginia Gazette*, December 1774.

30. H. Trevor Colbourn, *The Lamp of Experience: Whig History and the Intellectual Origins of the American Revolution* (Chapel Hill: University of North Carolina Press, 1965), p. 50.

31. "American Liberty: A New Song," from a broadside reprinted in Lawrence, 51.

32. "The Old Woman Taught Wisdom," reprinted in Moore, 33–35.

33. "The Mother Country A Song," reprinted in Lawrence, 43.

34. *OED*, s. v. "rattan."

35. Louis B. Wright, *The Cultural Life of the American Colonies, 1607–1763* (New York: Harper and Row, 1962), pp. 95–97.

36. "The Proselyte. A New Ballad, on a new Occasion," *Boston Gazette*, 9 May 1768.

37. John Tasker Howard and George Kent Bellows, *A Short History of Music in America* (New York: Thomas Y. Crowell, 1957), pp. 50–54.

38. "Chester," reprinted in Lawrence, 81.

39. Lawrence, 46.

40. "Lamentation over Boston," reprinted in Lawrence, 46.

41. "A New Song," *Pennsylvania Packet*, 29 August 1774.

42. *OED*, s. v. "bantling."

43. *OED*, s. v. "lawn sleeves."

44. "Tea Destroyed by Indians," a broadside reprinted in Ola Elizabeth Winslow, ed., *American Broadside Verse* (New Haven, Conn.: Yale University Press, 1930), p. 139.

45. "A New Song," reprinted in Lawrence, 45.

46. The best volume for locating original song sources is Gillian B. Anderson, ed., *Freedom's Voice in Poetry and Song* (Wilmington, Del.: Scholarly Research, 1977). The editor also includes a songbook containing Tory as well as liberty songs.

2

Melodies of Battle

The largest group of songs written during the Revolution comprises the broad category of liberty songs featuring several subordinate themes. The two most prominent of these themes are the belief in America's cause and the tyranny of Britain and those who serve her; these two themes form the basis for most war songs of the American Revolution. The topics within this category are many and generally range from songs affirming Americans' right to freedom to American prisoner-of-war songs.

After liberty songs, the largest category is those about battles. The American battle song begins with the appropriation of "Yankee Doodle" by American patriots after the Battle of Bunker Hill. The phrase "Yankee Doodle" came to represent the new American nationalistic spirit, and the melody was used for numbers of songs celebrating American victories.

Even before the formal creation of a navy, Americans composed naval songs; perhaps because America had such a new and small navy and won few outstanding victories, not many naval songs were written. Those that do exist, however, indicate Americans' pride in their naval skills. The young navy, like the young army, was ready to fight for liberty.

Many songs written during the war continued the tradition of pre-war American liberty songs in their accusations of British tyranny and corruption. Before the war and early in the war, some American composers implied that Scottish leaders in the British government might not have the best interests of England and King George at heart. Some of these composers regarded the Scots as little better than the detested Hessian mercenaries. The sentiments expressed in these songs might well have been intended also as a warning to colonists of Scottish origin with Tory leanings.

American songwriters showed confidence in the volunteer army and its leadership. Even some foreign songwriters shared their American counterparts' belief that America was the guardian of liberty. Like songs written to encourage Americans to volunteer, the songs purportedly composed by two Dutch supporters of America declared that America would undoubtedly defeat Britain. The final confirmation of optimism in the patriot cause is found in songs composed by Americans held as prisoners of war in British prisons. The prisoners' disdain for Britain and undiminished support of rebellion showed the strength of American faith, even under adverse conditions. The prisoners' sentiments mirror those in earlier liberty songs.

Many war songs printed shortly after the beginning of the hostilities between England and America are reminiscent of pre-war liberty compositions; at least one was written before the first shots were fired. "A Song, composed at a town meeting" was printed in June 1775, though ostensibly written eleven months before its publication. The song qualifies as a transition piece, written between the bitter period of the Intolerable Acts and the start of the war. The colonists are bold in their defiance of Britain, for their "firelocks are good,"[1] and they are ready to fight not only for freedom, but also to establish "the bright star" of a fledgling empire. A song published the following week, also in the *Virginia Gazette*, indicates that some Englishmen sympathized strongly with the American rebels. The tune, titled "The Sailors Address," is critical of the British ministry, scornfully labeling the ministers "courtiers."[2] Originally published in a London paper and set to the melody of "Hearts of Oak," the song clearly indicates the degree to which many Britons felt kinship with the Americans, "for the blood of GREAT BRITAIN flows warm in their veins." To kill the colonists in battle would be tantamount to "murder." In the attempts of those who would divide the colonies from the mother country, the author sees a plot to subdue Americans by those who harbor hidden Jacobean sympathies: "They roar out for George but are for James in their hearts." The author alludes to the year 1745 and the Stuart Pretender; 1745 was the year that Charles Edward Stuart led his followers in rebellion in Scotland against the Hanoverian King George, the father of George III, king of England at the time of the song's composition. The reference to James is either erroneous or the author is referring obliquely to James II or his son James, known as the Old Pretender. In any case, the rebel Charles was defeated at Culloden in 1745.[3] The composer ultimately declares his support for the king and hopes for peace.

"An extempore Song" was probably written after the fight at Bunker Hill because it mentions "Gage"[4] and "our forces." The song concludes with the usual resolution to fight to the finish; and it demonstrates a high degree of confidence in American political leadership, strongly asserting, "Our congress will plan out our courses/We cheerfully take up our guns."

"A New Song," published in Pennsylvania, a colony with a large population of settlers with Scottish ancestry, also makes a derogatory reference to *"Charlie,"*[5] the Stuart Pretender mentioned above. It is apparent from references in several tunes to the defeated Pretender and to other Scotsmen, that Scotland shared, in at least some American minds, with England the blame for the crisis in the colonies. An untitled song printed in 1776 scornfully refers to "Britannia's haughty Lairds,"[6] surely using the Scottish word "lairds" for "lords" as an intended criticism of British leaders of Scottish blood. The popular and sentimental ballad "Banks of the Dee" was parodied in a song that urged Scots soldiers in America to return home to sit by the banks of the river Dee and "upon your own land be valiant and free."[7] These criticisms likely indicate American anxiety about fighting efficient Scottish battle units like the Black Watch; they may also constitute a warning to the many transplanted Scots who remained loyal to the king. Although a large majority of Americans of Scottish ancestry supported America and were especially influential in intellectual circles, a sizeable portion of Scottish Americans (especially those with connections in the Highlands) remained fervently loyal to Britain.[8]

Apart from disparagement of the enemy, one of the most frequently used devices in the general war song is the recognition of one or more American heroes. In a popular piece printed in late 1775, these include "brave doctor Warren,"[9] the Boston patriot and physician killed at Bunker Hill, and "brave Washington," whose leadership inspires confidence in American generals. As a measure of his already prominent stature, the song alludes to Washington's valor during "Braddock's defeat." When Edward Braddock and his force of British regulars and Virginia troops were ambushed by a force of French and Indians near Fort Duquesne during the "Seven Years' War," Braddock was killed and the British routed. As the song tells it, Washington and his men held fast, preventing a total annihilation of the British forces. Washington's courageous "conduct" will inspire other American men at arms, and, under his leadership, "the Boston men will beat all the regulars back" in the same fashion and with the same results as twenty years before.

The 1776 song entitled "Off from Boston" honors no single American hero, but it does villify two leading British figures. The song is different from its companion pieces in several regards. First, it is one of the initial popular songs to openly condemn the king. It further aspires to a literary tone in its Miltonic comparison of General William Howe with Satan, for like Satan, Howe is "banished from heaven,/never to see the smiling shore,"[10] and so he will be from America, the patriot's heaven. Third, the song offers a rare geographical catalogue, describing in general terms how in each colonial region the British will be defeated in a different way. Finally, it is possibly the first song to mention Hessians, reputedly savage mercenaries who were believed by American warriors to enjoy their murderous duties.

A number of unusual compositions are found among the many war songs composed between 1775 and 1781. One of them is "The New Recruit, or the Gallant Volunteer, A New Song." The song is obviously a musical call for enlistment in the Continental army; it provides a convincing list of reasons for joining the army. The song is gently persuasive, emphasizing the virtues found in a soldier's character. It declares "a soldier is a gentleman,/His honor is his life."[11] To encourage prospective fighters to leave their wives and sweethearts to serve their country, the song equates "love and honor." Further enticements include liberty and a place in history for "A thousand years to come." While it may be merely coincidental, additional encouragement to enlist appears in the same issue of the *Pennsylvania Packet* in the form of a long poem in praise of America and a battle song exalting Washington, combat, and the American soldier.

Although the Dutch, like the Scots, were divided in their loyalties, Americans were not without supporters in Holland.[12] "A Song, made by a Dutch Lady at the Hague" is a respectful piece on American heroes and American victories. Written in English and published in Pennsylvania, its sentiments could as easily have been expressed by an American composer. This song might have been authored by an American rebel seeking to demonstrate foreign support for the patriot cause. The song refers to "our States"[13] and "our Country's Cause"; it evidences a sound general knowledge of the Revolution from Warren's death to the deeds of "Brave Stark at Bennington." Perhaps the most peculiar feature of the song is its use of the phrase "United States." The ostensibly Dutch author apparently believed that American victory was ultimately certain and so acknowledged the birth of a new country, the United States. The same paper contains a similar but shorter piece written, according to the introductory material above the untitled song, by a Dutch man. In a reference to the Stamp Act, the author rejects the king's authority with a directness like that of Thomas Paine. The song echoes Jefferson's views on nature and God as found in the Declaration of Independence:

> Now are our only Laws
> Those God and Nature hath
> Laid on mankind.[14]

Like the first Dutch song, it sounds as though it could have come from the pen of an American writer.

Not all European nations were sympathetic to the American cause; the Hessians, for example, fought viciously against the Americans. In "A New Privateering Song: Concluding with some Remarks upon the cruelty exercised by the Regulars and Hessians, British, and Tories upon our poor prisoners in New York," the American author describes how captured soldiers were placed in a "stinking dungeon,"[15] had their "cash and clothes" taken from them, "bore the want of food," "pinching cold," and "small-pox." American condemnation of Hessian treatment of prisoners is concluded with the standard comparison of the enemy with the devil.

Though prison life was difficult, it did not exclude the singing of war songs. An American held at Forton Prison in the vicinity of Portsmouth, England, left behind him a diary containing two such songs (the author of

the tunes and date of composition, probably 1777 or 1778, remains unveri-
fied).[16] The first of these works, called "A New Liberty Song #44," refers
to King George, Lord North, and the English libertarian John Wilkes. Its
theme concerns "free trading in North America."[17] The final stanza was
likely written to bolster American prisoners' defiance, wishing for "bad luck
to the King and Queen/And all the Royal family." The second song, called
"American New Song #39," is a standard liberty piece dated 5 September
and details the oppression of America from the Stamp Act to the Battle of
Bunker Hill. Although this song was probably first published in an American
broadside, apparently no copy exists in that form. Because of references to
"Washington"[18] and "Bunkers Hill," the second song is probably newer than
the first prisoner-of-war song discussed and is even more rousing and patriotic
in nature than its companion piece. Both songs imply that American morale
remained strong under these most trying circumstances. As song collector
George Carey writes, these songs provided prisoners with both a way to
pass the time as well as a release from the agonies of prison life by reinvig-
orating patriotic spirits.[19]

Americans' patriotism was fired by one of the most widely performed
tunes of the war, "Yankee Doodle." As a battle song "Yankee Doodle" was
doubly important. First, it became symbolic of Americans' justified confidence in themselves. Second, the term "yankee doodle," formerly a phrase
Britons derisively applied to Americans, became a source of pride to patriots
after the Battle of Bunker Hill. The melody became the inspiration for
countless numbers of American war songs.

Throughout the Revolution, Americans continued to sing and play the
quintessential war song, "Yankee Doodle," in various forms. The history of
this song until shortly before its use in the Revolution is mysterious. It has
been conjectured that the first appearance of the song in America was in a
version written by a British doctor, Richard Shuckberg (one of many spell-
ings), to ridicule the ragged dress of colonial troops in the 1750s during the
French and Indian War. Shuckberg's version uses the word "Yankee" as a
term of derision. The word was possibly first employed in Europe with
pejorative connotations and brought to the colonies by the Dutch, who used
it to refer to New Englanders.[20]

The tune was later applied to a musical lampooning of Isaac Sears, a well-
known New York patriot, in a Tory ballad opera entitled *The Disappointment*.
This 1767 play, replete with Loyalist songs, also mocked the patriots' devotion to the liberty tree or liberty pole.[21] Thus, while the tune was used to
ridicule Americans and American beliefs before 1775, it was not until after
the opening shots were exchanged that the melody was first used with patriotic compositions. The British, however, continued their use of the tune
well into the war; it served as accompaniment for parodies such as "The
Lexington March" and "Yankee Doodle's Expedition to Rhode Island." As
the war progressed Americans made greater use of the tune until it became,

primarily because of its association with American victories, essentially an American song.

The earliest widely circulated version of "Yankee Doodle" is a long, puzzling song called "The Farmer and his Son's return from a visit to the Camp." According to Oscar Sonneck, the most notable critic of the song, it describes the various and sometimes confusing scenes of a military training camp.[22] The song reports, among other memorable sights, "Captain Washington,"[23] large and noisy cannon, and multitudes of men engaged in various military tasks.

The music itself was frequently used as a marching tune by both sides; the British played it at Lexington as a sign of their disdain for the colonials, while Americans laid claim to it as a martial song after their strong stand at Bunker Hill. British feelings regarding the American use of the song after Burgoyne's surrender to Horatio Gates in 1777 at Saratoga are clearly illustrated in Thomas Anburey's remarks. Anburey, who served with Burgoyne, writes:

The name of Yankee has been more prevalent since the commencement of hostilities. The soldiers at Boston used it as a term of reproach, but after the affair at Bunker Hill, the Americans gloried in it. Yankee Doodle is now their paean, a favorite of favorites played in their army, esteemed as warlike as the Grenadier's March—it is the lover's spell, the nurse's lullaby. After our rapid successes, we held the Yankees in great contempt, but it was not a little mortifying to hear them play this tune, when their army marched down to our surrender.[24]

Despite Anburey's statement, the British and Americans shared "Yankee Doodle" along with many other songs like "The White Cockade."[25]

According to music historian Raoul F. Camus, when the disgusted and shamefaced British troops turned away from the Americans in an attempt to surrender to the French at Yorktown, Lafayette ordered the American band to strike up "Yankee Doodle."[26]

"The Irishman's Epistle to the Officers and Troops at Boston" was the first major war song published as well as the first to "sing [of] how the Yankees have beaten the Doodles."[27] Printed in May of 1775 and sung to the tune of "The Irish Washerwoman," the song playfully accuses royal troops of having "your bums in your skulls," for fruitlessly trying to impress the Americans with firepower and reputation. The author expresses his confidence in a smoothly turned phrase, assuring the British that Americans will organize and fight together, "For Concord by discord will never be taken." (At Concord, Americans proved themselves as able as their British opponents.) British tactics are questioned as the composer asks, "is it not, honeys, a comical crack,/To be proud in the face, and be shot in the back?" British stamina is ridiculed in the last verse, which accuses the king's troops of resting on their "bums" and becoming fat and unfit for combat. The composer's advice to

British soldiers regarding their physical condition reads: "I'm sure if you're wise you'll make peace for a dinner,/For fighting and fasting will soon make ye thinner." Obviously the author doubts neither the will nor the ability of American soldiers to best their British enemies in combat. As Moore indicates, American confidence grew with each British step back toward Boston.[28]

In 1775 and early 1776 much of the war was fought around Boston. While the Battle of Bunker Hill was a technical defeat for the Americans, who fled in confusion, they emerged victorious in terms of casualties inflicted. Because of their success, the Americans won grudging respect from the British and gained even more self-respect. The most carefully composed American song about the struggle was authored by New England theologian Nathaniel Niles, with music supplied by one of the more competent Amrican composers, Andrew Law.[29] These two men were the first important team of American war song composers. The song, first published in a broadside and titled "The American Hero," was later printed as sheet music. The battle is mentioned specifically only in the subtitle, "Made on the battle of Bunker-Hill, and the burning of Charlestown." The song somberly glorifies God in Old Testament style; "Good is Jehovah"[30] and "Forever praising God our Creator." Also included are allusions to Greek mythology, including references to "Mars" and "serpents fiercer than Medusa's." The song warns the British to beware of the patriots' devotion to their cause; the theme is poignantly stated in the final lines:

> Life for my country and the cause of freedom,
> Is but a trifle for a worm to part with;
> And if preserved in so great a contest,
> Life is redoubled.

The British retreat from Boston in March 1776 inspired two imaginative songs on the sudden British departure, both untitled and printed in the same broadside. Carrying out detailed plans to gather a strong force of approximately 10,000 men in early 1776, Washington decided to fortify Dorchester Heights, making certain that his gun emplacements and trenches were thoroughly protected from an expected British attack. Though the first song to treat this encounter describes none of the movements to fortify the heights (such as the transporting of cannon from Fort Ticonderoga to Boston), it is clear that the Americans held a well-defended location. Other elements of the song are accurate; for example, the "wind and weather which often occurred"[31] did indeed delay Howe's attack. The "hilter skilter" of the British troops in retreat is a correct appraisal of British action. Howe's frustration upon seeing the American works is clear: "in three months, all my men with their might,/Cou'd not make such Forts as they've made in a night." Howe is quoted by Revolutionary War historian Christopher Ward as saying "The rebels have done more in one night than my whole army could do in months."[32] Yankee songwriters must have seemed privy to British thoughts. As they departed, the redcoats destroyed their stronghold, Castle William, by "burning the Castle." Although the Americans sent the enemy packing, Washington feared, contrary to the song's optimistic conclusion, that the British would strike at American positions.[33] The second untitled song composed after the British retreat covers much the same subject matter as the first, though it also expresses the concern of Boston residents in its final lines: "May all our heads be covered well,/When cannon balls do fly."[34]

As the war shifted to the South, it carried with it American confidence and the irrepressible Yankee sense of humor clearly revealed in the well-written comic ballad "A New War Song" (see appendix), purportedly composed by British admiral Sir Peter Parker. The obviously American author uses the first person point of view to describe the Battle at Sullivan's Island, and he is quick to emphasize his own part in the engagement. As in many war songs, the complex action of the battle is omitted. A brief summary of the battle will explain some of the references in the lyrics. The fort at Sullivan's Island, later called Fort Moultrie, having only a small force of men protecting it with thirty operating cannons, was weakly defended. In June 1776 the British planned an attack on the island with ten well-armed vessels under Parker's command and 6,000 men under the command of General Henry Clinton. The army floundered in the seven-foot-deep waters surrounding the island, which had been reported as eighteen inches deep near shore. Meanwhile, a portion of the fleet ran aground. American cannon fire, at first sporadic and undisciplined, later became deadly and severely damaged some of the finest ships in the British fleet, the heavily armed *Experiment* and the flagship *Bristol*, Parker's boat. Parker literally had his pants shot off, and he also received wounds in the knee and thigh. Parker later followed the already departed Clinton in retreat.[35]

The author of the ballad ridicules the British admiral by having him unwittingly compare himself with "Falstaff or Pistol,"[36] two of Shakespeare's bragging but cowardly and clownish soldiers. Parker sees himself as "bold as a Turk." Clinton is predictably assigned the unfavorable role of a do-nothing who chooses to "peep/And not venture over the water." Parker's embarrassing fate is chronicled in the line "I've the wind in my tail,/And am hoisting my sail." The tune closes with Parker's ironic promise that he will win the war in the following year if permitted by the "cowardly Yankees." The rebels sang this ballad, often in unprintable versions, to cheer their flagging spirits with laughter.[37]

The next important war song to appear was another humorous piece set to the tune of "Yankee Doodle." "The Battle of the Kegs" has a unique place among Revolutionary War songs for several reasons: it was composed by a professional American songwriter, Francis Hopkinson, a man of many talents who actually helped produce the event about which he wrote. Hopkinson was adept as a writer, inventor, lawyer, philosopher, and artist. His two most notable accomplishments in American history are his reputed design for an American flag and his signing of the Declaration of Independence. He numbered among his friends Washington, Jefferson, and Franklin, men with whom he was on equal terms.

Hopkinson worked with inventor David Bushnell to help devise a plan to stun the British in their comfortable winter quarters in Philadelphia. By the time the two conferred on a method of surprise, Washington was already entrenched at nearby Valley Forge.[38] With Washington's approval, Bushnell set out to disrupt the British navy at Philadelphia harbor on 5 January 1778. His plan was to use infernals or floating mines that might have caused more damage had British ships not been docked because of floating ice.[39]

The attempt was given a lively, humorous treatment as a news story written by Hopkinson and published in the *New Jersey Gazette*.[40] *The Pennsylvania Ledger*, on the other hand, played down the incident, mentioning it only because two boys (the article claimed) were killed when they fished one of the curious objects from the river. A letter written in Philadelphia indicates that a great deal of confusion and fear was created by the multitude of barrels sent down the Delaware by Bushnell. Some British partisans believed the kegs were filled with patriots invading Philadelphia. Another report portrayed them as filled with enough powder to set the entire river aflame and destroy all the ships thereon. A third and even more absurd version endowed the barrels with the supernatural power to roll out of the river and ignite everything they touched as they rolled down the city streets.[41]

Hopkinson used this marvelous material to ridicule the British in song. Although the ballad covers most of the action at Philadelphia, it is purposely vague. The tone is pompously ironic. The song capitalizes on the British fear that a secret invasion was being launched against them, and Hopkinson draws comic scenes of British panic, referring to the enemy as "men almost distracted."[42] General Howe, sleeping peacefully with his mistress, "Mrs. Loring" (the wife of one of General Howe's officers),[43] and General Erskine are awakened by a frantic subordinate and, in mock heroic lines, order the troops to defend "British Courage" by making a stand against the invading kegs. With intense rifle fire, the redcoats give the invaders a terrific pounding. The sound of battle penetrates even the depths of the river, as Hopkinson wryly notes:

> The fish below swam to and fro,
> Atta'k'd from every quarter:
> Why sure, thought they, The devil's to pay,
> 'Mongst folks above the water.

The author observes that the British will reflect on this magnificent victory with the pride of accomplishment. Hopkinson's satiric ballad is certainly one of the finest literary contributions to the patriotic cause.

Though many songs were written about the Revolution's battles, most are of little value in studying American music because their descriptions of the fighting are strictly formulaic. Other fine songs, such as those about the battles of Saratoga and Yorktown, treat British personalities in greater detail than they do the combat. Songs about these two conflicts are discussed in chapter four, which will examine British and American personalities in the music of the war.

A somewhat different approach to the war song, both in content and method, is shown in naval songs of the Revolution. No important navy song appeared in America before 1777, despite the chanty tradition of the English navy and America's establishment of a fledgling and struggling sea force. When they were written, American naval songs boldly stated that American boats would not hesitate to take on the powerful British fleet. Privateers like the *General Mifflin* were celebrated in song as were the accomplishments of American commanders Abraham Whipple and John Paul Jones. Songs about both of these men praise American sailors; the songs about Jones add personal praise for America's most famous Revolutionary War seaman. The song "Capt. Paul Jones's Victory," the best naval piece of the war, is especially notable for its realistic dialogue and accurate description of naval combat. While the song exalts American valor, it does not diminish the difficulty the *Bon Homme Richard* had in winning its victory over the powerful British vessel *Serapis*. American naval songs add a new theme to American liberty and war songs.

One of the first songs to salute American seamanship was "Song on the *General Mifflin* Privateer." This liberty song is set to the popular melody "War and Washington." It is also the first song to order the British navy out of American waters. In a stern remonstrance the author writes,

> Let England's boasted Navy,
> Return to guard their coast;
> For while they War in Foreign Climes
> Their native wealth is lost.[44]

The tune lists none of the missions of the ship mentioned in the title, but the vessel did remain in American service for more than six months. This fact is confirmed by an advertisement in the *Connecticut Gazette* of 5 August 1778 declaring that the schooner *Mifflin* with four guns would be sold on 21 August 1778.

"The Cruise of the *Fair American*" is the first of many songs to describe American attempts to disrupt British commerce. The song remained a part of oral tradition for many years after the Revolution and was finally "taken down from the mouth's [*sic*] of [Captain Daniel] Hawthorne's surviving shipmates early in the last century."[45] The song is especially clear on several minor details such as the sailing date, given as "the twenty-second of August," probably in 1778, although the year is omitted. It also gives geographical and course measurements such as "the Gulf of Florida" and a "Longitude of twenty-seven." The ballad describes in general terms an encounter with the British navy that might have applied to any sea battle during the war. It does not mention the name of the British vessel, but does note an attempt at boarding it. Those killed are mentioned by name, and the number of wounded is listed. Though the song ends with the usual good wishes for the ship, it is not a liberty song, but an honest appraisal of the voyage. The realism of the narrative is sustained in its carefully controlled tone.

"The Yankee Privateer," a song glorifying Captain Abraham Whipple and one of his most famous exploits, is distinguished mainly by its large number of errors. For example, as naval historian William Fowler notes under his copy of the song, the ship was a Navy vessel, not a privately commissioned one. Whipple's daring deed was not accomplished alone but with the help of two other boats; the feat was performed in one afternoon, not ten nights. The adventure began when the *Providence* and her sister ships accidently encountered a British merchant fleet near Newfoundland that was bound for Jamaica. With silent and careful dispatch of superior crews, the Americans captured eleven vessels, three of which were taken as prizes.[46] The song accurately points out that the ships were taken "Beneath the Lion's nose,"[47] since the Americans were not immediately discovered by armed British escorts. After the surprise seizures, the song claims the Americans bested "the biggest British frigate" that followed them; American seamanship was superior to English skills, as American sailors "raked her fore and aft" before fleeing with extraordinary speed from their pursuer. The tune boasts that Americans are heroes who "swept the seas clear" of the bumbling British.

"The Yankee Man-of-War," likely written in late 1778 or early 1779, is a song about John Paul Jones' voyages near the coasts of England and Scotland. Though it does not describe all of his adventures there (which included a visit to the Earl of Selkirk's home on St. Mary's Isle near Scotland), it is probably the finest naval song of the Revolution.[48] Featuring uncommonly long lines for a war ballad, much like the fourteeners[49] used by William Blake, the song shows traces of the style that was to become characteristic of the Romantic period. Images like "the fiery waves she spread"[50] and a "white and silv'ry track" are faintly reminiscent of Samuel Taylor Coleridge's famous "Rime of the Ancient Mariner," one of the great English Romantic ballads. The song's lively and light tone makes Jones' voyage sound much like an adventuresome pleasure cruise. Another song about John Paul Jones' exploits, "The Stately Southerner," was published about 1780. The southerner of the title is Jones himself; according to Coffin, Jones was so identified because he was a Virginian—a "southerner" in contemporary speech.[51] This somewhat lyrical song, like the one above, in one of its many printings mentions the havoc that Jones' presence created in Scotland.[52] Samuel Eliot Morison quotes a Scots preacher's tale of a prayerful effort that turned the feared Jones away from a possible ransom of the village of Leith. The village was saved from American invasion through the stormy intervention of God.[53]

The song "Capt. Paul Jones's Victory" describes how, with a small fleet of four ships, among them the *Alliance*, whose name reflected America's wartime agreement with France, Jones challenged a British merchant fleet of forty-one ships. The fleet was guarded by the forty-four-gun *Serapis* and the twenty-gun *Countess of Scarborough*.[54] The song is memorable for its imaginative use of dialogue between Jones, captain of the *Bon Homme Richard*, and Captain Richard Pearson of the *Serapis* to describe the events of the battle. As is characteristic of the naval ballad, much of the action is described in terms of the commands shouted by Captain Jones to his sailors. (This feature is central to many naval ballads because the immediate orders of the ship's captain and the speed of their execution might well affect the outcome of the battle.) Jones' determination is implied in lines such as "stand firm to your quarters, your duty don't shun/The first man that quits them thro' his body I'll run." It is interesting to note that the famous claim "I have not yet begun to fight" appears nowhere in the song.

The song "Capt. Paul Jones's Victory" is particularly accurate in its account of the fighting in several important respects. The length of the battle was remarkable, as the song correctly notes: "We fought them eight glasses, eight glasses so hot."[55] In naval terms this means four hours; Fowler declares that Pearson, erroneously called "Percy" in the broadside, surrendered after more than three hours. The piece also notes the extraordinarily high number of casualties: "Seventy bold seamen lay dead on the spot/And ninety brave seamen lay bleeding in their gore." Almost half of each crew, a surprising number for battles of the period, were wounded or killed.[56] The broadside does not describe the additional damage caused by the *Alliance* to the *Richard*, but Neeser's version (which might well have been written much later) mentions it,[57] and Morison indicates that the *Richard* was shelled not once but twice by the French-commanded vessel.[58] The British "their colours pull'd down" essentially because Pearson's courage failed him. The song claims that Americans will find a glorious example in this hard-won victory, and so they must have, judging from the numerous repetitions of this battle song.[59]

With the outset of the Revolution many Americans wrote war songs. The majority of these were liberty songs with a number of varying but related themes. Usually only two or three songs were written about a subject, but nearly all of them share the twin themes of Americans' determination to fight for their undeniable rights and the British intention to conquer and oppress America. For the first time in the liberty song, foreigners were given a place. The Dutch enthusiastically supported the Americans while the Hessian mercenaries appeared a mere tool of their British employers. For the first time Americans became prisoners of war in British prisons; not only were they mentioned in American songs, but they also composed and sang patriotic songs while in captivity. This activity indicated the strength of the rebel spirit.

The patriotic impulse was also found in the most notable American battle song of the Revolution, "Yankee Doodle." The use of the melody for many American war songs was an indication of its popularity; it came to symbolize the power and enthusiasm of the patriot cause. The religious aspect of the Revolution was not lost on Andrew Law and Nathaniel Niles; together they composed a battle song firmly declaring the patriots' unwavering devotion to the right. The battle song also featured the use of humor in some of its finest examples. Humor was to become a part of songs celebrating American military triumphs in several wars. The use of humor in the battle song became a measuring stick of American confidence. One of America's ablest Revolutionary War writers, Francis Hopkinson, took an actual event and added imaginative touches to it while keeping the essential elements of the story. The same thing had been done earlier without Hopkinson's wry humor by the anonymous composer of two songs on the British evacuation of Boston.

Like battle songs, American naval songs were born during the Revolution. The pride in American seamanship was celebrated in song as was the first authentic naval hero, John Paul Jones. One naval song added a realistic dimension to the war song; "Capt. Paul Jones's Victory" shows the actual rigors of naval combat.

American war songs served as both inspiration for and commemoration of victory in battle. Probably for this reason few were written after 1781. Their ultimate purpose was to lift American spirits and to raise consciousness about the significance of the conflict and the potential for a victorious resolution. At the same time, they have proved to be an important measure of the development of American culture in general and specifically of the evolution of one area of the American popular song. The variety of topics, styles, and themes that made up the war song helped further the American musical experiment.

NOTES

1. "A Song Composed at a town meeting in Chester, Burlington County, July 1774," *Virginia Gazette*, 22 June 1775.

2. "The Sailor's Address," *Virginia Gazette*, 29 June 1775.

3. *Penguin Encyclopedia*, s. v. "Jacobites."

4. "An Extempore Song," *Virginia Gazette*, 29 June 1775.

5. "A New Song, Fair Liberty Now," *Pennsylvania Packet*, 14 September 1775.

6. Untitled song, *Pennsylvania Packet*, 13 May 1776.

7. "Banks of the Dee," reprinted in Frank Moore, *Songs and Ballads of the American Revolution* (Port Washington, N.Y.: Kennikat Press, 1964; originally published in 1855), pp. 81–82.

8. Robert Kelley, *The Cultural Pattern in American Politics: The First Century* (New York: Alfred A. Knopf, 1979), pp. 65–66.

9. "A New Song, Fair Liberty Now," *Pennsylvania Packet*, 14 September 1775.

10. "Off from Boston," reprinted in Moore, 122–125.

11. "The New Recruit or the Gallant Volunteer," *Pennsylvania Packet*, 8 April 1778.

12. Kelley, 38.

13. "A Song, made by a Dutch Lady at the Hague," *Pennsylvania Packet*, 1 June 1780.

14. "Another, made by a Dutch Gentleman at Amsterdam," *Pennsylvania Packet*, 1 June 1780.

15. "A New Privateering Song: Concluding with some Remarks upon the Cruelty exercised by the Regulars and Hessians, British, and Tories upon our poor prisoners in New York," reprinted in Vera Brodsky Lawrence, *Music for Patriots, Politicians, and Presidents: Harmonies and Discords of the First Hundred Years* (New York: Macmillan, 1975), p. 69.

16. George A. Carey, ed., *A Sailor's Songbag: An American Rebel in An English Prison* (Amherst: University of Massachuusetts Press, 1976), p. 19.

17. "A New Liberty Song Number 44," reprinted in Carey, 121–122.

18. "American Liberty Song Number 39," reprinted in Carey, 110–111.

19. Carey, 18–19.

20. Tristram P. Coffin, *Uncertain Glory: Folklore and the American Revolution* (Detroit: Folklore Association, 1971), pp. 91–92.

21. Lawrence, 41.

22. Oscar George Theodore Sonneck, *Report on "The Star-Spangled Banner," "Hail Columbia," "Yankee Doodle"* (New York: Dover Publications, 1972; originally published in 1909), p. 141.

23. "The Farmer and his Son's return from a visit to the Camp," from an undated broadside reprinted in Ola Elizabeth Winslow, ed., *American Broadside Verse* (New Haven, Conn.: Yale University Press, 1930), p. 141.

24. Excerpted in Coffin, 101.

25. Lewis Winstock, *Songs and Music of the Redcoats: A History of the War Music of the British Army, 1642–1902* (Harrisburg, Pa.: Stackpole Books, 1970), p. 69.

26. Raoul F. Camus, *Military Music of the American Revolution* (Chapel Hill: The University of North Carolina Press, 1976), p. 163.

27. "The Irishman's Epistle to the Officers and Troops at Boston," reprinted in Carolyn Rabson, *Songbook of the American Revolution* (Peaks Island, Maine: NEO Press, 1974), pp. 30–31.

28. Moore, 74.

29. Lawrence, 59.

30. "The American Hero, made on the battle of Bunker-Hill and the burning of Charlestown," from an undated broadside reprinted in Lawrence, 64.

31. Untitled song, from an undated broadside reprinted in Lawrence, 64.

32. Christopher Ward, *The War of the Revolution*, ed. John Richard Alden (New York: Macmillan, 1952), 1:128.

33. Ibid., 1:125–132.

34. Untitled song, from a broadside reprinted in Lawrence, 64.

35. Willard M. Wallace, *Appeal to Arms: A Military History of the American Revolution* (Chicago: Quadrangle Books, 1964), pp. 92–95.

36. "A New War Song," reprinted in Moore, 135–137.

37. Oscar Brand, *Songs of '76: A Folksinger's History of the Revolution* (New York: M. Evans and Co., 1972), p. 65.

38. Lawrence, 76–77.

39. Moore, 217–218. For a detailed description of Bushnell's contribution to the American Revolution see Jack Coggins, *Ships and Seamen of the American Revolution* (Harrisburg, Pa.; Stackpole Books, 1969), pp. 60–63.

40. Paul M. Yall, ed., *Comical Spirit of Seventy-Six: The Humor of Francis Hopkinson* (San Marina, Calif.: Huntington Library, 1976), p. 38. Yall's collection of Hopkinson's works is the best one-volume edition available.

41. Moore, 215.

42. "Battle of the Kegs," reprinted in Moore, 209–214.

43. Lawrence, 77.

44. "Song on the *General Mifflin* Privateer," *Boston Gazette*, 29 December 1777.

45. "The Cruise of the *Fair American*," reprinted in Robert Neeser, ed., *American Sea Songs and Ballads* (New Haven, Conn.: Yale University Press, 1938), pp. 9–12.

46. William M. Fowler, Jr., *Rebels Under Sail: The American Navy during the Revolution* (New York: Charles Scribner's Sons, 1976), pp. 48–49.

47. "The Yankee Privateer," reprinted in Neeser, 20–23.

48. Fowler, 154–156.

49. *Princeton Encyclopedia of Poetry and Poetics* defines a "fourteener" as a line of fourteen syllables.

50. "Yankee Man-of-War," reprinted in Neeser, 25–26.

51. Coffin, 117.

52. "The Stately Southerner," reprinted in Neeser, 25–26.

53. Samuel Eliot Morison, *John Paul Jones: A Sailor's Biography* (Boston: Little, Brown and Co., 1959), 217–218.

54. Ibid., 225.

55. "Captain Paul Jones's Victory," from a broadside reprinted in Winslow, 155.

56. Fowler, 168.

57. Neeser, 28.

58. Morison, 234–235.

59. Ibid., 237.

3

Heroes, Villains, and Democrats

For the first time in the brief history of American war music, a number of men and a woman had been the main subjects of songs. The major figures in these American war songs are George Washington and British generals John Burgoyne and Lord Cornwallis; around them are clustered the minor figures Nathan Hale, Jane McCrea, British major John André, and American soldiers John Paulding and Sergeant John Champe. Just why many more notable figures than these five are not celebrated in American song is a mystery.

As might be expected, Washington is the most widely mentioned figure in American Revolutionary War music. Although he is the subject of only one song, Nathan Hale's name was probably almost as well known as Washington's; Washington is the quintessential hero, while Hale is the Revolution's most recognized American tragic figure.

Sir John Burgoyne, whose surrender at Saratoga gave America its first major victory of the war, is the subject of several songs, some of which mock the British leader. Linked with his name is the American tragic heroine Jane McCrea, killed by Indians serving the British during the campaign that led Burgoyne to Saratoga.

Benedict Arnold's treasonous conspiracy with the British produced two songs, neither of them featuring the traitor as its main character. John Paulding, one of three New York militia men responsible for the capture of Major John André, Arnold's British contact, is the hero of a ballad about the event; the song ends with regrets for André's death and a wish that Arnold had taken his place on the American gallows. John Champe is the central character in a long ballad about a frustrated attempt to capture Arnold from the British, to whom he had defected.

The final songs deal with Lord Cornwallis, along with Burgoyne the only British general to be the central figure in a number of American war songs.

Considering the magnitude of his defeat, he is mildly lampooned. American composers do not roundly condemn him but treat his defeat as inevitable; the writers are gracious in victory but undeniably proud of America's triumph at Yorktown. For Cornwallis and Britain, Yorktown was a final major defeat; for Washington, it was the crowning glory of his military career and inspired many songs about the triumphant warrior.

Washington was the figure most frequently glorified in American popular song, not only during the Revolution, but until his death in 1799; Washington's prowess as a soldier was heralded throughout the colonies shortly after the war began. Early songs cite his bravery and leadership abilities during the French and Indian War, as noted in chapter three. This reputation, no less than his Virginia citizenship, which helped to solidify support for the war in the southern colonies, was likely responsible for Washington's selection as commander in chief. American confidence in Washington is affirmed in a brief piece titled "Follow Washington," written after the battle at Trenton, which describes the soldiers' loyalty to a leader they "will obey,/Through rain or snow, by night or day."[1] A song printed in several papers and broadsides in 1775 accurately predicts Washington's future role in governing the country. Called "A New Song" in the *Virginia Gazette*, the song claims that Americans are "inspired by Washington"[2] and warns the British, "ye shall share an Asses fate, and drudge for Washington." The ordinary American soldier is proudly described as "him who humbly guides the plow," while Washington himself is "god-like," "great," "conqu'ring," and "glorious." In a clever play on names, the author writes that America must be ruled by "a George or WASHINGTON." (Washington's name appears in capital letters throughout the twelve stanzas of the song.) He concludes that Spain, France, and England's George III cannot fail to recognize Washington's superior ability.

In almost all the songs describing battles in which he took part, Washington is praised as the force behind American victories, from Trenton to Yorktown. For example, in the broadside "Washington and De Grasse, A New Song," he shares with the "Valiant"[3] French Admiral Comte De Grasse and "Warlike" General Greene the credit for the victory at Yorktown. The description of his character is unchanged from 1776; again he is contrasted with the anonymous "Patriot Sons" who helped achieve the victory. It is noteworthy that, in true democratic fashion, ordinary soldiers are mentioned in the same lines with the finest American military leader of the war. The French, called in this tune "the Blue and White," are also accorded well-deserved praise.

After the Revolution, Washington's considerable fame grew; in a 1784 song commemorating his birthday, he is called "The scourge of George and North/and tyrants all."[4] With his abilities and "honest mind," Washington is described as chiefly responsible for American liberation from English oppression. A 1788 song continues the glorification begun in 1776, again

referring to the soon-to-be president as "Godlike."[5] In song he has become
the savior of the budding nation and will henceforth deserve "virtuous praise."

One of the most famous heroes of the Revolution was Nathan Hale, pop-
ularly known for his alleged last words, "I regret that I have but one life to
give for my country." Hale was educated for the ministry at Yale, but shortly
after his 1773 graduation the war began, offering him the chance to serve in
the Connecticut Rangers with the distinguished Lieutenant Colonel Thomas
Knowlton. After Washington's fortunate strategic retreat at Long Island,
Hale volunteered to serve as a spy. Although ill-suited for the job because
of his easily recognizable scarred face, he was accepted for a mission. The
two most popular stories of his capture concern his betrayal by his cousin
Samuel Hale and his fatally mistaking a British boat for an American rescue
ship.[6]

Hale is accurately described as a captain in a song about his capture,
fittingly titled "Nathan Hale." In a rare touch in American song, the youthful
spy is described as embraced by nature, which conceals him from his enemies:
The breezes mutter 'oh Hu-ush"[7] while a thrush warns "Keep still." Hale
attempts to escape "thro' the wood." Hale's trip with his captors is made in
a "rude launch," presumably the boat he has mistaken for an American craft.
According to the tune, the imprisoned Hale's trust in God led him to believe
"In his heart, all was well," perhaps meaning that he had reconciled himself
to whatever awaited him and so was at peace with himself. Nature empathizes
with the unfortunate youth, as "An ominous owl with his solemn base voice,/
Sat moaning hard by" the doomed patriot. The "tyrant's proud minions"
are juxtaposed with the brave soldier who "must soon die."

The song states that Hale confessed his mission and was captured with
undeniable evidence of his work. The "cruel general" of the British forces
who authorized Hale's punishment, William Cunningham, would die himself
on the gallows in 1791 for forgery. If the song's account of his condemnation
of Hale can be believed, then his reputation for ferocity seems justified. His
harshness is matched by his disdain for the rebels, whose "cause [he] did
deride." Before his execution Hale was allowed a brief time to reflect on his
life and his immediate destiny: "Five minutes . . . no more" he was given to
prepare himself for death. If indeed he did pray for his mother, as the song
suggests, it was not for her welfare in this world, for she had died four years
before.[8] The British will "shudder" at the memory of Hale's death because
they will recognize in his courage the American determination to triumph.

The last stanza, containing Hale's "last words," is a curious mixture of
neo-classical form with Romantic content:

Thou pale king of terrors, thou life's gloomy foe,
Go frighten the slave, go frighten the slave;

Tell tyrants, to you, their allegiance they owe.
No fears for the brave, no fears for the brave.

This verse not only echoes Romantic sentiments toward death, written here in neo-classical form, but it also prefigures the gothic impulse in American literature. The repeated half lines in each stanza are dramatic because they imitate the slow, dull thump of footsteps to the gallows. This rare artistic tune points toward a competence in American arts that will result in an American Renaissance in the mid-nineteenth century. It is interesting that no mention is made of Hale's famous "regret"; nonetheless, the song accords Hale the stature of a folk hero. American song had achieved a new purpose: to acknowledge the sacrifice of the common soldier.

Among the most notable patriotic songs are those that record not the successes of noteworthy Americans but rather the failures of British leaders and Americans linked with them. One of the most inauspicious of these was John Burgoyne, whose defeat at Saratoga, New York, in 1777 first made Britain aware of the strength of the American rebels. The victory over Burgoyne led the Americans into a treaty with France, which helped to sustain the new republic. Burgoyne's defeat at Saratoga renewed American confidence; the rebels had defeated one of England's finest generals at the head of a major British army. Moreover, the Hessian general Baron von Riedsel lost his fearsome Hessian contingent to the Americans in a fierce wilderness conflict.

The many American songs composed after the Saratoga battle include several fine tunes and poems, the majority of which attribute the British defeat to General Burgoyne himself. Burgoyne was a man of high reputation whose interests included such diverse subjects as literature and politics. Burgoyne, a soldier's general, was a member of Parliament, a fine statesman, a playwright, and a man of ideas somewhat ahead of his era. Thus, as a man of no little fame and substance, his defeat represented a fine plume in the ragged American cap.[9]

Burgoyne's name appears in several songs, and two offer contrasting views of the American perception of this significant leader. "A song for the Red-Coats," as it is cited by Moore, is a piece also published under other titles. The song, written probably in 1777 or 1778, is classically patriotic, obviously composed to inspire the rebels as well as to commemorate their victory with unusually close attention to details such as time. It mentions such prominent American generals as Arthur St. Clair, Benedict Arnold, and Horatio Gates as well as the British generals Baum (a Hessian commander) and Burgoyne. The song consists mainly of a tribute to American bravery and fortitude; the most prominent reference to Burgoyne calls him "the king's commander."[10]

Burgoyne receives a great deal more attention in a song composed in 1777 called "Titled John. A New Song." This song also describes the battle at

Saratoga, where "mighty"[11] Burgoyne "did let the Yankees fright him." He and his army are ridiculed as cowards, for his soldiers are glad

> to yield to terms so clever;
> No doubt they all rejoice
> to quit the war forever?

Though only fragments of this satiric composition have survived, the intent of the song is clear. In the third verse Burgoyne's "Quixotic scheme" to subdue the American rebels is attributed to his desire for "promotion," but in verse four he is described as wishing to escape the battle (not necessarily in an honorable fashion) in order "to grow older." Verse six claims that "against a cause that's right," Burgoyne's eloquence is like that of "Demosthenes." (This reference is probably to Burgoyne's parliamentary speeches in defense of the Tory position.) Burgoyne's reasons for coming to America were "*Knighthood, Fame*, and *Guineas*." The British leader is urged not to worry about this failure in the 1777 campaign because his

> zeal in George's cause,
> Tho' with defeat attended,
> Will meet with his applause.

His immediate reward will be "cash in plenty" and an attendant knighthood. The song's mocking tone is supported by a unique device; in the margin opposite each stanza is a brief comment about Burgoyne, reflecting the sentiments expressed in the previous verse. For instance, some of the marginal notes read "Valiant John," "General John," "Fluent John," "Matchless John," and "Esquire John." These comments help reinforce the song's already strong satiric tone.

In "Song" Burgoyne is once again simply referred to as "Jack the King's Commander."[12] Indeed, King George had chosen him to head a British army to invade New England from Canada and to formulate a plan of attack. The song correctly claims that Burgoyne courted the king's favor by visiting him.[13] As the song delicately puts it, Burgoyne visited "Hampton Court . . . To kiss great George's Hand." Burgoyne's remarks to Parliament are scored as a "harangue" and a "grand oration." In 1777 Burgoyne issued a proclamation to the rebels famed more for its pomposity than its content. In Britain, too, figures like the English writer Horace Walpole remarked on its overblown rhetoric.[14] The song quotes the text of the proclamation concerning two subjects wildly unpopular with the former colonists, "submission" and the "Savage Bands" of Indians employed as British mercenaries. The song turns to the fate of Burgoyne's troops; their leader is mocked as "This boasted Son of Britain" and "a second Alexander," who, since he is both "humane and tender/thought it best . . . to surrender." The song concludes with more bad wishes for the enemy, hoping all British troops will meet an end "the same as here recorded."

In a song titled "The Gamester," likely written in late 1777, the flamboyant Burgoyne is portrayed as a confident card player (a recreation he indeed enjoyed).[15] The song's title is appropriate. Burgoyne gambled that his mission would result in America's surrender and thus bring an end to the war, and it is likely that Burgoyne expected his own political ambitions to be fulfilled as a result of a successful military campaign of such magnitude. If his victory had ended the war or helped bring about its conclusion, Burgoyne would likely have been credited with putting down the American rebellion; his already considerable reputation as a military leader would have been greatly enhanced. "The Gamester" summarizes the "stakes" as follows: "A great bet depending on that single game;/Dominion and honor—destruction and shame."[16] The ferocity of battle between royal forces and the dogged Americans is described metaphorically: "twas diamond cut diamond." In the final count Burgoyne lost his "hearts," and the rebels showed him that "clubs were trumps." Believing that he might be saved by reinforcements, the English leader balked at the surrender terms he had accepted. After four meetings with his commanders, Burgoyne finally agreed to capitulate.[17] This delay for discussion is mocked in the song's declaration that Burgoyne "pompously talks." Burgoyne is described as a sullen child who "Quit the game with a curse." At the final surrender, however, the general's behavior actually dignified his rank and position.[18] After the description of the battle, the remaining portion of the song is a strange composition depicting England and her king as bullies, comparing Benjamin Franklin with Moses, and praising the American forces. Only the final two lines continue the card-playing theme initiated in the middle portion of the song. The last line in particular illustrates American sentiments; the rebels want "To cut and turn up all the knaves in the pack." This allusion includes not only Burgoyne but all others who support the court and thus the king's position on the war.[19]

For Burgoyne the most unfortunate incident of his career after the defeat at Saratoga (at least as chronicled in American song) was his responsibility for the death of young Jane McCrea. Jane McCrea was a twenty-three-year-old American woman whose brothers fought for America but whose fiance served Britain with Burgoyne's army. In spite of his proclamation to Britain's Indian allies cautioning them against savagery, Burgoyne was unable to control his native charges or prevent their depredations in the wilderness. After the murder of McCrea, Burgoyne was of a mind to punish the chief villain in the crime, Wyandot Panther, but one of his commanders persuaded him to overlook the deed, claiming that the Indians might desert if Burgoyne pressed the matter. General Gates presented the American view of the case in a strongly worded letter to Burgoyne critical of his use of Indian mercenaries and his handling of Indian atrocities, citing in particular the McCrea matter.[20]

"The Ballad of Jane McCrea" is a vague, Romantic song, featuring, as did the one on Nathan Hale, much nature imagery. The song opens with a warning about "the Indians in the van/And the Hessians in the rear."[21] Natural images are invoked in the phrases "brilliant autumn," "the eagle," "the gray wolf," and "the cool spring." Into this rich, lovely atmosphere "bold Burgoyne" brings his forces "to do battle with the people"; his employment of Indians might well have turned some Americans toward the patriot cause who might otherwise have been neutral or even sympathetic to Britain. With the stage set for tragedy, Jane awaits her lover, unaware of her fate but naively certain that "her lover's name would guard her" from harm. Jane's fiancé, David Jones, is described as a sensitive, reflective soul[22] who "thought about the madness/And the fury of the strife."

Eager to protect Jane from the possibility of harm, Jones sends an Indian messenger with a letter instructing her to come to him under the protection of the friendly Indians he has sent to her. A lone survivor of Jane's Indian escort watches helplessly as another band of Indians captures Jane and slaughters her, taking her scalp as a trophy. She dies with a mysterious joy appropriate to the Romantic nature of the song, expiring as she "breathed her lover's name,/Blessed him with her last sigh." One verse describes Jones' reaction when he is given the scalp, which he recognizes as Jane's:

> He received it, cold as stone,
> With a ghastly stupid stare;
> Shook not, sighed not, asked not,
> Oh, he knew that yellow hair!
> And he never smiled again,
> Nor never did he weep;
> And he never spoke her name aloud
> Save when muttering in his sleep.

This verse is unique among colonial war songs in that it artistically recounts the personal impact of the death of a loved one. No date of authorship is available for this song, but this version may well have been written some time after the Revolution, since it is clearly marked by Romantic conventions (including a description of the place of death, replete with nature imagery). Even if this particular version postdates the Revolution, it is likely modelled on one or more similar tunes composed at the time of the incident. If this ballad is a post-war composition, it is an indication of the lingering sense of tragedy that remained after Jane's death. The song ends on a melancholy note: "Beauty, innocence, and youth/Died in hapless Jane McCrea."

Jane McCrea became a symbol in the New England mind; her untimely end represented the tragedy perpetrated on Americans by British mercenary soldiers, the Hessians, and Indians. According to historians John Fiske and

George Trevelyan, her death inspired New Englanders to defend their country more vigorously than ever. Because of the melodramatic nature of her death, it might well have fed the anger that impelled Americans to victory over Burgoyne and his paid allies at Saratoga.[23]

One of the most complex stories of the war is the tale of American general Benedict Arnold. The story of Benedict Arnold's treasonous attempt to surrender the fort at West Point in exchange for 10,000 pounds and a British command is one of the most well known episodes of the war, and it seems certain that Arnold should have been made the subject of a number of derisive songs. No specific song about Arnold's treason seems to exist, though at least one poem villified his character after the event; Arnold received favorable if slight mention in a few songs written before his controversial actions of 1780.[24]

It is interesting to note, however, that songs were written about other figures who took part in either Arnold's treason or his capture. Major John André, the British spy who served as Arnold's contact with General Henry Clinton, was later executed for his part in the conspiracy; John Paulding was the New York militiaman who captured André. Both are treated in the 1780 song, "Death of Major André," subtitled "Brave Paulding and the Spy." The song begins with a brief description of Paulding's background; Paulding was erroneously called "John Spaulding"[25] in a broadside version of the song probably published immediately after André's death. The young patriot, "whose age was twenty-two,"[26] had been once captured by the British but "soon . . . ran away." The young man then returned to the American side and again took up arms in New York. As the song states, André was indeed stopped near Tarrytown by three New York militiamen, Paulding, Isaac Van Ward, and David Williams, who were watching the road. When André first encountered the three men, he believed them to be Loyalists. In the song (which, unusually, features much conversation), he remarks to them, "You're of British cheer"; "the young hero," Paulding, suspiciously inquires, "Sir, tell us where you're going,/And also, whence you came?" André replies that he represents "the British flag," a statement that confirms for the trio that "he was a spy." They further verify their suspicions by searching their prisoner, finding enemy papers hidden upon him. In addition, he bears Arnold's pass for an American called John Anderson, which he tried to use upon realizing that his questioners were American. The song indicates, as historian Carl Van Doren confirms, that André offered his captors payment for his freedom and promised them an additional sum when he reached his destination.[27] The song emphasizes the unselfish nature of the rebels in Paulding's reply: "I want not the gold and silver." Paulding offers André his freedom if he can best the young American in face-to-face combat. André politely refuses on the grounds that "the time . . . is improper," perhaps because the contest is not on the field of battle. After his capture, André wishes

to write
A line to General Arnold,
to let him know his fate,
and beg for his assistance.

In fact, André wrote to Washington informing him of his true identity
and his mission, without revealing Arnold's name. The request to write to
Arnold would not have been logical as it is represented in the song, since it
would surely have provoked the Americans' suspicions. As it happened,
messengers were on their separate ways to both Arnold and Washington
with news of the treasonous plot André had revealed, creating for the two
unsuspecting principals a contest of speed which Arnold would ultimately
win by a hair's breadth, allowing him to escape with his life.[28]

The final verses lament "poor Major André," who was hanged as a spy.
He is represented by the sympathetic composer as a man "meek and mild"
with a pleasant smile. His death "moved each eye with pity/[and] Caus'd
every heart to bleed," while Arnold's name was heaped with disgrace. Many
Americans "wish'd him released/and Arnold in his stead." He probably
would have saved his own life had he followed Clinton's orders and disre-
garded Arnold's request to dress in civilian clothes.[29]

Washington, angry with Arnold's betrayal, ordered Arnold kidnapped and
brought back alive to American lines. He relied on the dragoon Colonel
Henry Lee to supply him with a man for the job, and the hero of the ballad
"Sergeant Champe" was provided. After devising a plan, Lee sent the athletic
young John Champe on his mission. The first and major portion of the song
details Champe's antics on horseback after his pretended desertion from the
rebel army and escape toward British lines. Since Lee apparently wrote his
memoirs long after this episode, his account may contain a mixture of fact
and imagination. It is, however, Lee's account that provides history with
some of the details of this unusual story. Lee's memoirs, for example, describe
the heated and sometimes confusing chase of Champe by his own troops,
who were unaware of the sergeant's assignment.[30] According to the song,
Champe owed his escape, as might be expected of a dragoon, to the superior
qualities of his horse, "old Rip."[31] Upon reaching British lines, Champe was
taken to Clinton. The British general, called with good-natured contempt
"Sir Hal," is taken in by the sergeant's ruse; Clinton has the would-be
kidnapper taken to Arnold. With glee, "Arnold grinn'ed and rubbed his
hands" at "the recent prank." Arnold was, in American eyes, also congrat-
ulating himself on attracting a following of deserters, of which Champe would
be the first. Although Champe had carefully planned his moves and Arnold
was not aware that "Champe was all the while/A taking of his measure," the
plan failed when the "British fleet set sail." The song follows Lee's re-
membrances in mentioning Champe's ill-timed and unexpected voyage to
Virginia, where he "join'd his friends/Among the picininni," probably mean-

ing that slaves friendly to the American cause hid Champe from British forces. He finally escaped into Virginia and later slipped into North Carolina, where he rejoined American forces. The song closes by lamenting André's untimely end, blaming Arnold for "André's fame." The ballad has one peculiar but insightfully humorous note. The "troopers" who lost the fleeing Champe did not return immediately to camp but stopped to enjoy "gingerbread/and cider from the neighbors." This reference to rural New Yorkers indicates some support of rebel forces in a divided state. When the "cornet" conducting the operation returns to Lee, he tells all with the exception "of the cider."

Arnold's escape was soon put aside when Americans began to fight successfully against Lord Charles Cornwallis in the South. After some initial victories against the Americans, Cornwallis slowly but surely worked himself into an inextricable position in Virginia, which resulted in his dramatic surrender at Yorktown.

Cornwallis began his long army career as an ensign; after twenty-two years he had attained the rank of lieutenant general. He served in the House of Lords as a Whig and offered some support to the Americans in their prewar struggle against taxation. He was a thoughtful, compassionate man of great physical vigor, and in battle he was fearless.[32]

In America Cornwallis was not met with the derision and outright hatred that greeted some British commanders like Gage. Under the circumstances, he was treated rather gently in American song. In "Cornwallis Burgoyned" Cornwallis' surrender at Yorktown is compared with Burgoyne's humiliating defeat at Saratoga. At the start of the campaign in Virginia, Cornwallis believed "he would soon her conquerer be,"[33] as did Lord North ("So was North's opinion"). His past successes contributed to his false sense of security "till quite elate with martial pride,/he thought all dangers o'er." Cornwallis' position became clear in the course of the battle until, like Burgoyne before him, he "cursed his fate." Finally, like a true gentleman, "his martial pride he laid aside,/And cased the British standard." For the first time in American song, "the glorious end of war" is celebrated.

In "The Dance, A Ballad, to the tune of Yankey Doodle" (see appendix), Cornwallis is compared to a dancer worn to weariness by a clever but contrary partner. Cornwallis' position is parodied in a song that consistently and smoothly preserves the metaphor of the dance with relation to Cornwallis' southern campaign (the treatment is similar to that of Burgoyne in "The Gamester"). His offensive position at the start of his march is in the first line: "Cornwallis led a country dance"[34] (likely an allusion to the many skirmishes fought in the wilderness). The British general's dance appears to be uncontrolled as he moves about the dance floor of the American South, changing partners, but never finding a satisfactory companion. After rounds with Generals Greene and Layfayette, Cornwallis decides that his best dance is a

parade
on park's smooth green,
Or a masquerade.

He favors the "red heels" and "long lac'd skirts," and reference to the Continental battle formation; he prefers a formal ball to the "hunting skirts" of the rugged American from the backwoods who shot at his formations from behind trees. Seeking his own terms of combat, he challenges the rebels to a "minuet or all'mande." Cornwallis draws three willing partners in Comte De Grasse, General Rochambeau, and General Washington, whose "gentle movements soon confound/the Earl as they draw near." Finally "his feet can move no more," and Cornwallis and his forces "must pay the piper." This artful tune gracefully mirrors the intricacies of military strategy and troop movements in the subtle rhythms of the dance.

With the exception of Washington, the American personal ballad featured a strange and unlikely cast of characters. Major American heroes like Nathaniel Greene and Anthony Wayne are praised, but only in passing. Instead, relatively minor figures like Nathan Hale, Jane McCrea, and John Champe have been made famous in American song. Only the predictable candidates among the British generals appear in American music, however, probably because their defeats were so important to American morale. Why is this peculiar assortment of personalities celebrated in the rebel war song? Perhaps the most likely answer is that all share one characteristic. Each of these characters is subjected to sudden and often capricious twists of fate: a tragic death, a fall from greatness, or the frustration of a heroic mission by an unforeseen circumstance. Of all the major figures in American war music, only Washington is consistently praised.

The second notable characteristic of the American ballad is its emergent literary quality. "Nathan Hale," "The Ballad of Jane McCrea," and "The Dance," in particular, mark the growing artistic impulse in American composition. In "Nathan Hale" and "The Ballad of Jane McCrea," a new, Romantic sensibility is exposed. Tragedy and the use of nature are the two literary characteristics shared by these songs. In "Nathan Hale" nature is sympathetic with Hale's plight but cannot directly help him. In Hale's case evil has temporarily won a victory over good, but ultimately Hale's brave sacrifice will only serve to fan the flames of liberty. Hale's personal tragedy therefore becomes a gloriously Romantic triumph because it shows the magnitude of the patriot spirit, victorious over death. Jane McCrea's death offers no evidence of heroic sacrifice; she is a true tragic figure. Nothing comes from her death but her lover's shock and anguish. The song closes with a sense of loss softened only by its contrast with a peaceful nature.

In "The Dance" fitting metaphor is consistently employed with a clever and mildly humorous effect. The tone of the song is carefully controlled, indicating a high degree of artistry. "The Dance" does not villify Cornwallis.

Instead, he appears as a foppish character who is contrasted with the humble Americans dressed in homespun clothes. Yet the simple rebels and their French allies manage to control Cornwallis as if their dance had hypnotized him. The artistically detached author does not dramatically conclude his song but smoothly brings it to an end, somehow leading the reader to believe that the conclusion of the battle at Yorktown was predetermined.

Although these three songs are distinctly different from other American war songs written during the Revolution, they are closely related to the traditional English ballad. For the first time American composers had skillfully adapted the ballad form to the content of the war song. The revolution that created an independent nation thus contributed to the early growth of American music.

NOTES

1. "Follow Washington," reprinted in Edward Arthur Dolph, ed., *"Sound Off!"*: *Soldier Songs from the Revolution to World War II* (New York: Farrar and Rinehart, 1942), p. 498.
2. "A New Song," *Virginia Gazette*, 24 February 1776.
3. "Washington and DeGrasse," a broadside reprinted in Vera Brodsky Lawrence, *Music for Patriots, Politicians, and Presidents: Harmonies and Discords of the First Hundred Years* (New York: Macmillan, 1975), p. 90.
4. Untitled song, reprinted in Lawrence, 96.
5. Untitled song, "Hail Godlike Washington," reprinted in Lawrence, 96.
6. Tristram P. Coffin, *Uncertain Glory: Folklore and the American Revolution* (Detroit: Folklore Association, 1971), pp. 164–166.
7. "Nathan Hale," reprinted in Frank Moore, *Songs and Ballads of the American Revolution* (Port Washington, N.Y.: Kennikat Press, 1964; originally published in 1855), pp. 37–39.
8. Coffin, 65.
9. Christopher Ward, *The War of the Revolution*, ed. John Richard Alden (New York: Macmillan, 1952), 1:60–61.
10. "A Song for the Red-Coats," reprinted in Moore, 176–184.
11. "Titled John. A New Song," *Boston Gazette*, 23 November 1778.
12. "Song," *Boston Gazette*, 1 December 1777.
13. Ward, 1:399–400.
14. Ibid., 1:404–405.
15. Willard M. Wallace, *Appeal to Arms: A Military History of the American Revolution* (Chicago: Quadrangle Books, 1964), p. 165.
16. "The Gamester," reprinted in Moore, 191–194.
17. Ward, 2:537–538.
18. Wallace, 167.
19. Moore's note, 195.
20. Ward, 2:496–497.
21. "The Ballad of Jane McCrea," reprinted in Harold W. Thompson, *Body, Boots,*

and Britches: Folktales, Ballads, and Speech from Country New York (Syracuse, N.Y.: Syracuse University Press, 1979), pp. 328–333.

22. Ibid., 326.

23. Ward, 2:497–498.

24. Wallace, 221–222.

25. "Death of Major André," a broadside reprinted in Ola Elizabeth Winslow, ed. *American Broadside Verse* (New Haven, Conn.: Yale University Press, 1930), p. 157.

26. "Brave Paulding and the Spy," reprinted in Moore, 316–321.

27. Carl Van Doren, *Secret History of the American Revolution* (New York: Viking Press, 1968), p. 340.

28. Ibid., 342–346.

29. Wallace, 233.

30. Van Doren, 392–393.

31. "Sergeant Champe," reprinted in Moore, 322–329.

32. Ward, 1:382–383.

33. "Cornwallis Burgoyned," reprinted in Moore, 368–369.

34. "The Dance," *Pennsylvania Packet*, 27 November 1781.

4

Star-Spangled Melodies

Although the newly formed United States signed a peace treaty with Britain to end the American Revolution in 1783, feelings between the two powers remained somewhat strained. The provisions of the Treaty of Paris were not completely honored by either nation, and American ministers to Britain were often treated with the disdain that a mighty power reserves for an insignificant one. Jay's Treaty of 1794 did not solve the problems between the two countries, although it did help ease the relationship between the United States and the former mother country during John Adams' administration.[1] France, America's Revolutionary War ally, created difficulties in the 1790s, first in an unofficial war over American commercial rights and again after 1800 as a result of Napoleon's battle with England for European supremacy. Thus the early years of the nineteenth century saw the United States caught in the struggle between the two most powerful nations in the world. Not only was American commercial freedom and prosperity threatened by this conflict between the military giants, but sailors' personal rights were violated by English sea captains who did not hesitate to remove from American ships those sailors they deemed English deserters. Of course the Royal Navy sometimes made errors using this policy; some American seamen were forcibly employed in the British service. In the years following 1803, the number of impressments of American sailors rose rapidly, as did American outrage with British indifference to this procedure.[2]

The difficulties of finding qualified seamen, punishing deserters, and discouraging desertion were the most serious problems facing the undermanned Royal Navy.[3] An official English government measure helped to foster the impressment dispute; orders in Council forbade neutral ships to trade in enemy ports (meaning those of France), and consequently British captains often stopped ships apparently bound for those destinations, using this tactic to "recruit" sailors for British vessels. Napoleon's decrees prohibiting trade with England, a measure intended to close the European continent to England, merely served further to curtail American freedom of the seas and presented the United States with discomforting commercial restrictions.

Under this intense pressure two important incidents occurred involving the American and British navies. The first of these conflicts took place near Norfolk, Virginia, in June 1807. The British frigate *Leopard* stopped the American frigate *Chesapeake* to search that vessel for deserters, but the American captain refused to allow the search. The *Leopard* then fired on the *Chesapeake*, killing and wounding several sailors. After the crippled American boat surrendered, the British search party impressed four men. Americans were naturally incensed over British actions, and British-American relations remained tense until 1812.[4] In 1811 the American navy repaid the insult to national pride in an exchange between the United States frigate *President* and the British corvette *Little Belt*. The American ship, on a mission to protect commercial vessels from British harassment, spotted the *Little Belt* and mistook her for the powerful frigate *Guerrière*. Darkness and confusion resulted in a battle that lasted less than an hour, and more than thirty seamen on the British vessel were killed or injured. The *Little Belt* affair helped to prepare the Americans psychologically for war.[5]

The most prominent theme in liberty and war songs written during the War of 1812 is the conflict between a fledgling United States representing the ideal of freedom and powerful Britain representing European corruption. Many songs written during the struggle either explicitly or implicitly contain this theme.

The evident ability of the small United States to contest British might is found in the largest and most important category of songs, those treating naval combat. Some American songs, in fact, were composed prior to the declaration of war. Naval victories were especially important to Americans because Britain's fleet represented her claim to world power. The first type of naval song, which treats ship-to-ship combat, reflects America's pride in her ability to defeat the finest British vessels. The second type of naval song is a general victory song, usually reciting past victories or celebrating American seamanship. The third and final type of naval song praises American sailors for their fresh-water victories.

The second type of song discussed in this chapter, the liberty song, was prominently featured in the War of 1812. The war gave birth to "The Star-Spangled Banner," a song that eventually became the United States national anthem. Although many similar liberty pieces were written, Francis Scott Key's song won a place in history as one of America's best-known tunes. Two unusual liberty songs written during the war warn Americans to beware of their unpatriotic fellow citizens who would betray the republic and sell American liberty to Britain.

A third type of song written during the War of 1812 was the personal ballad; few were written about soldiers but those that were are unusual and interesting. A melancholy ballad was written about James Bird, a deserter who served under Oliver Hazard Perry during the dramatic Battle of Lake Erie. James Wilkinson, a general whose connections with Spain gave him an unsavory reputation, is the hero of another ballad. Andrew Jackson, America's most celebrated hero from the War of 1812, is the subject of several songs, most of them inspired by his victory at New Orleans after the war had formally ended. One of them, "The Hunters of Kentucky," became a well-known song because of its use in the 1828 presidential campaign. With the exception of Jackson, much of the glory in songs composed during the War of 1812 is reserved for American seamen.

The first songs written about the naval conflict with Britain are filled with praise for the sailor's life and the glory of the *President's* victory over the *Little Belt*. A piece titled "Naval Recruiting Song," probably published in 1811, showed not only the writer's enthusiasm for combat, but also indicated the immediate need for sailors to man American naval vessels. The first line of the song refers to the *President* but does not describe the action between the American ship and the *Little Belt*. A poem printed as a companion piece in the original broadside also alludes to the encounter. The tone of "Naval Recruiting Song" is carefree, and the piece promises adventure and glory without describing the hazards of naval combat. The mood of the song is captured in the first two lines of the chorus: "With a light heart we'll sail away jolly boys,/In search of good fortune to go."[6]

An 1811 song entitled "Rodgers and Victory" is a standard battle piece of the period appropriately set to the tune of "Yankee Doodle." In it the British, called "John Bull"[7] (a figure symbolic of England), are condemned as enemies who "kill and press" innocent American sailors. The *Chesapeake* incident is mentioned, as are two other minor British attacks that receive cursory attention. The Americans, "finding injuries prolong'd," are finally avenged under Commodore John Rodgers, "who whipped the Turks"—a reference to Rodgers' service in the conflict with the Barbary coast pirates of Africa.[8] According to the song, the *President's* battle with the *Little Belt* began when Rodgers hailed the British ship and she "with a gun . . . quick replied." The song states that the British vessel "struck" and then was given "leave to go"; more than likely the song exaggerates the American victory because the *Little Belt* apparently broke off the fight and fled into the night.[9]

A unique French-dialect song, also titled "Rodgers and Victory," ostensibly put in the mouth of Napoleon's barber, also treats Rodgers' victory over the *Little Belt*. The dialect is fairly well done in spots, and the humorous touches are effective. Set to the melody "Yankee Doodle," the song remarks on British ineffectiveness against the Americans, and Britain is ultimately called "a ninny."[10] The angered Rodgers and his crew fire telling cannon shots "stronger than French brandy." The use of a French character to relate Rodgers' victory might well have been the composer's ploy to remind the sometimes troublesome French that America had an effective navy.

Naval songs about battles that took place after the declaration of war fall into three categories, two of which correspond (predictably) to significant American victories. The first group treats the fierce single-ship battles that were responsible for most of the American victories in the first year of the war. One such battle was the encounter between the *Constitution* and the *Guerrière*, about which many poems and songs were composed. Most of these pieces tell the same story in essentially the same fashion. For example, in the lively "The American Constitution Frigate's Engagements with the British Frigate *Guerrière*," the *Constitution* is glorified, the American captain, Isaac Hull, is saluted, the British captain, James Dacres, is ridiculed, and American seamanship is lauded. The song also traces the history of the *Constitution* from its departure upon completion of construction to its conquest of the *Guerrière*. The song describes the ship's dramatic escape from a threatening British squadron: "five British ships/unto her gave a chace [sic]".[11] It tells how Hull's masterful handling of his ship and crew in a difficult situation (a few minutes' lost time and a few hundred yards' distance could have meant capture) saved his reputation and his boat. On a still sea, tactics such as wetting his boat's sails and discharging 20,000 pounds of drinking water enabled Hull to escape the desperate "quips and cranks" of his pursuers. According to the song, the *Guerrière* was defeated within "half an hour." Historian Alfred T. Mahan's account of the action indicates that this time span is fairly accurate. He says that the battle was initiated at 6:00 P.M. on 19 August 1812 and by 6:30 the British frigate was completely crippled; the *Constitution* moved away from the immediate battle area to make repairs and at 7:00 P.M. was again ready for action. At that time the *Guerrière*, under "poor Dacres," surrendered to the American ship.[12] The American sailors are described as a "noble crew" of whose accomplishments American women will be proud: "Our girls with smiles shall greet us."

This victory and successive American triumphs inspired scores of such songs. No matter how inconsequential the victory, American valor was praised and British seamanship was discredited. The best of these songs are characterized by at least one unconventional feature; for instance, a song entitled "Cash in Hand" celebrates the unusual capture of a packet vessel carrying a large amount of gold, a victory celebrated in the repeated phrase "jingling cash."[13] The composer makes a play on the British boat's name, declaring that Commodore Rodgers "will give [them] pills/the British cannot *Swallow*." In another song, "*Wasp* Stinging *Frolic*" an insect metaphor (suggested by the name of the American boat) is used to describe the encounter between the American *Wasp* and the British *Frolic* in 1812. The American vessel is compared to an angry wasp whose sting has crippled the British sloop. Both sloops were slowed by the combat, and the victorious American boat and its prize were consequently taken by the seventy-four gun British vessel *Poictiers*, a fact noted in several contemporary poems. Nonethelss, the song closes with the hope that "our Navy will have a few *Frolics* more."[14]

Unfortunately for the Americans, the *Wasp* was sent to sting her former masters when she was commissioned as a British warship.[15]

The undated ballad "The *United States* and the *Macedonian*" commemorates the victory of the American frigate *United States* over its British counterpart, *Macedonian*, in 1812. The song offers some standard American sentiments in its glorification of "brave Yankee boys"[16] fighting for "free trade and sailor's rights," a widely used slogan. The song also includes references to military and naval devices not mentioned in other American war songs, such as "tompions," wooden plugs used as wadding in some muzzle-loading guns,[17] and "chain-shot, grape, and langrage." Langrage is a shot of irregular size designed to destroy rigging and sails. Chain shot features a chain suspended between two missles. Grape shot is composed of a number of grape-sized shots loaded into one shell.[18] It is significant that the greatest damage in the encounter was to the *Macedonian*'s sails and rigging; indeed, it was this damage that forced her to surrender.[19] The two ships' respective casualty figures reflect the amount of physical damage each suffered. Describing the casualties, the song tells that "ten to one their blood was spilled," which is roughly accurate; the Americans reported twelve men killed or wounded, while the British lost approximately 100 men.[20] *United States* commander Stephen Decatur knew the propaganda value of his capture of an important British warship and so brought the "noble prize" into port as a tribute to American seamanship.[21]

By the time the *Constitution* under Commodore William Bainbridge met the British frigate *Java* on 29 December 1812, American songwriters were already compiling long lists of American victories in their ballads. A group of these conquests, including some of those discussed above, are given cursory treatment in an undated broadside titled "Bainbridge's Victory or Huzza for the *Constitution*, Once More." The unusual feature of this song is not its catalogue, but the metaphorical treatment of the *Java* as a loose woman; the British boat is rudely described as "a brazen-faced hussey."[22] The metaphor is continued in the following stanza with the curt reference to the enemy vessel as "Miss *Java*," roughly handled by the Americans who "cut up her dress." In another ironic reference to a well-known British symbol, the bulldog, the American composer declares, "and now did our bulldogs most merrily bark." In song Americans did occasionally call themselves "bulldogs," probably to irritate their enemies.

After the American ship *Hornet* defeated the *Peacock* on 24 February 1812, the United States Navy had no major single-ship victory for fifteen months. The American triumphs in one-to-one combat ended for two reasons. First, after a number of shocking losses, the British Admirality ordered its commanders to avoid single-ship encounters with American vessels of corresponding strength; British ships were organized into combat squadrons to discourage bold American hunters. Second, the British blockade effectively bottled up most of the powerful American frigates in or near port. Only

Captain David Porter and his lightly armed vessel created problems for British shipping with his attacks on English whaling fleets; later, however, his ship was captured.[23] Another American captain attempted to reestablish the American reputation for single-ship combat in spite of the blockade; his mission resulted in a fierce and futile battle against a well-prepared British captain and crew. The experienced American commander James Lawrence sailed out of blockaded Boston in the *Chesapeake* on 1 June 1813. At sea Lawrence engaged the British commander Philip Vere Broke of the *Shannon* and his well-drilled crew in ship-to-ship combat. Broke had earlier issued a sharp challenge to Lawrence, who had not received it; nonetheless, the two aggressive seamen found each other just outside of Boston. Broke and his men quickly outmaneuvered and outgunned the Americans. Lawrence was mortally wounded in the encounter, and the American vessel surrendered after about fifteen minutes.[24]

The battle resulted in patriotic compositions on both sides of the Atlantic, sad and angry songs from the Americans and jubilant songs from the British, the latter much like earlier American victory songs. A "Song," ostensibly written by a sailor on the frigate *Constitution*, is a melancholy piece set appropriately enough to the melody "The Disconsolate Sailor." The song praises the sacrifice of "brave Lawrence"[25] and Charles Ludlow, his second in command. In contrast, the composer cites various examples of British malice. He reminds Americans of

> those fields that were ravag'd,
> those town that were fir'd;
> [and] . . . those wrongs which your females endur'd.

The song ends on a rare egalitarian note in the final two lines, which may reflect the author's opposition to slavery. The lines read, "what'ere be man's tenets, his fortune, his hue,/He is a man and therefore shall be free."

A second song published under the imposing title "Offset for the *Chesapeake*, or the Capture of Fort George, and Repulse of the Enemy from Sackett's Harbor" describes the American dismay at the British victory, but declares that the loss of the *Chesapeake* has been avenged. The composer probably expressed the feelings of many Americans in the lines, "We wonder'd, besure, for we ne'er saw the like,/That a Yankee should e'er to an Englishman strike."[26] Despite their loss, Americans could draw inspiration from Lawrence's last words, "Don't give up the ship. Fight her 'till she sinks,"[27] which are echoed in the song: "Lawrence . . . would ne'er think/Of striking 'till his frigate should sink." (The *Chesapeake* did not sink, but was taken by a British boarding party.) The Americans have evened the score, the author claims, because "to balance the ship, we have taken a fort." The reference is to the capture of Fort George and the defense of Sackett's Harbor, which (peculiarly enough) took place in late May, before the loss of the *Chesapeake* on 1 June

1813. Also, it must be noted that both Fort George and Sackett's Harbor were on the American side of Lake Ontario and thus the actions there constituted, respectively, a recovery of United States territory and the defense of an American fort. The song optimistically declares that Americans will triumph because of their love of freedom and prophesies that "Canadians shall gladly share." The prophecy, of course, has never been fulfilled. In the song America's inability to take Canada from the British is attributed to the fact that Britain has gained her victories "not by fair play." But "Columbians" will finally win the war because they are "brave, generous, and noble, and happy and free."

The British, who for so long endured ridicule in numerous American war songs, quickly responded with a song of their own, probably rousingly sung by British tars. "*Shannon* and *Chesapeake*" is modeled on American naval songs (with which English sailors were probably familiar), even to the point of making telling use of the tune "Yankee Doodle." The song mocks the American spectators of the battle, who "came out to see the sport."[28] The onlookers did not see what they expected; the British composer notes that while the American ship was suffering a disastrous defeat, "the bands were playing 'Yankee Doodle Dandy.' " Actually, it is unlikely that anyone on shore could see the combat because, as Mahan states, the British captain "stood out to sea" between Cape Cod and Cape Ann; the battle took place at a distance from the position initially taken by Broke to show the *Shannon* to Lawrence. Had the battle taken place on a relatively calm sea on a clear day, the distance of the ships from port would still have rendered observation of the battle nearly impossible.[29] The song also describes American boasts of victory before the battle. In the song American sailors claim that "after [the conquest] they'd dine,/[and] treat their sweethearts with wine." But the Americans lost their courage in the fight, for "from their guns they run" before the British "hearts of oak." The phrase "hearts of oak" represents the British regard for themselves; it is also the title of a well-known English patriotic melody. The author also takes this occasion to counter American composers' claims that American seamen excel Britons in romance and battle skills; he declares

> that in fighting and in love
> the true British sailor
> is the dandy.

During the lull in open-sea victories, a second form of American naval song appeared. Many of the songs of this period (early 1813), like the tune titled "Stanzas," simply recount in brief, general terms the major sea victories achieved in the early period of the war by the once formidable "MOSQUITOE FLEET." "Stanzas" compares Decatur with Caesar; the brave American captain might well say of his victory over the British *Macedonian*, "veni, vidi, vici."[30] "Yankee Tars," published in 1813, also recapitulates some of the major American victories, but its significance to the development of the American song lies in its melody and its use of Romantic conceits. The song borrows the old melody "Derry Down," an English tune sung often during the Revolution; it may have supplied the melody for "The World Turned Upside Down," the song played at Cornwallis' surrender to Washington at Yorktown. Second, "Yankee Tars" makes use of definite Romantic conventions such as the treatment of Nature as a deity. This "Nature, kind goddess,"[31] is America's patron, who "one fav'rite land with all blessings endowed." Through her guidance, the United States has reached the pinnacle of civilization; this favored country is "the asylum of laws—/The refuge of Liberty, Science, and Arts." Another song in the same category is "Yankee Thunders," published in 1813. The song is somewhat lofty in tone and, as the title indicates, emphasizes America's military power. It does give credit to the defeated British sailors, who are called "bolder warriors" and "braver seamen."[32] Unfortunately, they must surrender to the superior Americans. Most other general war songs are like "Yankee Frolics," which avers: "No more of your blathering nonsense/'Bout the Nelsons of old Johnnie Bull."[33]

The third type of sailor's song about fresh water battles appeared in 1814. The first of these victories was also the most musically celebrated; Oliver H. Perry's victory over British captain R. H. Barclay on Lake Erie on 10 September 1814 produced a new American hero for the slowly growing pantheon. Captain Perry led his men to victory over the British fleet with a combination of luck, skill, daring, and the poor judgment of his English opponent. Barclay's failure to act against Perry's fleet while it crossed a sand bar into the lake proper was the first British mistake. Barclay had ceased to follow American movements before the crossing, when the American squadron was most vulnerable. When Barclay finally arrived, much of the American flotilla was already on Erie; his own fleet was too ill-fitted to attack the Americans, and he retired. But the aggressive Perry sought him out and fought him on a windy day, with a breeze favoring the American attack.[34]

"The Battle of Lake Erie" is primarily distinguished by its unique form. The song consists of four verses alternating with four short prose passages. It contains historical narrative intertwined with the usual praise for American valor, paying special tribute to Perry. In the first stanza the position of the *Lawrence*, Perry's flagship (named for the ill-fated commander of the *Chesapeake*), is correctly described, for it was indeed the boat that "led on the van."[35] As the prose section correctly notes, the "*Lawrence* fought on until she was completely disabled."[36] Most historians of the War of 1812, especially Mahan and C. S. Forester, disagree with some of the statements made in the second verse. For example, the *Niagara*, one of the largest boats in the American fleet, did not create "destruction around her" until Perry took command of the ship after his own was disabled. Whether "Elliot led so boldly" is a matter of much dispute. Lieutenant Elliot, appointed commander of the *Niagara* by Perry, apparently hung back from the battle (Mahan has documented this fact in detail).[37] The second prose section is generally faithful to historical fact in its statement that Perry "board[ed] the *Niagara* with a determination to conquer or die." Fortunately, he was able to find an undamaged life boat on the crippled *Lawrence* and under heavy fire safely made his way to the *Niagara*. The one object that he took with him when he abandoned the *Lawrence*, the ship's flag, is perhaps the best indication of his determination. Ironically, the flag was emblazoned with James Lawrence's famous last words, "Don't Give up the Ship." However, Perry did give up the crippled flagship, but only for the purpose of continuing the battle. Perry then took the *Niagara* into combat against the largest British vessels, the *Queen Charlotte* and the newly built *Detroit*. His determination, combined with solid gunnery from his crew, carried the day.[38] As the composer declares, in a play on Perry's name ("perry" is a strong drink derived from fermented pears),[39] "They [the British became] all drunk adrinking [and] down went their flags."

The ballad "American Perry: A Song" is perhaps the most interesting song written about the battle; it contains a number of puns on Perry's name, but the purpose of the song is to provide a broad description of the action at Erie. In the song the British claim that they are "tir'd of Jamaica and Sherry"[40] and want something spicier, like the "taste of American Perry." The song adds a problematical detail to what is known about the British-Indian allies. The author asserts that during the naval contest, "the Indians on shore/made a horrible roar." While their shouting might not have occurred then, it likely did later when they fought fiercely in a devastating defeat by American forces. Perry's victory allowed General William Henry Harrison to move against the British under General Henry Proctor and defeat them at the Battle of the Thames in Canada on 5 October 1813. Proctor's force included a large contingent of Indians under the powerful Shawnee chief Tecumseh. The Americans killed the Shawnee leader during the battle, destroying the effective British-Indian coalition and driving the British back into Canada.[41]

Two other songs celebrating Perry's victory are also noteworthy. Though it does not describe the action in any detail, "Brilliant Naval Victory," published in a broadside in 1814, names the boats in the American fleet, offering a word or two of praise for each ship. The second song, "Naval Victory on Lake Erie," also written in 1814, does not name each boat in Perry's fleet, but it does commend earlier victories.

This ballad also offers one piece of intelligence information, an unusual revelation in war songs. The final lines of one of the last stanzas read: "[The British] will pour down their troops, thro' the Canadas all,/and make winter-Quarters at Isle Montreal."[42] As the song correctly states, the British did indeed move south; they had planned a campaign in 1814 to move from Canada through New York, although not necessarily by way of Montreal. To carry out this plan, the British government ordered Sir George Prevost to attack Plattsburgh with his force of about 11,000 men. After some delay

Prevost finally launched his attack on 1 September 1814. Prevost's goal was to capture Plattsburgh while a small naval squadron under Captain George Downie secured Plattsburgh Bay. The town was defended by General Alexander Macomb, who was holding Plattsburgh with a small and unimpressive force (approximately 3,000 men), mostly composed of local militia units. The American fleet on Plattsburgh Bay was commanded by Lieutenant Thomas Macdonough and roughly equaled Downie's squadron in fighting capability.[43]

The two most notable songs written about this American victory do not provide any detailed descriptions of the actual fighting. "The Battle of Plattsburgh," composed in 1814 and sung to the old Scots melody "Banks of the Dee," mentions only the names of the American leaders and the occupations of the defenders: "M'Comb, and M'Donough/the farmer, soldier, sailor, and gunner,"[44] indicating that a diverse collection of Americans was hurried into battle. The striking feature of this tune is the speaker's persona; unlike the Revolutionary War tunes "A Song Made by a Dutch Lady at the Hague" and "The Ballad of Jane McCrea," "The Battle of Plattsburgh" is clearly narrated by a woman. Like many traditional folk songs, "The Battle of Plattsburgh" focuses on a young woman's concern for her sweetheart's safety and excludes details about the battle in which "Sandy" is involved.

A second song written about the fight at Plattsburgh is a black-dialect piece composed several years before the rise of the minstrel show, which popularized the dialect form.[45] The dialect is less sophisticated than that of later tunes in this genre, but it does offer a white man's conception of black speech. For example, in speaking of Macdonough's fleet, the writer declares, "Uncle Sam set he boat,/Massa M'donough he sail 'em."[46] The song features several instances of a rare, gentle humor. Prevost, called "gubbener Probose," has "come to Plat-te-burg a tea-party courtin' " (an allusion to the Boston Tea Party). In a satirical note impugning Macomb's valor, the composer claims, "he always a home" instead of performing his military duties. A mostly accurate (if unconventional) description of the battle is given in these lines:

> Gubbener Probose try he hand 'pon de shore
> While he boat take he luck 'pon de water—
> But Massa M'Donough,
> Knock he boat in the head,
> Break he heart [and] break he shin.

The song may exaggerate Prevost's fear of battle in the line "Probose scare so," but he did retreat quickly, destroying some of his supplies. The song correctly states that these were "lef all behime."[47] As noted in the piece, Macdonough's victory over the British pushed Prevost and his army from the town of Plattsburgh, ending the threat to upper New York and terminating Prevost's invasion.

Like a number of navy songs published during the war, many liberty songs simply celebrated American glory while condemning British corruption and tyranny. Some liberty songs, however, offer a bit more variety and some food for thought. The first of these, "Union and Liberty," is set to the melody "Anacreon in Heaven" (later made famous when it was used for "The Star-Spangled Banner"). Biblical imagery, found less frequently in songs of the War of 1812 than in those of the American Revolution, is important in this tune. The reference to "our Moses"[48] is clearly meant as an allusion to George Washington. The phrase "thousands of Joshuas" is more vague, but can be interpreted to mean that America has produced many capable generals, who, though lesser heroes than Washington, may nevertheless "proudly conduct us to glory eternal." (Joshua was one of Moses' several generals.) The War of 1812 produced no composer of religious war songs of William Billings' stature, possibly because New England, with its strong religious tradition, was not united in support of the war and thus did not totally commit itself to the cause. "Union and Liberty" is among the first of many songs to refer to "Old England" as the "east."

The differences between east and west are made clearer in "New Song, Written for the Fourth of July, 1812, By a Female." "New Song" is set to the melody "Anacreon in Heaven" and distinctly associates "the WEST" with all that is just and good.[49] In anticipation of "The Star-Spangled Banner" and in a tribute to the tradition of American liberty, the composer declares that, despite Washington's death, the flag continues to "wave o'er the SONS OF THE WEST."

Another "New Song" written at approximately the same time emphasizes the differences between America and Europe while lamenting the borrowing of tunes from European countries. The composer declares,

> 'Tis not a good thing that the songs that we sing
> Should be imported from Britain or France;
> Where worshippers flatter the idols we batter,
> And monarchy pipes and the multitude dance.[50]

The American advantages listed in the song are several: the first is "Nature's Abundance from Orleans to Maine"; second, in America no "parasites [are] cringing in black or in red," a reference to the king's clergy (the black) and the standing military (the red), both of whom serve monarchy's tyrannous control of the people; third, "no fiscal state-doctor" exists to plunder the people's wealth; and fourth, "No elder son beggars the next or a daughter," a criticism of the English custom of primogeniture. In declaring this custom acceptable in the United States, the author proudly states that America is a "republican land" based on "virtue with talents."

Two songs represent the urgent pleas of Virginians to their countrymen to defend Virginia during the disastrous months of August and September of 1814. By the time the song "Virginians to Arms" was published on 30 August 1814, the British had captured and burned Washington. The first three lines indicate the urgency of the American position:

> Virginians to arms: 'tis our country demands us;
> Our mothers, our daughters, our sisters, our wives,
> every tie that is dear constrains us.[51]

Another call for aid titled (unoriginally) "A New Song," published on 17 September 1814 in the *Richmond Enquirer*, three days after the British ceased their efforts to capture Baltimore, reveals the American fear of continued invasion. Virginians are asked, in a reference to the Revolution, to "fight as your ancestors gallantly fought,/unmindful of veteran odds."[52]

The most celebrated liberty song of the War of 1812 (or for that matter, in American history) later became the U.S. national anthem. Francis Scott Key wrote the lyrics for "The Star-Spangled Banner" (see appendix) in the early morning hours of 14 September 1814 after learning that the Americans at Fort McHenry near Baltimore had survived a savage bombardment intended to reduce the fort and force a surrender. This song was inspired by the continuing invasion that had already alarmed Virginians as noted earlier. The preface to the "Defense of Fort McHenry," the original title of the song later known as "The Star-Spangled Banner," supplies the details of the action that inspired the composition. Key wrote:

> The annexed song was composed under the following circumstances—a gentleman had left Baltimore under a flag of truce for the purpose of getting released from the British fleet a friend of his who had been captured at Marlborough. He went as far as the mouth of the Patuxent, and was not permitted to return lest the intended attack on Baltimore should be disclosed. He was therefore brought up the mouth of the Patapsco, where the flag was kept under the guns of a frigate, and he was compelled to witness the bombardment of Fort M'Henry, which the Admiral had boasted that he would carry in a few hours, and that the city must fall. He watched the flag at the fort through the whole day with an anxiety that can better be felt than described, until the night prevented him from seeing it. In the night he watched the Bomb Shells, and at early dawn his eye was again greeted by the proudly waving flag of his country.[53]

A more complete account of the events triggering Key's epic composition is found in a letter from Supreme Court Justice Roger B. Taney to a correspondent, H.V.D. Johns, written in 1856. According to Taney, Key himself told his story to the justice.[54] In his letter Taney writes that Key presented his verses on 15 September 1814 to Judge Joseph Hopper Nicholson of Baltimore, who immediately had them printed on a broadside.[55] Nicholson apparently designated the melody "Anacreon in Heaven" as the one to be printed with Key's lyrics. Key nowhere specifically stated that the song should be set to that tune;[56] he might well have had this melody in mind, however, since a poem he had written sometime after 1805 and dedicated to Stephen Decatur was supposedly set to that tune. In late 1814 Key's publisher titled the song "The Star-Spangled Banner" in his printing of the piece.[57]

The melody, like the lyrics, has an interesting history. The song originated with an eighteenth century British dinner and drinking club, the Anacreontic Society, which completed its celebrations with bouts of group singing.[58] The favorite concluding song was "To Anacreon in Heaven," with lyrics by Ralph Tomlinson and music by John Stafford Smith, both of whom were members of the club. The society was named for the sixth century (B.C.) Greek poet Anacreon, who wrote verses about the pleasures of drink and romance.[59] Despite the song's overwhelming popularity as a patriotic song and war tune, "The Star-Spangled Banner" did not become the national anthem of the United States until 1931.[60] The sentiments expressed in "The Star-Spangled Banner" are little different from those of many other liberty and patriotic tunes; the language of the song is stirring, but hardly varies from that of other patriotic compositions of the time, especially those written during the British invasion of 1814. The contemporary popularity of the piece is obviously due to Key's skillful rendition of the drama he had observed. The continuing appeal of "The Star-Spangled Banner" undoubtedly owes much to the time and place of its composition. Perhaps the most likely reason for the song's longevity is its universal theme of the promise of hopes fulfilled in the morning after a particularly dark and danger-filled night.

Not all Americans shared Key's patriotic fervor. In New England, which escaped the British blockade until 1814, many Americans opposed the war. Their opposition resulted in the formation of the Essex Junto and the Hartford Convention, both groups containing well-known figures who supported peace with England. Although the war's opponents published no antiwar tunes in the leading New England papers, countless numbers of editorials were written to protest the conflict.[61]

Those patriots who feared that some Americans would overtly or covertly aid England published songs about the need for vigilance against treason. "A New Song" of this period warns, "the times are portentous when traitors are bold."[62] A subtle criticism of merchants (usually New Englanders) who continued to trade with the enemy can be inferred from the lines "What dust can be thrown in the eyes of the Fold/more hard to expel than the dust of her Gold." The pronoun "her" clearly refers to England. Another "New Song" urges loyal Americans to overlook the "sneer of *old* Tories or new."[63] The composer's emphasis on the word "old" may refer to some older Americans who, at the beginning of the American Revolution, took the British side. These traitors would "condemn a just war or discolor the facts." An untitled song published in Washington's *National Intelligencer* includes the following preface, which specifically identifies the group that its author finds injurious to the American cause.

The following little song from the opera of "Paul and Virginia," shows in a striking manner the difference there is between those would be Englishmen, "the Federalists of the Boston Stamp," and the true sons of Albion, by whom they are as much despised as they are by their own Countrymen.[64]

The song itself mentions only the pride of "Albion's crew." Southern song-writers condemned those New Englanders who did not support the United States.

A third type of song, the personal ballad, has both villains and a hero as its subjects. The main character in one of America's best-known folk ballads is James Bird, a deserter who had served honorably with Perry at Lake Erie. Bird was unusual because he was one of the few individuals about whom a song (titled "James Bird") was written and the only American traitor who was represented as a tragic figure. Early in the song Bird is depicted as

> tall and graceful in his mein;
> firm in his steps, his looks undaunted—
> Ne'er a nobler youth was seen.[65]

He fought on the heavily pounded *Niagara* with Perry, continuing to fight even after "a ball struck him." Bird refuses (in the song) to go below with the wounded, exclaiming "I'll stand by the gallant Captain/'till we conquer or we die"; his words sound much like those attributed to Perry in a song discussed earlier. Suddenly the tone of the song shifts from that of praise for a hero's glorious performance to regret when Bird informs his parents in a letter, "I must suffer for deserting from the brig *Niagara*." Bird was shot for his transgression, despite the composer's plea for leniency: "Let his courage plead for mercy,/Let his precious life be spared." New York folk tradition has it that Bird was given leave to go home to allow his wound to heal and to visit his lady love. He inadvertently failed to return to duty on time because of impassable roads near his New York home. When rewards were posted for his capture, he was spotted by a citizen who offered him a place to stay for the night and a ride to his unit the following morning. Instead, his host delivered him to the military authorities for the reward of thirty dollars (the reference to the sum of Christ's betrayal is surely intentional). Although Perry gallantly hurried to Bird's rescue (it is said that he rode two horses to death), he was too late, for Bird was executed as he arrived.[66]

Historical fact disagrees with legend in some particulars. Bird had indeed served admirably under Perry; however, he was far from a model soldier, and as a discipline problem he had been placed in the marines. When his wound was healed, he was assigned to guard government supplies. He immediately deserted. President James Madison declined to halt his scheduled execution, and Bird with two fellow deserters met death in October 1814. In a last letter to his parents, Bird blamed no one for his conduct and lamented his behavior. He offered his life as an example of unworthy conduct.[67]

General James Wilkinson, a highly unlikely choice for the subject of a patriotic song, is the hero of a short piece titled "The Veteran," which was published in 1813. He received high praise in the lines, "his word . . . was our leading star."[68] He is depicted as the dreaded foe of his enemies: "Spaniards with thrice his numbers fled." Such accolades are strange in view of historians' condemnations of Wilkinson's conduct. Wilkinson at one time conspired with former Vice-President Aaron Burr to cause, in historian Marshall Smelser's words, "the secession of the western states." Despite his intrigues against the Spanish, such as his plan to invade Mexico, he managed to maintain his connections with Spanish agents.[69] If the Spanish ever fled from him, it was probably because Wilkinson, once known as Spanish agent 13, had made a bargain with some corrupt Spanish commander to further his own reputation among Americans. Wilkinson's dubious record may not have been known to the composer, who declares, "May Wilkinson our leader be,/and may that day come speedily." Wilkinson did eventually receive a command during the War of 1812, but he did not enhance his reputation while serving in this capacity.[70]

Certainly the most musically celebrated hero of the war was General Andrew Jackson. In little more than a month after the Battle of New Orleans, songs about Jackson's post-war defeat of the British began to appear across the country. The battle took place on 8 January 1815, after the Treaty of Ghent had been approved by both belligerents, and ended in an overwhelming defeat for the British, who lost about two thousand men, including their commander.

In "Jackson is the Boy," the general is called "ever brave"[71] and referred to as "immortal Jackson," indications of his already significant reputation. His opponents are lampooned in a line obliquely praising Jackson, the man "the British turned their backs on." This reference is to the hurried British retreat from the battlefield. The most famous song about Jackson was written sometime after the battle, when Jackson's reputation as a military leader was approaching legendary proportions.[72] Samuel Woodworth, a well-known poet of the time, composed the lyrics as a ballad; the tune was written by Noah Ludlow for the comic opera "Love Laughs at Locksmiths" and was called "Miss Bailey."[73] The fortuitous combination of lyrics and music was first performed in May 1822.[74] The song actually says little of Jackson, referring to him only twice; the work emphasizes the contribution of the Kentucky riflemen, who were so hardy and tough that every man was "half a horse,/and half an alligator."[75] The lyrics accurately describe the action at New Orleans because the sharp-shooting abilities of Jackson's troops were the main cause of the heavy British casualties. The song won a place in history for its wide popularity in Jackson's successful presidential campaign of 1828.[76]

Since the Treaty of Ghent had been signed before the final battle, Jackson's overwhelming victory at New Orleans gained no concessions at the bargaining table, but it did provide Americans with an authentic hero who was to be celebrated in song for many years after his achievement. Jackson's victory also helped the United States to retain possession of the coastal area along the Gulf of Mexico; it effectively voided a British claim to the region and thus gave the young republic a sound basis for the validity of the Louisiana Purchase.[77] Neither side gained anything of note from the peace treaty except the end of the war. The American relief at the conclusion of the conflict is reflected in the "Ode for the Return of Peace." The sentiments of many Americans are expressed in the line "Peace hath illumin'd a nation in tears."[78] Americans had finally won their freedom from Great Britain.

The War of 1812 produced an unusual pattern of songs. Navy songs were in the preponderance, not only because most of America's outstanding and sometimes surprising victories took place on the water, but also because America had developed a flourishing sea commerce and thus a powerful interest in nautical strength. Much of the country's economic life depended on both fresh and salt water industries. The apparent absence of songs written to celebrate land combat, despite such outstanding victories as the Battle of the Thames or the triumph at Chippewa, remains a mystery. Indeed, the most likely answer is that no land victory represented a significant permanent gain of territory; the few American land victories served mainly to recapture territory from British forces. In view of American hopes of capturing Canadian ground early in the war, an ambition often expressed in song, the minor territorial gains must have seemed inconsequential.

The absence of songs that might have made important contributions to American music poses other questions. First, it seems strange that the opponents of the war were not musically opposed to the conflict in view of the strong sectional affiliation of the northeast with Britain, especially in the early phase of the war. It may be that New England merchants were still making a profit from the enemy and thus saw no need to protest against a war that did not adversely affect their commerce. Moreover, when the British did invade New England, past economic friends of the empire were treated no differently from any other British enemies. New Englanders saw that they had only two options; either fight for their lands or surrender separately from the remainder of the country. Protest songs had no place in this peculiar situation. A second mystery—why so few American war heroes received tributes in song—is a little easier to solve. First, no Washington, with a well-known and well-deserved accumulated reputation, emerged from the War of 1812. Madison, the first president to preside over an American war, exhibited no particularly outstanding leadership abilities and so went uncelebrated in tune. Only Andrew Jackson achieved a heroic standing in popular opinion, but his late victory did not allow him time to develop a carefully documented reputation over a considerable period of time. Finally, no leader, on sea or land, was able to link his name with consistently brilliant strategy or numerous important victories, or even one crucial triumph that turned the tide of war.

Liberty songs of the War of 1812 are much like those of the American Revolution with the exception of three new variations. First, America is linked with the west, and the use of the word "west" in this connection clearly means freedom from oppression and a land where liberty is sacred. Second, the tone of the liberty song is one of urgency; moments of crisis are depicted. The dramatic setting of Francis Scott Key's "The Star-Spangled Banner" is a classic example of the trials Americans faced during the War of 1812. This song and other liberty songs call to Americans to resist foreign invasion. It is likely that because the song shows Americans' determination to protect land and liberty, "The Star-Spangled Banner" captured its significant place in American patriotic song. Third, for the first time in song, U.S. citizens are warned to protect themselves from their fellow countrymen who would betray America to England.

As a whole, the songs of the War of 1812 did not depart from the European tradition and take an original form. Even though at least one composer recognized that American music should seek its own distinctive voice, it continued to feed primarily upon the tradition of new lyrics set to existent popular tunes. While most songs written during the War of 1812 followed the traditional pattern set during the American Revolution, American liberty and war music developed in two new directions.

The most outstanding advances in liberty and war songs were the expansion of older themes and, more important, the growth of dialect song, because it constituted an experimental technique in American music. The black dialect song was used to a much greater degree in the next two wars. By the time of the Mexican War in 1846, the minstrel show had become well established, and dialect tunes were widely popular. The use of a French dialect song in the War of 1812 was the first example of foreign dialect in the war song. It was the only example of the use of foreign dialect in a naval song; it heralded songs written during the Civil War when Irish and German speech patterns were copied. The dialect song was usually, until the Civil War, used as a comic device. The lighthearted tone not only served to note a casual disregard of the enemy's might, but the distortion of language also demonstrated a mocking disregard for an opponent. Unlike British war music, which remained almost exclusively traditional, American war music had made an important advance, but it had not yet taken its own course.[79]

NOTES

1. Harry L. Coles, *The War of 1812* (Chicago: University of Chicago Press, 1965), p. 1.

2. Reginald Horsman, *The War of 1812* (New York: Alfred A. Knopf, 1969), p. 7.

3. C. S. Forester, *The Age of Fighting Sail: The Naval War of 1812* (Garden City, N.Y., Doubleday, 1956), pp. 15–16.

4. Coles, 5–7.

5. Ibid., 15.

6. "Naval Recruiting Song," from a broadside reprinted in Robert Neeser, ed., *American Sea Songs and Ballads* (New Haven, Conn.: Yale University Press, 1938), p. 80.

7. "Rodgers and Victory. Tit for Tat or the Chesapeake Paid for in British Blood!!!!" from a broadside printed in Neeser, 82.

8. James Ripley Jacobs and Glenn Tucker, *The War of 1812: A Compact History* (New York: Hawthorn Books, 1969), p. 19.

9. Coles, 19.

10. "Rodgers and Victory," reprinted in Neeser, 85–87.

11. "The American Constitution Frigate's Engagement with the British Frigate *Guerrière*," a broadside reprinted in Neeser, 102.

12. Alfred T. Mahan, *Sea Power and Its Relation to the War of 1812* (New York: Charles Scribner's Sons, 1903; reprinted, Cambridge, Mass.: The University Press, 1905), 1:232–234.

13. "Cash in Hand," reprinted in Neeser, 111–114.

14. "*Wasp* Stinging *Frolick*," from a broadside reprinted in Neeser, 117.

15. Mahan, 1:415.

16. "The *United States* and the *Macedonian*," reprinted in Neeser, 118–119.

17. *Oxford English Dictionary* [hereafter cited as *OED*], s. v. "tampions."

18. Ibid., s. v. "langrage."

19. Mahan, 1:419–420.

20. Forester, 108.

21. Ibid., 111.

22. "Bainbridge's Victory: or Huzza for the *Constitution*, once more!" a broadside reprinted in Neeser, 135.

23. Coles, 84–88.

24. Mahan, 2:133–140.

25. "Song," reprinted in Neeser, 160–161.

26. "Offset for the *Chesapeake*, on the Capture of Fort George, and Repulse of the Enemy from Sackett's Harbor," reprinted in Neeser, 173–175.

27. Quoted in Coles, 86.

28. "*Shannon* and *Chesapeake*," reprinted in Neeser, 169–170.

29. Mahan 2:135.

30. "Stanzas," printed in the *National Intelligencer*, 22 March 1813.

31. "Yankee Tars," reprinted in Neeser, 135–136.

32. "Yankee Thunders," reprinted in Neeser, 137–139.

33. "Yankee Frolics," reprinted in Neeser, 154–157.

34. Forester, 75–83.

35. "Battle of Lake Erie," reprinted in Neeser, 192–193.

36. Horsman, 106.

37. Mahan, 2:82–88.

38. Forester, 180–185.

39. *OED*, s. v. "perry."

40. "American Perry: A Song," *Baltimore American and Daily Advertiser*, 6 October 1813.

41. Forester, 186–187.

42. "Most Brilliant Naval Victory on Lake Erie," reprinted in Neeser, 202.

43. Horsman, 184–189.

44. "The Battle of Plattsburgh," reprinted in Neeser, 232–233.

45. Harold W. Thompson, *Body, Boots, and Britches: Folktales, Ballads, and Speech from Country New York* (Syracuse, N.Y.: Syracuse University Press, 1979), p. 351.

46. "The Seige of Plattsburgh," reprinted in Thompson, 351–352.

47. Horsman, 192.

48. "Union and Liberty. A Song for the Fourth of July," *Baltimore American and Daily Advertiser*, 3 July 1812.

49. "New Song Written for the Fourth of July, 1812, By a Female," *National Intelligencer*, 4 July 1812.

50. "New Song 'Tis not a good thing," *Richmond Enquirer*, 5 February 1814.

51. "Virginians to Arms! A Song for 1814," *Baltimore American and Daily Advertiser*, 30 August 1814.

52. "New Song," *Richmond Enquirer*, 17 September 1814.

53. "Defense of Fort McHenry," *Baltimore American and Daily Advertiser*, 21 September 1814. This is perhaps the earliest newspaper printing of the song, appearing seven days after its composition. The song was printed, however, after Key's poem was set to the melody "Anacreon in Heaven."

54. National Committee for the Preservation of Existing Records of the National Society of the Colonial Dames of America, *American War Songs* (Philadelphia: privately printed, 1925), pp. 34–35.

55. Ibid., 40.

56. Joseph Muller, ed., *The Star-Spangled Banner: Words and Music Issued between 1814–1864* (New York: G. A. Baker, 1935), p. 25.

57. David A. Randall, ed., *"Yankee Doodle" to the "Conquered Banner" with Emphasis on the "Star-Spangled Banner"* (Bloomington: Indiana University Press, 1968), p. 4.

58. Muller, 13–14.

59. *Oxford Companion to Classical Literature*, s. v. "Anacreon."

60. Muller, 36.

61. The best recent book on the New England Federalists' opposition to the war is James M. Banner, *To the Hartford Convention: The Federalists and the Origin of Party Politics in Massachusetts, 1789–1815* (New York: Alfred A. Knopf, 1970). In his bibliography Banner cites the *Columbian Centinel* as one of the two best newspaper sources for information on the Federalists. Neither this paper nor the *Connecticut Gazette* or *Boston Spectator* printed any antiwar songs; on the contrary, the *Centinel* and the *Gazette* occasionally printed standard war and patriotic tunes.

62. "New Song. Americans awake. . . . " *Richmond Enquirer*, 6 January 1814.

63. "New Song. Raise song for the country. . . . " *Richmond Enquirer*, 13 January 1814.

64. Untitled song, *National Intelligencer*, 28 February 1814.

65. "James Bird," reprinted in Louise Pound, ed., *American Songs and Ballads* (New York: Charles Scribner's Sons, 1972), pp. 93–96.

66. Thompson, 344–345.

67. Ibid., 347–348.

68. "The Veteran," *National Intelligencer*, 20 August 1813.

69. Marshall Smelser, *The Democratic Republic, 1801–1815* (New York: Harper and Row, 1968), pp. 114–115.

70. Ibid., 112. A good biography of James Wilkinson is James Ripley Jacobs, *Tarnished Warrior: Major-General James Wilkinson* (New York: Macmillan, 1938).

71. "Jackson is the Boy," reprinted in Robert V. Remini, *Andrew Jackson and the Course of American Empire, 1767–1821* (New York: Harper and Row, 1977), p. 296.

72. Vera Brodsky Lawrence, *Music for Patriots, Politicians, and Presidents: Harmonies and Discords of the First Hundred Years* (New York: Macmillan, 1975), p. 226.

73. Ibid., 212.

74. John William Ward, *Andrew Jackson: Symbol for an Age* (New York: Oxford University Press, 1962), pp. 13–15.

75. "The Hunters of Kentucky or the Battle of New Orleans," from a broadside reprinted in Lawrence, 212.

76. Ibid., 212.

77. Remini, 299.

78. National Committee . . . "Ode for the Return of Peace," Colonial Dames, 47–48.

79. Lewis Winstock, *Songs and Music of the Redcoats: A History of the War Music of the British Army, 1642–1902* (Harrisburg, Pa.: Stackpole Books, 1970), p. 86.

5

Rough and Ready Singers

The years 1815 to 1845 were a time of growth for the United States. Most of her problems, those solved and those temporarily resolved, were related to American expansion. For some years after the War of 1812, the United States remained, for the most part, at peace with foreign nations; her relations with her former enemy, Britain, were cordial. The Transcontinental Treaty of 1819 ended a dispute with Spain and added Florida to American territory. At home, however, the slavery issue made relations between North and South difficult. The unresolved question of slavery and its connection with the admission of new states into the Union was temporarily settled by the Missouri Compromise in 1820.

A few years later Andrew Jackson's election to the presidency in 1828 gave America a new direction. He regarded his victory as a mandate to pursue his brand of democracy; his goal was to extend economic opportunity to all Americans. Jackson's rise to the highest office in the land from humble origins created a "log cabin" syndrome in American politics that remained strong through Lincoln's election in 1860. By the time of Jackson's death in 1845, America had become a thriving nation rapidly expanding both economically and geographically. As the country moved west, many Americans came to believe that the United States had a manifest destiny to expand from Atlantic to Pacific; this belief helped bring America into conflict with Mexico.

The failure to negotiate a mutually agreeable settlement of the annexation of Texas, combined with the American desire to gain western lands for future settlement, brought the United States to the brink of war in early 1846. The movement of American troops into southern Texas and Mexico's counter movement of troops into the Rio Grande area ultimately led to the first military actions of the war.[1]

After Texas won its independence, the attitude of Mexico toward the United States became one of mistrust and wariness; many Mexicans were aware that most Americans clearly favored the cause of the Texas rebels.[2] United States annexation of Texas sent war fever in Mexico to new heights in July 1845.[3] Further complicating diplomatic problems between the two countries was the Mexican government's lack of cohesion and stability, factors that made predictable negotiations nearly impossible. Mexican regimes were often threatened when they took unpopular actions, and when in danger of falling, they pursued the course their leaders deemed necessary to retain power.[4]

The shooting war started primarily over the southernmost Texas boundary, an area in dispute since the establishment of the Texas Republic in 1836. The fledgling Texas government insisted that its territory extended to the Rio Grande; the Mexican government claimed that the Texas boundary was the Nueces River more than one hundred miles north of the Rio Grande. As did many Americans, President-elect James Polk believed that the Texas border was the Rio Grande, and he urged Texas before annexation to declare so, believing such insistence would force Mexico to make a territorial settlement.[5] When the Mexican government refused to discuss the boundary dispute with the United States in late 1845 and early 1846, Polk sent General Zachary Taylor with an army from Corpus Christi to a point near the Rio Grande on 13 January 1846.[6] Two months later Taylor occupied a position close to the river, and on 24 April hostilities commenced when General Anastasio Torrejon crossed the Rio Grande and clashed with American dragoons under Captain William Thornton.[7]

The most noticeable change in American liberty and war songs written during the Mexican War is the confident, aggressive air that they project. The optimistic belief that America would conquer Mexico pervades virtually every war song written during the conflict and is reinforced in Americanisms present in some tunes. The first group of songs examined is entirely devoted to promoting an aggressive war as the best means for preserving liberty. The concept of manifest destiny is an integral part of these songs; an unpleasant characteristic of some of these songs is the ethnic bias they contain. A second group of songs is closely tied to the first. Texas, whose border was the immediate cause of the dispute, is the topic of many songs that describe the ferocity of Texans and their desire to contribute to American prosperity by defeating Mexico.

Another important category of songs treats the military aspect of the war. Several good songs were written about Zachary Taylor, the most musically celebrated American general since Washington. Some anonymous battle songs offer enlightening comments on Americans' views of the Mexican enemy. A few good comic pieces add a humorous side to the battle song. For the first time in the history of the American war song, a few tunes tout the merits of volunteer units. The war in Mexico featured little naval action, but the few songs written about the navy describe its part in the conflict. Even American women appear aggressive in songs of the Mexican War;

women totally support their men and believe that they are superior to any women in the world.

Some Americans, many of them New Englanders, did not support the war or accept American cultural or ethnic superiority. Fearing the expansion of slavery into conquered and annexed territory, American protestors wrote the first antiwar songs. These pieces also criticize Americans who see the enemy as inferior or subhuman. A New Hampshire soldier, however, chose to protest against the protestors.

The war also inspired a few songs in the sentimental vein, a form that had become popular long before the war. So widely accepted was this type of song that a Mexican composer's sentimental work was printed in the United States. The use of sentiment in Mexican War songs prefigured the sentimental war song vogue, which reached its peak during the Civil War.

For the first time the United States cheerfully entered a war believing that humbling an inferior and despotic enemy would establish the United States as a power that would protect liberty in North America. Americans were not only eager to liberate territory controlled by Mexico but also warned Britain in song not to support Mexican tyranny. Using historical references, American composers reminded the British of American might, which had twice frustrated them.

To show American superiority further, some composers condemned Mexicans as genetically inferior. Mexicans were thought to be cowards because of their mixed Indian and Spanish blood. American chauvinism was heightened by the realization that a nation conscious of its primarily Anglo-Saxon origins faced a power culturally and ethnically different from itself.

The first published song of note discussed here is a rather standard liberty song titled "Strike, Columbia, Strike the Foe!" set to the melody "Rule, Britannia." The music provides a counterpart to the lyrics. The major theme of the piece is "that Freedom must prevail."[8] The title of the song, repeated in its chorus, reveals the militant attitude of many Americans who unwaveringly believed that "Freedom spreads with ev'ry blow." "Song" continues this theme of Americans as undaunted fighters for freedom when its author claims that "if their rights invaded be/they'l [sic] drub their foes severely."[9] In an aside to the British, with whom the Americans were diplomatically contending for an advantagous settlement of the Oregon border dispute, the composer reminds England of her unsuccessful efforts to curtail American liberty: "Johnny Bull, he tried it twice,/and both times had to knuckle." American soldiers are ready, not bashful or hesitant about conquest, for, "if Poke [sic] says go!" the troops will "march straight on to Montezumy." Not only will the North Americans defeat their enemies, they will also force tribute from the conquered nation to satisfy the urge to move the United States westward:

> But best it were for Jonathan
> to peddle through the nation,

for Californ and Yucatan,
will soon go for annexation.

The enthusiastic composer sees possibilities for the United States to expand
south of the Rio Grande as well as west toward the Pacific.

"Strike for Your Rights: Avenge Your Wrongs" offers several examples of
Mexico's wrongdoing as reasons for acquiring Mexican lands. Listeners are
urged to

think of the jails of Sante Fe [sic];
where freemen in captivity,
felt Mexico's foul tyranny.[10]

This phrase may refer to the imprisonment of members of a Texas expedition
sent to Santa Fe in 1841 to negotiate with the Mexican government for the
addition of New Mexico to the Texas Republic. The Texans were forced
into hard labor under miserable conditions.[11] With this thought in mind
Americans are asked to

strike by noble Taylor's side
till Freedom's stars in triumph wide,
shall float from the Pacific's tide,
unto the Rio Grande.

For many Americans liberty meant not only defending their territory and
the right to acquire more, but also freedom from the interference of European
nations in the affairs of the United States. With the Oregon question unsettled
and Mexican agents meeting with British diplomats, some Americans feared
that Britain would aid Mexico. The British wanted the Mexican government
to avoid war with the United States unless a shooting conflict arose over the
Oregon boundary dilemma. The annexation of Texas had upset the English
government, and the London *Times* declared in 1845 that Mexico would be
the next territorial goal of the United States; the London *Standard* affirmed
that only the power of Britain and France would halt American territorial
gains.[12] On the other hand, many American government officials thought
that Britain wanted California as well as Oregon, and a British fleet near
Mazatlan in February of 1846 appeared to reinforce this view.[13] Concern
about British interference in the war with Mexico was openly voiced in
"Uncle Sam to Texas" in the lines "Johnny Bull's fat greedy boys/about our
union grumble."[14] The implication of "greedy" is that Britain might take
Mexico's side to gain North American territory. The writer of this song,
like many during the Mexican War, overstates his case when he declares "if
Mexy backed by secret foes" still has the desire to take Texas, as the author
and probably others think, then the United States will "lick 'em all" and
"then annex 'em too."

Many Americans believed that the glory which would elevate them to the ranks of military heroes would be easy to achieve. In the United States many Americans considered Mexicans upstarts, bullies and mixed-blood cowards.[15] A portion of an untitled song published in Washington shortly after the declaration of war bears out this view, using the epithet "vile crew"[16] for Mexican soldiers. Courageous Americans would "punish them for all their sins,/by stripping off their yellow skins." A piece titled "Way Down in Mexico" not only impugns the courage of the enemy, but also offers an ethnic slur as well. The American army will have little trouble quickly ending the war because they will simply "take the greasers now in hand/And drive 'em in the Rio Grande."[17] Furthermore, the victors will "hang Old Santa Anna soon." "Come Raise Aloft the Red, White and Blue" contains a short phrase that conveys the composer's opinion of the enemy, whom he calls the "Mongrel Spaniard."[18] "The New York Volunteers Camp Song" demeans Indians and explains the reason Americans cannot fail to win the war with Mexico. The author proudly states that

> We chill the false heart of the red man with fear;
> The blood of the Saxon flows full in the veins
> Of the lads who will lord over Mexico's plains.[19]

Since the war started over the Texas border, it is apparent that Texas and Texans would become the subjects of many songs. Texans joined in large numbers to fight with Taylor and showed an enthusiasm for combat; they looked forward to destroying an enemy who had shown himself capable of extreme savagery, as indicated by Mexican actions at the Alamo and Goliad. The revenge-minded, heavily equipped Texans were not, however, fond of military regulations. They had little use for drill, discipline, military organizations, or the system of ranks.[20] In "Remember the Alamo," in which the title is repeated at the end of every verse, the Texans' desire for revenge is catalogued in several places. For instance, one verse reads:

> For every wound and every thrust
> On prisoners dealt by hands accurst
> A Mexican shall bite the dust.[21]

The composer indicates a dire fate for the enemy: "Woe to every Mexican brigand." And the Texans did carry out their threats; of all the troops who committed illegal acts and foul deeds against the Mexicans, they were unquestionably the most profligate.[22] The Texans ultimately became such a discipline problem that Taylor ordered some Texas units to be disbanded and returned to Texas.[23]

"The Song of Texas" gives a brief general history of the state and shows Texans' pride over their state's annexation to the United States. The opening lines indicate the relief from foreign interference that Texans felt at having joined the Union, for Texas will "fear no haughty nation though foes all 'round are plied."[24] The security coming from statehood is evident in the belief that "Young Texas now is free" from all threats of foreign intrigue and domination from both England and Mexico.[25] Texans quickly adopted a belief in manifest destiny, as the song clearly illustrates: "Texas will aid his [Uncle Sam's] cause, now,/for Sister Oregon." Further and stronger reinforcement for this sentiment is revealed in the thought,

> We'll clear our own rightful bond,
> [because] From Atlantic to Pacific
> Is Uncle Sam's own ground.

A more direct statement of manifest destiny is impossible.

Military songs constitute a large and significant body of war tunes. Military songs range from affirmations of confidence in Zachary Taylor to discussions of naval actions during the war. Taylor's career is presented and his homespun manner is prominently featured; songs about Taylor show his military prowess and indicate a great affection and respect for him. Many battle songs make American victories seem easy and predictable; some demonstrate an anger with Mexican treachery. Most battle songs exhibit an arrogant disdain for the enemy, a disdain particularly evident in the comic battle pieces of the war. These songs mock the enemy with humorous descriptions of combat and its consequences for the Mexican army. Songs about volunteer units, composed for the first time during the Mexican War, depict the eagerness American volunteers evinced for combat and the desire to win glory for themselves and their country. A punishment song written during the war indicates that some high-spirited soldiers, many of them no doubt volunteers, were overzealous in seeking out an enemy to humiliate or destroy; some soldiers were also punished for unruly behavior. Two naval songs indicate the minor part American sailors played in the conflict. The first song conveys the boredom many American soldiers experienced during a war in which naval combat was almost nonexistent. The second song, a serio-comic piece, describes a rare naval victory accomplished by a small group of men and for which the unfortunate hero was discharged from the service. Despite the sailor's fate, the ease of his victory mirrored American sentiments about the optimistic prosecution of the war. In a strange conjunction of fates neither the young officer nor General Zachary Taylor would retain their commands. The seaman was to end his military career in misfortune; Taylor's was to lead him to the presidency.

Taylor, the first commander of United States forces in combat, was known to his men as "Old Rough and Ready." Taylor became the subject of more songs than any general since Washington. His fame may in large part be attributed to his striking victories early in the war at Palo Alto and Resaca de la Palma; each victory thereafter served to enhance his reputation. These unexpected triumphs brought him acclaim from the people and earned him a message of gratitude from Congress.[26]

"Huzza for Brave Zac and his Bayonet Boys" is a tribute to Taylor's courage as well as that of American troops. As a note appended to the song declares, the tune was sung on the occasion of the presentation to Taylor of a ceremonial sword.[27] The most notable feature of the song, however, is a sardonic remark about the quality of the Mexican artillery at Palo Alto. The contest was fought primarily with artillery, and the Americans for the first of many times, showed themselves to be more efficient and accurate than their counterparts. Mexican artillery skills were so poor that some of their cannon balls rolled harmlessly among the American troops, who simply stepped out of the missiles' paths.[28] The song refers humorously to this portion of the action in the lines.

the balls flew so hot,
they made dodging a science on that busy spot
For the copper they threw will not soon be forgot.

As if to make sure that his meaning is not misconstrued, the composer adds, "Sublime to all gazers, their show and their art/but sublime and ridiculous ain't far apart."

Three songs about Taylor detail his appearance and his character. The first—"With Him We'll Bivouac"—tells of Taylor's disdain for heavily decorated uniforms or shows of rank; Taylor personally felt no need to wear his uniform on a regular basis and wore it only occasionally.[29] As the song relates, the general's "regimental suit [was] plain as that of some raw recruit."[30] The song "Taylor, the Fine Old Southern Gentleman" confirms the picture of a man who was no "dandy Broadway beaux"[31] he never "cut a swell," a nineteenth-century phrase for dress that was always immaculate and appropriate to the occasion.[32] The song tells of Taylor's valor at Fort Harrison during the War of 1812 when the fort was under Indian attack. His quick thinking and courage helped to save the fort, and the author states, "he stood midst death and blood,/and earned his laurels well." Taylor was promoted to brevet major for his bravery.[33] The remark "he never stood, in time of war, for holiday parade" is entirely accurate, for Taylor's relaxed, informal approach to dress was reflected in his indifference to ostentatious martial displays.[34]

A piece simply titled "Zachary Taylor" lists, without giving details of the battles, the location of every American victory from Palo Alto to Buena Vista. The general whom the soldiers knew and the man celebrated as a great American hero is depicted in one of the final stanzas:

In the thickest of the fight old Zachary appeared,
the shot flew about him as thick as any hail,

and the only injury that he received there
was a compound fracture of his brown coat tail.[35]

This description of Taylor agrees with Brainerd Dyer's in his biography of
the commander.[36] The one inaccuracy in the song—a standard one in American war tunes—is the number of enemy casualties listed in one of the four
major battles. According to the piece, Mexico lost "four thousand" at Buena
Vista. Neither Taylor nor General Santa Anna offered this number; Taylor
guessed the figure to be fifteen hundred to two thousand, while Santa Anna
claimed approximately a thousand of his men fell.[37] The song "Rough and
Ready" adds a few interesting facts about Taylor while briefly outlining his
military career. The piece explains the origin of his nickname, mentioning
that while an Indian fighter "so hardy and so prompt was he/we called him
"Rough and Ready."[38] Dyer believes that the appellation resulted from Taylor's rumpled outfit and his willingness to share hardships and danger with
his men.[39] He is pictured wearing his "brown surtout [while riding] an old
white horse" named, appropriately enough, "Old Whitey." Taylor's kindness
and his regard for his men are shown in his action of stopping to "wipe the
drops of pain" from the forehead of one of his wounded men while he
"proffered from his own canteen/a drink."

An important song about Taylor called "A Little More Grape, Captain
Bragg" contains a remark erroneously attributed to the general. The title is
based on the words he supposedly uttered to Captain Braxton Bragg, one of
his artillery officers during the battle of Buena Vista. The phrase "A little
more grape"[40] fittingly serves as the chorus. Historian Justin Smith asserts,
however, that General S. E. Chamberlin, who was present when Taylor
gave his orders to his batteries, remarked that Taylor actually said, "Double-
shot your guns and give 'em hell."[41] Historian David Lavender believes that
the legendary phrase was actually coined during Taylor's presidential campaign in 1848.[42]

Taylor was not the only officer to be enshrined in song. Major Samuel
Ringgold, an artillery commander under Taylor, was killed at the battle of
Resaca de la Palma and shortly after was mourned in two songs, although
only one of them mentions him by name.[43] In an untitled song published in
New Orleans, he is called "our gallant chief"[44] and is made to sound like an
infantry or cavalry officer in the song; he is the man who "led [his troops]
to dash on the foe." The tune is a tribute and a lament for an officer who
"fell in the noon of his glorious fame." The second song, "Fire Away,"
captures the sensations of firing an artillery piece with its descriptions of
"smoke-wreaths uprising,"[45] "belching flames," and "thunders." The title is
repeated in each chorus, and the final one sadly proclaims "Ringgold was
summoned/to fire-fire away," dying like a cannon's fading roar. Ringgold
was hit with a cannon shot that injured both legs. He probably died from a
ruptured artery.[46]

Four of the battles fought during the war are the subjects of several songs. The interesting song "Battles of the 8th and 9th of May" refers, respectively, to the battles at Palo Alto and Resaca de la Palma; the piece does not give many of the details of the actions, but it does show the scorn Americans rapidly developed for Mexican leaders. In this case, "old Arista and Ampudia"[47] are Generals Mariano Arista and Pedro Ampudia, two undistinguished Mexican commanders, as their actions would continually prove.[48] The Mexican army is also disdainfully called "a motley crew"; this was the opinion of supposedly knowledgeable European observers about the American army. Before the war began, much European opinion held that the Mexican army was a remarkably competent fighting force.[49] Thus, despite foreign opinion, and that of some Americans, United States troops, many of them volunteers, proved their mettle under fire.[50] The writer makes the victories appear to be much more easily attained than they actually were when he asserts that the Mexican forces were "scattered . . . like children's toys." The song, probably unintentionally, makes the victors sound like heartless criminals who "killed their [Mexican] men and took their money." Of the battle of Resaca de la Palma, the author states: "Old Vega fixed behind his fort,/Just thought he'd have some noble sport." General Rómulo Díaz de la Vega was not in command of Mexican forces during this Battle [Arista was], but the song correctly notes that the Mexican position was well fortified. Vega and some of his officers were captured in an American charge, as the song tells, by the "gallant May," Lieutenant Colonel Charles May, a flamboyant cavalry leader widely regarded as a hero by the American public. "Ampudia ran and left the ground" as the song accurately relates, but so did the remainder of the Mexican contingent, carrying little of their equipment with them. Their confused retreat resulted in a number of deaths from drowning, as the Mexican forces hurriedly crossed the Rio Grande back into Mexico.[51] "The Fall of Matamoros" is actually about the Battle of Resaca de la Palma, which led to the fall of Matamoros. The song decries enemy general Ampudia's attempt to cover the Mexican left, whose weakness he had discovered just before the onset of combat. For this reason, plus the hidden position of the Mexican force, the Mexicans are called "Ampudia's sly minions,/in dastardly ambush concealed."[52] Arista's men did indeed "mangle the forms of our true [men]" when his cavalry unnecessarily killed some American stragglers after the Mexican forces had been pushed away from the battlefield.[53] The Mexican army retreated south beyond "Rio's swift wave," possibly so characterized because many Mexican troops were drowned.

Perhaps the best battle song, in terms of pure military details and accuracy of account, written about any battle in any American war between 1775 and 1865 is "Buena Vista."[54] The Mexican troops are made to look impressive, as indeed they did with "their great standards in the sun like sheets/of silver shine,"[55] while "their blood-/red pinnions stream." As the song describes, when the battle heatedly rages, "a portion of our line . . . is broken and dismayed; /a regiment of fugitives is fleeing from the field." This description is absolutely correct, for the second Indiana regiment ran from a portion of the battlefield, leaving Captain P. J. O'Brien to hold the enemy back with his artillery. He could not, and in his retreat, "one of his guns [was] gone." O'Brien lost a four-pound piece when he pulled back. American problems were compounded with "Lancers . . . passing round our left." However, Captains John Washington and Thomas Sherman made the "roar of battle . . . more terrible and loud" from the American side with their accurate and rapid artillery fire. Although the Americans had been pushed back partially from the positions they had held at the beginning of the fight, they still were in a solid defensive location. Because of "stout Mississippi, the bold Lancers/ charged in vain." The action of the Mississippi rifles, plus that of other American units throwing themselves fiercely into the battle, helped to wrest the field from the enemy. When Bragg came "thundering to the front" with his deadly artillery, enemy hopes of victory were completely demolished. The battlefield is pictured as the sun falls and the action has ceased. The composer poetically states,

> An o'er the dead and dying came the evening shadows fast,
> and then above the mountains rose the cold moon's silver shield,
> and patiently and pityingly looked down upon the field.

Santa Anna was "careless of his wounded," leaving them to be taken care of by the victors. The final verse offers praise to the army for "another battle won" and solemnly offers "honor to the brave and gallant/dead."

The Mexican War spawned a number of comic and dialect battle songs, probably influenced by the development of the minstrel show and its most popular songwriter, Daniel D. Emmett. The dialect song may well have appealed to whites because it pictured blacks as sentimental yet cheerful people ready to sing enthusiastically about a variety of subjects. Perhaps the dialect song owes its great popularity to its comic appeal. "The Siege of Monterey" is unmistakably in the comic vein; the piece is ostensibly about the experiences of a black combat veteran from Ohio who enlisted in Alabama. It is not likely that a black composed this song because the few blacks who served in the Mexican War were in naval units and were not present at Monterey.[56] In addition, the melody is by Daniel Emmett; although the exact title is not given, it is listed only as "Original by old Dan Emmit [sic]" under the song title. Finally, the song openly pokes fun at the black speaker. The composer has his persona claim that he was requested by Taylor "Bekase he wants dis niggar's mouth to stow de prisoners in."[57] A comic touch is found in the lines, "de Mexicans dey run/dey saw de banjo stickin' out—dey tink de debble come." Obviously the songwriter believed that the banjo was unfamiliar to the Mexican soldiers, and he stereotypically placed this musical instrument in the hands of his stock figure.

The song accurately depicts Taylor's battle plan, a pincer movement. The lines detailing the troop movements read, "Worth he march aroun' de town, de Mexicans to bodder." General William Worth was to take a western approach to the city of Monterey while Taylor planned to move straight toward the town from his position behind it. His hope was to "fotch up de rear, to starve dem [the Mexicans] out deyre fodder." The ferocity of the battle is summed up in the metaphor of two snakes battling, as the writer states, "When dey look 'roun for deyre heads—de foun'um both missin'/For 'Pudia [Ampudia] bite of Taylor's—an' Taylor swaller'd hissin." Despite the heat of the combat, the speaker declares that he has found time to relax for a few moments. He says,

> I brace my back agin a tree—my heel stuck in de ground
> I wasted all my powder [so] I shoot de old banjo
> You orter see his nigger run when he charge de ranchero.

The soldier did finally get into action as he proudly stated. Ampudia, who at last surrendered to Taylor, probably did so more solemnly than the colorful language that the song attributes to him: "I now gibs up de corn."

Another dialect song, titled "Uncle Sam" and sung to Emmett's "Old Dan Tucker," is a standard battle piece, but with a few linguistic points of interest. Coining the word "gunpowderation"[58] to rhyme with "annexation" is the most unusual twist of the language in the tune. The word "bullgine," usually spelled "bulljine," was American slang for a locomotive engine.[59] The phrase "called out" is rhymed with the old variant spelling "sour crout." With a reference to two Mexican generals, the composer discusses some surgery on these commanders: "Since Texas cut off Sant' Anna's peg,/We'll *amputate* Ampudia's leg." Santa Anna did indeed lose a leg at the knee when the Mexican army was involved in a conflict with the French in 1838.[60] Ampudia's major loss was not physical, but involved his surrender to Taylor at Monterey. Santa Anna's leg is the subject of a comic song entitled "The Leg I Left Behind Me" sung to the old marching tune "The Girl I Left Behind Me." The artificial leg was a part of the general's personal effects the Americans recovered when Santa Anna's belongings were abandoned in the Mexican army's uncontrolled flight from their decisive defeat at Cerro Gordo. The last lines put into the Mexican commander's mouth the fear that "in the museum, I will see/The Leg I left behind me."[61] He probably did not see his leg on display, but it was kept at the capitol building in Springfield, Illinois.[62] The song "Santy Anno" is a fairly ordinary tale of the defeats Santa Anna suffered, but it is unique in two respects. First, after working its way from the land war to the sea, it was transformed into a sea chantey, as is clear from the use of the phrase "heave away"[63] scattered throughout the text. As the song passed from American sailors to their British counterparts and back again, the outcome of the battle at Monterey, at which Santa

Anna did not command, is changed—the Mexicans are made to triumph over Taylor at Monterey. Whether this was done on purpose by the British for comic effect and sung in ignorance by American sailors will probably remain a mystery. As an example of the reversal of the battle's outcome in song, one verse is clear.

> Oh, Santa Anna gained the day,
> Heave away, Santy Anna,
> He gained the day at Monterey,
> All on the plains of Mexico.[64]

The army that was to fight the land war under Zachary Taylor and Winfield Scott was made up mostly of enthusiastic but untrained volunteers. The regular army had only seven thousand men shortly before the initiation of the conflict, and Congress was debating the elimination of West Point, as they saw little need for professional officers.[65] When war was finally declared on 13 May 1846, Congress provided for a force of fifty thousand volunteers to supplement the regular army and ten million dollars with which to wage the war.[66] The volunteer force created problems from the start because the men chose their own officers, a practice that did not often make for an efficient officer corps.[67] Furthermore, the volunteers were sometimes difficult to control. They lacked military discipline and occasionally committed crimes, ranging from theft to murder, against Mexican civilians.[68] The outstanding positive feature about the volunteers was their enthusiasm.

The song that epitomizes the volunteer spirit and outlook is the aptly titled "We're the Boys for Mexico," sung to "Yankee Doodle." The first two lines are indicative of much American sentiment about the war's ultimate outcome: "The Mexicans are doomed to fall,/God has in his wrath forsook 'em."[69] Since victory is certain, the volunteers believe that "All their goods and chattels call/on us to go and hook 'em." Many of those attractive objects are located in "Churches grand with altars rich"/[where figures of] saints with diamond collars" are also available. Besides diamonds, "gold and silver images are also plentiful and handy." Fortunately for the reputation of the United States, American soldiers did not often plunder the churches, although occasionally property was taken from them; individuals did not fare as well,[70] losing "lots of bright new dollars." Occupation troops were, however, sometimes critical of the Catholic church and its rituals. General Caleb Cushing's aide, Lieutenant W. H. Davis, wrote, "You have no idea of the flummery that we see here every day, all of which the Mexicans call religion."[71] Tales of Mexico's riches were widespread and undoubtedly the composer believed them, as he declares that after the conquest of Mexico is completed, "We'll vote ourselves extensive farms,/Each one as big as Texas."[72] The soldiers' celebration after Mexico City falls will be "free and easy" as a large convivial gathering that includes such pleasures as tobacco and strong drink.[73] Of this uncontained joy in the expected final victory, historian Justin Smith says, "Stranger than all else perhaps, the vague but romantic idea of 'revelling in the halls of the Montezumas' exercised a perfect fascination."[74]

Eager enlistees sang many of the plentiful volunteer unit songs composed during the war. "The Printer Volunteers" sang their song to the interestingly titled melody "The Teetotal Society." The piece playfully mentions the courage and energy of printers, while punning on words in the song related to the printers' trade. Words such as *"leader,"*[75] *"matter,"* and *"headlines"* were set in italics so that those unfamiliar with the printers' vocabulary would not miss the puns. The cleverest pun in the song is found in the lines "The *Incas* of Mexico soon/will find that our *inkers* are knowing."

The Hickory Blues, a New York unit, was named for Andrew Jackson, commonly known as "Old Hickory." One of the last stanzas of the song "Join the Hickory Blues" confirms this connection as a portion of it reads,

> Brave Hickory rests in heaven,
> But from aloft his views
> In grateful pride his ready sons.[76]

Jackson had died in 1845, and his recent death combined with his military reputation clearly inspired this unit's name as a tribute to the departed hero. The song indicates that the men wanted to be identified with their home state when they brought home wartime laurels for "the name and fame of New York's sons." The practice of choosing officers through approval of the men is shown in the lines, "Colonel Ming . . . is our leader/A better one we can't choose." Like "Join the Hickory Blues," the central message of the "Song of the Memphis Volunteers" is that this unit is destined to reach the apogee of glory and honor. The peculiar fact about this song, which distinguishes it from other unit songs, is its inconsistent and unnecessary use of dialect. For example, a typical stanza reads,

> We are waiting for our orders
> To shake our true lub's hand
> To shed a tear-then haste away
> To rescue Rio Grande.[77]

The dialect does not add any of the usual effects, sad or comic, to the song.

A tune that is certainly appropriate for some of the volunteers is a song about soldiers' punishments, titled "Buck and Gag Him" and sung to the old tune "Derry Down." The undisciplined volunteers were often punished for such offenses as gambling, which they considered inconsequential. The severity of punishments varied from whipping to hanging, depending on the nature of the crime.[78] Bucking was one of those punishments and was relatively easy to apply; the unfortunate offender was staked to the ground and tightly gagged. The punishment was both painful and effective.[79] The composer, perhaps a soldier who had suffered the penalty himself, believed that men in the ranks were unmercifully disciplined for "each trifling offence,"[80] "usually out of malice or spite." The soldiers' view of the army's unfairness is evident in the composer's declaration that soldiers were punished merely for "whipping the foe." Sometimes the soldiers' and their commanders' opinions of who constituted the foe differed measurably. The author also accuses officers who chastised their men for aiding the enemy, when he asserts, "the Mexicans' ranks they have helped to fill." For the most part, this is an exaggeration; relatively few American soldiers deserted to the enemy. Nonetheless, at Churabusco a number of deserters who fought against their former comrades were captured, and fifty of them were executed.[81]

Naval songs describe the primary concerns of sailors in a war that featured little naval action. For many sailors who served in the Mexican War, the song "The Coast of Mexico" included some sentiments that were undoubtedly true. A problem for many seamen was not fear of death but the boredom of sailing endlessly with no apparent destination. The author writes that many ships sailed "without an aim or object and roaming to and/fro."[82] Clothing and food were the sailors' primary concerns because "clean shirts are a premium"/[and] 'duff' is all the go." "Duff" was the Mexican War sailors' slang for food.[83] American sailors, eager to win their share of honors, were forced, as they complained, to "cruise inglorious[ly] on the coast." The song mentions the "*Albany*," one of the ships assigned to render aid to land forces during Scott's attack on the Mexican port of Vera Cruz. The piece was clearly written before 29 March 1847, because that was the date of the surrender of Vera Cruz. The composer asserts that " 'San Juan' grimly/stands." San Juan de Ulua was a granite walled fort, well constructed, capable of holding twenty-five thousand soldiers, and with cannons covering all likely landing areas. This massive structure was the strong point of a city well prepared for naval attacks.[84] By the end of the song, having been cheered at the possibility of action at Vera Cruz, the composer heartily declares, "we'll give them fits, ere long,/on the coast of Mexico."

By the time "Alvarado" had been written, Vera Cruz had fallen to Scott's assault. Alvarado, a smaller port than Vera Cruz, had escaped capture, and in the song, Scott, as commander of American forces, found it unacceptable "to teach the castle who was who,/and fail at Alvarado."[85] Commodore William Connor, the first commander of American naval forces in Mexico, tried twice to take Alvarado but was unsuccessful both times. He had hoped to capture the small Mexican fleet and use those ships in his own flotilla. As the song says,

And Perry, too, his anchors weighed
His heart within him glad,

To put poor Connor in the shade
by taking Alvarado.

Perry is Matthew Perry, who took over for Connor as commander of the American fleet in Mexico.[86] Major General John A. Quitman was to combine with Perry in a land-sea operation to take Alvarado in order to acquire a harbor for the American fleet's small boats, supply drinking water for the men stationed there, and provide cattle and horses for American forces. But "ahead went Hunter with his crew" and accidently foiled the elaborate operation. When the joint commanders arrived a day after Lieutenant C. G. Hunter and his tiny force landed, they found that "five sailors sat within the fort/in leading of a lad." Hunter, the youthful commander of a small boat, violated his orders to remain near the town. Instead of being congratulated for a successful mission, he was expelled from the service. His capture of the position allowed Mexican forces to take the livestock from the village, and a Mexican fleet, of possible use to the American navy, was destroyed. Finally, Hunter forced the town to surrender at gunpoint, alienating the citizens from their conquerers.[87]

For the first time in the American war song, women take an assertive attitude. Women, as portrayed in war tunes, completely mirror men's views toward combat. Some American women want a military hero as a lover; they believe that they have every right to wed a military hero because American women are the fairest and finest in the world.

The most unusual song about warriors in the Mexico campaign is a piece entitled "Female Volunteer for Mexico," expressing the desire and indeed the right of women to serve in the armed forces against the enemy. Women have the right to fight beside their men, and the composer states,

Then arouse man and maid,
Fair Mexico to aid
Grasp rifle and blade.[88]

Usually, however, the only females found in American-held areas were the Mexican women who were camp followers; on rare occasions an officer's wife joined him. At least one American officer's mistress, dressed as a man, marched with the troops and carried a gun.[89] The idea that a man with military honors was especially attractive to women was widespread during the war,[90] and true, according to the composer of the "Female Volunteer." The song's persona says of her ideal beau, "I'll give him *eclat*/for his bravery."

Certainly some American women, or at least some American men in the editorial guise of women, believed the American woman deserved a hero and had one in the American man. The final stanza of "Song of the American Girl" shows the superiority of both American men and women over all others in the world. The speaker declares,

> They tell of France's beauties rare,
> Of Italy's proud daughters'
> Of Scotland's lasses—England's fair,
> And nymphs of Shannon's waters;
> We need not all their boasted charms,
> Though Lords around them hover;
> Our glory lies in freedom's arms—
> A freeman for a lover.[91]

In "My Daddy to My Mammy Said," the attractiveness of the American woman is shown through a speaker who proudly proclaims her own loveliness, "My beauty is . . . great and grand."[92] A true American girl, she calls herself the "right charming Yankee Doodle." The confident representative of American womanhood makes it clear that she wants a uniformed hero, as she phrases it, "a captain millintary."

A different portrait of the war is found in the work of protestors who wrote and published songs marked by a self-righteous tone and clearly ironic sentiments. The protestors saw the war as a savage and unfortunate conflict demeaning Americans who participated in it. Much of New England, center of a group called Conscience Whigs, led by ex-President John Quincy Adams, was absolutely opposed to the war. Other Whigs and some Democrats were also against the war. The notion that united these forces was a fear that acquisition of new territory where slavery would be instituted was the underlying motive for the conflict.[93] One of the most influential voices in print against the war was William Lloyd Garrison, the publisher of the antislavery newspaper *The Liberator*. It was *The Liberator* that had the honor of printing the first group of antiwar songs in the United States.

"Mexico: An American National Song" opens with the usual enthusiastic and lighthearted tone of many early war songs, but the last three lines in the first stanza are unmistakably pointed. The Mexicans

> From all their poor slaves . . . have torn their strong fetters,
> A hateful example annoying their betters,
> And clouding the light of Religion and Letters.[94]

The second verse is filled with sarcasm. Hurry on to the conquest, the writer advises, for "there are maidens to ravish and churches to plunder." The reason for destroying the Mexicans is that "We are strong-they are weak." Following this thought is the caustic parody, "Hurra for the land of the brave and the free." So powerful are American warriors that "the nations in quiet behold us enslave them—/God's right arm is shortened—he never can save them." The last line is a firm ironic message to rabid patriots to beware of the unfettered ego of the conquering tyrant; danger lies in the presumption that mortals are more powerful than the Almighty. Printed below this song in the same column is an Englishman's poem decrying slavery. It is likely that this poem was strategically placed to reinforce the idea that the war was one of the conquest of new slave territory.

"Battle Hymn" (see appendix), the second protest song that *The Liberator* published, continues the irony found in the first. The song declares that the war " 'Tis by Polk's particular order,"[95] paraphrasing a remark popular among New England Whigs that the conflict was "Mr. Polk's war."[96] The pro-war papers are encouraged with pretended enthusiasm to "publish the faster and brag the louder,/Mexicans always run away." The chorus mocks the concept of manifest destiny in the lines,

> This is the way,
> Our rules say,
> That the rule of the free,
> From sea to sea,
> Shall ever increase,
> In kindness and peace.

The would-be conquering heroes are compared to "the bandits of old." Two references depict the plight of the ordinary soldiers. The common soldiers' potential grievances, carefully stated for the first time during the Mexican War to discourage volunteers, would find a stronger voice in the Civil War. While the "officers get the glory," the enlisted men will "figure in the killed and wounded,/ Washington Union, column 3d." As a reminder of the veterans' fate, the composer proposes,

> See how the soldier will be befriended,
> When health and fortune are both a wreck.
> Plenty of shot, and plenty of powder,
> This is the soldiers' principal pay.

A third piece, "The Volunteers' Song," contains essentially the same sentiments as the first two, but with several slight but important variations. It urges the troops to forget their humanity and moral training and become complete savages. The volunteers should "stab their [Mexican] hearts and drink their blood."[97] The final verse offers a thought that borders on megalomania, as the composer declares with pretended sincerity,

> We are freemen by our birth;
> Free for madness or for mirth,
> Free to conquer all the earth—after Mexico.

Yet some New Englanders, like a lieutenant colonel from New Hampshire who wrote a song published in the pro-war magazine appropriately titled *Rough and Ready*, repudiated the Conscience Whig position. He implies that perhaps cowardice is the cornerstone of antiwar feeling. Mockingly debating himself, he says,

> I have a little fear which way is best to go;
> If I dared I would fight, but I hardly think its right,
> Because get killed I might in the war with Mexico.[98]

"Hidebound Whigs" claim that "our soldiers kill and rob, they ravish by the job." Whig politicians are opportunists when they speak ill of the army in their districts, knowing that "such talk answers for the stump." They culminate their strident speeches "with a thump" for emphasis. Thus the hypocritical Whigs can take advantage of the war and "fill . . . [their] sails all full, with a breeze from Mexico." The colonel playfully ends his song, deciding to take the road to honor, when he exclaims,

> If you think there is no glory
> to be got by being a tory,
> then I'll march to Mexico.

This officer's song is an attempt to warn volunteers of the pitfalls of Whig logic and the questionable motives of Whig politicians.

Like the protest song, the sentimental song often describes an unfortunate side of war. Sentimental war songs emphasize the pain and sorrow of war; many of them indicate the sadness caused by the loss of loved ones. Some of them describe the heroic defeats of aristocratic soldiers. The purpose of the sentimental song is to invoke in the listener reflections on the tragic nature of war.

Several developments occurred in the sentimental ballad during the Mexican War. In the song "Love and Battle," a maiden warns young men about the dangers of combat while making them aware of their lovers' fears when they hurry off to win honor and glory. In a line reminiscent of many folksongs with their fatalistic themes, the young woman speaker declares about her lost love, "Had he stayed here he'd not been shot,/So never go to battle."[99] Although as has been stated, many young ladies wanted soldiers and heroes for beaux, certainly some women felt as did the teller of this sad tale. The most peculiar aspect of this song is the use of the tune "Yankee Doodle" with the lyrics of this doleful ballad. "Yankee Doodle" with its lively rhythm seems strangely out of place here.

The song "Rio Bravo" was written by a Mexican composer but was printed in at least one newspaper in the United States. The text laments the loss of many gallant soldiers and especially leaders like Arista, called the "best and bravest."[100] The piece incorporates references to both Spanish and Indian cultures when it mentions that Mexican soldiers are descended from those explorers from "Castile on Montezuma's shore" and when we hear that Mexican troops fight with "Aztec valor." The lyrics mention "Paladin and Knight" and indeed the song is filled with references to medieval knighthood; each dead Mexican hero is compared to a "Martyred knight." The tune "Roncevalles" itself alludes to the spot where Roland, the tragic but magnificent protagonist of the Medieval saga *Song of Roland*, fell.[101] The North represents the Americans and their modern weapons of conquest, such as "Northern wing'd artillery" and the deadly "Northern bayonet." The song is a sorrowful one ending fittingly, "lady ne'er mourned such a knight/Since the fondest hearts were broken in the Roncesvalles fight."

Two other romantic songs are worthy of brief discussion because they are connected with the war in an interesting fashion. First, the folksong "Green Grow the Lilacs" sometimes titled "Green Grow the Laurels," has been the subject of a persistent myth. The first two words in the title (also found in the song) sounded like the word "gringo" when heard by the native Spanish speakers. Thus, according to legend, the epithet "gringo" was given to Americans because Mexicans who often heard the foreign soldiers sing this popular song misunderstood the lyrics. In actuality, the word "gringo" is a corruption of "griego," the Spanish word for a Greek, and hence from that meaning it generally came to mean all foreigners. Since the Mexican War, "gringo" has been an insulting term applied to citizens from lands north of the Rio Grande.[102]

As mentioned earlier, some women gave aid and comfort to the American soldiers; "The Maid of Monterey" is about just such a Mexican woman who tended American wounded. An angel of mercy, she slipped onto the battlefield and nursed some of the fallen men, who "blessed the *senorita*"[103] because she "dressed the bleeding wounded." An important note to this song is its method of composition; John Hill Hewitt, who would later write songs for the Confederacy, composed both the words and music, albeit in 1851. Although the song was written after the war ended, it was the precursor of the sentimental songs of the Civil War.

The Mexican War inspired fewer songs of high quality than either of the two wars that preceded it or the Civil War that followed. But the writers of war songs, if not distinguished, were certainly vigorous. With all its chauvinism and cheerfulness, the war song reflects the country's attitude about the first conflict in which the United States acted as an aggressive power. Antiwar songs of this period also have a fire, but their theme is one of indignation at a war pursued for territorial aggrandizement, especially since the slave states seemed so eager for the country to acquire new lands. Although American antiwar songs originated with this war, they offer another theme in addition to opposition to the war: they evince a concern for the fate of the common soldier.

Of the two uncommon soldiers most likely to be the subjects of songs, one is celebrated roundly while the other is ignored completely. Certainly the reasons for Taylor's melodic elevation are clear enough, but why was

Winfield Scott slighted? He was, after all, the commander of American troops
who brought the war to a conclusion. Perhaps the answer lies in the different
personalities of the two men, so appropriately characterized in their respective
nicknames. Taylor, who won the first victories, was named romantically
"Old Rough and Ready." Scott, on the other hand, had the unenviable
nickname "Old Fuss and Feathers." The answer to Scott's absence from the
war song may well rest here.

By the end of the Mexican War, the American liberty and war song had
diversified in theme, and by 1848 American war songs had spread across a
broad range of subjects from liberty to war protests. Among the most prominent new themes included in the liberty and war song were volunteer soldiers
and war protests. Women were given an expanded voice in war songs and
the use of black dialect in American song became more common. Liberty
songs had changed again from the exuberance of the Revolution and the
dramatic calls to arms of the War of 1812; the liberty song took on an
unintentionally ironic character because it proclaimed that American freedom
could best be preserved with the addition of new lands taken from an unworthy enemy.[104]

What remained ahead was a new pinnacle; liberty and war songs had not
yet linked up completely with the major genres in popular song, and compositions had not yet become original, unified, quality works of art. In less
than a generation after the Mexican War, however, American composers
would produce a distinctive American song during a conflict that would
ultimately forge a unified nation.

NOTES

1. Otis A. Singletary, *The Mexican War* (Chicago: The University of Chicago
Press, 1960), p. 14.

2. K. Jack Bauer, *The Mexican War, 1846–1848* (New York: Macmillan 1974),
pp. 3–4.

3. Justin H. Smith, *The War with Mexico*, vol. 1 (Gloucester, Mass.: Peter Smith,
1963; originally published in 1919), p. 87.

4. Singletary, 18.

5. Bauer, 11.

6. Singletary, 150.

7. Seymour V. Connor and Odie B. Faulk, *North America Divided: The Mexican
War, 1846–1848* (New York: Oxford University Press, 1971), pp. 30–31.

8. "Strike, Columbia, Strike the Foe!" *Richmond Enquirer*, 3 July 1846.

9. "Song," *Charleston Mercury*, 15 July 1846.

10. "Strike for Your Rights, Avenge Your Wrongs," printed in An Officer in
General Taylor's Army, *Rough and Ready Songster* (New York: Nafis and Cornish,
n. d.), pp. 83–84.

11. Smith, 1:2.

12. Ibid., 1:113–115.

13. Bauer, 165–166.

14. "Uncle Sam to Texas," *Rough and Ready Songster*, 54–55.

15. Untitled song, *Rough and Ready Songster*, 125–126.

16. Untitled song, *National Intelligencer*, 8 June 1846.

17. John A. Lomax, *Cowboys Songs and Other Frontier Ballads* (New York: Macmillan, 1925), p. 314.

18. "Come Raise Aloft the Red, White, and Blue," *Rough and Ready Songster*, 36.

19. "New York Volunteers Camp Song," *Rough and Ready Songster*, 182–183.

20. Connor and Faulk, 44.

21. "Remember the Alamo," *Rough and Ready Songster*, 47–48.

22. Smith, 2:212.

23. Singletary, 145.

24. "The Song of Texas," *Rough and Ready Songster*, 55–56.

25. Smith, 1:67.

26. Brainerd Dyer, *Zachary Taylor* (New York: Barnes and Noble, 1946), p. 179.

27. "Huzza for Brave Zac and His Bayonet Boys," *Richmond Enquirer*, 2 October 1846.

28. Dyer, 173–174.

29. Ibid., 184.

30. "With Him We'll Bivouac," *New Orleans Times-Picayune*, 19 August 1847.

31. "Taylor the Fine Old Southern Gentleman," *Rough and Ready Songster*, 93–94.

32. *A Dictionary of Slang and Unconventional English*, s. v "swell."

33. Dyer, 121–123.

34. Ibid., 186. See also Holman Hamilton, *Zachary Taylor: Soldier of the Republic* (New York: Bobbs-Merrill, 1941), pp. 191–192.

35. "Zachary Taylor," reprinted in *Rough and Ready Songster*, 8–10.

36. Dyer, 237–238.

37. David Lavender, *Climax at Buena Vista: The American Campaigns in Northeastern Mexico, 1846–1847* (New York: J. B. Lippincott, 1966), p. 213.

38. *Rough and Ready Songster*, 5–8.

39. Dyer, 126.

40. "A Little More Grape Captain Bragg," reprinted in Vera Brodsky Lawrence, *Music for Patriots, Politicians, and Presidents: Harmonies and Discords of the First Hundred Years* (New York: Macmillan, 1975), p. 316.

41. Smith, 1:559.

42. Lavender, 210.

43. Bauer, 55.

44. Untitled song, *New Orleans Times-Picayune*, 11 October 1846.

45. "Fire Away," *Rough and Ready Songster*, 90–91.

46. George Winston Smith and Charles Judah, eds., *Chronicles of the Gringos: The U. S. Army in the Mexican War, 1846–1848* (Albuquerque: University of New Mexico Press, 1968), p. 67.

47. "Battles of the 8th and 9th of May," *Richmond Enquirer*, 22 September 1846.

48. Bauer, 147.

49. Smith, 1:105–106.

50. Dyer, 179.

51. Bauer, 59–62.

52. "The Fall of Matamoros," *Rough and Ready Songster*, 74–75.

53. Smith, 1:174–175.

54. Bauer, 210–217. Bauer's account has been cited here because it is clear, detailed, and accurate.

55. "Buena Vista," *Rough and Ready Songster*, 23–28.

56. *Encyclopedia of Black America*, 1981, s. v. "Mexican War."

57. "Siege of Monterey," *New Orleans Times-Picayune*, 20 November 1847.

58. "Uncle Sam and Mexico," *Rough and Ready Songster*, 91–92.

59. *Dictionary of Slang*, s. v. "bulljine."

60. Smith, 1:48–49.

61. "The Leg I Left Behind Me," reprinted in Edward Arthur Dolph, ed., *"Sound Off!": Soldier Songs from the Revolution to World War II* (New York: Farrar and Rinehart, 1942), p. 392.

62. Bauer, 268.

63. "Santy Anno," reprinted in Irwin Silber and Earl Robinson, *Songs of the Great American West* (New York: Macmillan, 1967). pp. 53–54.

64. Ibid., 52.

65. Singletary, 24.

66. Bauer, 69.

67. Smith, 2:192.

68. Singletary, 143–147.

69. "We're the Boys for Mexico," *Rough and Ready Songster*, 20–21.

70. Smith, 2:459.

71. Smith and Judah, 411. Davis also mentions the Catholic church in W. W. H. Davis, *El Gringo: New Mexico and Her People* (Lincoln: University of Nebraska Press, 1982; originally published in 1857), pp. 256–263.

72. Smith, 1:125.

73. *Dictionary of Slang*, s. v. "free and easy."

74. Smith, 1:125.

75. "The Printer Volunteers," *The Rough and Ready*, 30 January 1847, 1. This is a periodical that is in no way connected with the *Rough and Ready Songster* except for a similarity in title.

76. "Join the Hickory Blues," reprinted in Dolph, 383–384.

77. "Song of the Memphis Volunteers," reprinted in Dolph, 384–385.

78. Singletary, 146.

79. Dolph, 394.

80. "Buck and Gag Him," reprinted in Dolph, 394.

81. Smith, 2:385.

82. "The Coast of Mexico," *Rough and Ready Songster*, 19–20.

83. *Dictionary of Slang*, s. v. "duff."

84. Smith, 2:18.

85. "Alvarado," *Rough and Ready Songster*, 10–11.

86. Smith, 2:197–199.

87. Ibid., 2:344.

88. "Female Volunteer for Mexico," *Rough and Ready Songster*, 190–191.

89. Smith and Judah, 303–304.

90. Smith, 1:124–125.

91. "Song of the American Girl," *Rough and Ready Songster*, 76–77.

92. "My Daddy to my Mammy Said," *Rough and Ready Songster*, 231–232.

93. Bauer, 358–359. Opposition to the annexation of Texas and to possible new slave territory is clearly documented in Fredrick Merk, *Slavery and the Annexation of Texas* (New York: Alfred A. Knopf, 1972) and in *Manifest Destiny and Mission in American History: A Reinterpretation* (New York: Alfred A. Knopf, 1963).

94. "Mexico. An American National Song," *The Liberator*, 29 May 1846.

95. "Battle Hymn," *The Liberator*, 10 July 1846.

96. Singletary, 23.

97. "The Volunteer's Song," *The Liberator*, 8 January 1847.

98. "The Bold Volunteer, or the War-Peace Man," *The Rough and Ready*, 6 March 1847, 4.

99. "Love and Battle," *Rough and Ready Songster*, 224–225.

100. "Rio Bravo," reprinted in Dolph, 391. The *Santa Fe Republican*, a newspaper published in both Spanish and English editions, reprinted the song in English. The paper is so badly faded and worn that the song is completely unreadable in parts; Dolph's version is cited here.

101. *The Reader's Encyclopedia*, s. v. "Roncevalles."

102. Silber and Robinson, 49.

103. "The Maid of Monterey," reprinted in Silber and Robinson, 56.

104. For an excellent, brief study of the music of the Mexican War, see Robert W. Johannsen, *To the Halls of the Montezumas: The Mexican War in the American Imagination* (New York: Oxford University Press, 1985).

6

Old Tunes for a New War

Robert E. Lee once remarked, "I don't believe we can have an army without music."[1] His sentiments were shared by the Union forces as well as by civilians on both sides. The Civil War inspired stirring marches, war hymns, and memorable songs designed to delight and entertain the populace and the armies, instilling in them the essential righteousness of the causes of both North and South. The music of the Civil War was so melodious and moving that soldiers were tempted to sing when they were in combat areas. They had to be ordered not to sing, since they risked the possibility of betraying their positions to the enemy.[2]

The war inspired a vast quantity of songs, perhaps more than any other war in American history; the majority of these songs were written by setting words to existing tunes. In the South where there were fewer composers of note than in the North, writers used this process a great deal, especially relying on such standard melodies as "Yankee Doodle" and "Dixie." "Yankee Doodle" was usually set to lyrics intended to ridicule or otherwise demean the North. "Dixie" and sometimes the melody known in the South as the "Bonnie Blue Flag" were used as the musical basis of southern liberty and patriotic songs. Occasionally the "Marseillaise" was translated and altered for use as a Confederate patriotic song.

For the first time in both the North and South, composers began to work together to produce one or two war songs. This process led to the production of a few high quality songs, but in most cases the compositions were not much different from the derivative songs; a poem was sometimes set to words with little consideration for the proper blending of lyrics and music. Most of these works lack the unified quality that is found when two trained composers work together over a long period of time, or better yet when one rarely gifted composer combines the twin functions of writing lyrics and music to create a smooth, attractive, and artistic piece.

Sectional patriotism is the most prominent theme in Civil War songs and is present in most wartime compositions. Southern patriotic and liberty songs are discussed in this chapter before northern patriotic and liberty songs because most southern pieces in this genre are derivative, like "Dixie," or are variations of contemporary popular songs. Many of them mention the nobility of the southern cause and the desire of southerners to escape from an oppressive Union. Some southern composers remained loyal to the Union and their songs serve as a bridge between southern and northern songs. The North's most widely popular derivative songs were "John Brown's Body" and its companion piece "The Battle Hymn of the Republic." These songs were the best northern patriotic pieces not written by the North's outstanding composers.

Wartime leaders, both civilian and military, were the major figures in a second group of songs treated here. The presidents of both sections were the subjects of a large but not always flattering body of songs; military leaders were key figures in some songs. The most highly praised Confederate generals were P.G.T. Beauregard, Robert E. Lee, "Stonewall" Jackson, J.E.B. Stuart, and John H. Morgan. The most notable figures among northern generals to be singled out for musical comment were George B. McClellan and Ulysses S. Grant. McClellan did not receive favorable mention in some songs largely because of his political views and ambitions.

Military songs fall into three secondary categories—battle pieces, soldiers' songs, and naval ballads. Battle songs demonstrate the pride in victory and the shock and anguish at the high casualty rate that marked Civil War battles. Soldiers' songs voice the common soldiers' two most persistent complaints, the lack of food and the unseemly behavior of the officer corps. Naval songs mention ironclad ships, whose first use in combat by Americans was during the Civil War, and the southern commerce raider *Alabama*, which became the subject of a popular folksong.

Another important category of songs treats slavery, black soldiers, and abolition; the common themes are freedom and the desire for an end to slavery in America. The liberty theme came to include in its newest variation freedom from physical bondage. Like blacks, women had a place in the war song. They were depicted as willing producers of military goods whose work was crucial on both sides of the conflict. The last group of songs shows how the sentimental tune became a major part of the music of the Civil War.

Some of the most popular patriotic lyrics were set to well-known melodies, and these songs often were as widely sung, sometimes more so, than the originals. The process of contemporary variation is evident in songs such as "Dixie," composed in 1859 and whose origins are connected with the development of American popular music; both the song and its composer, Daniel D. Emmett, have interesting histories.

Emmett was born and grew up in Ohio, leaving the state for the first time in 1835 to go to an army training camp in Missouri when he was eighteen.

By this time Emmett had learned the printer's trade. He was also an accomplished violinist.[3] His career in the army was short-circuited when it was discovered that he was not of military age. Upon being discharged from the service, Emmett became a circus musician and traveled around the country. It was as a circus performer that he published his first tune, a dialect song titled "Bill Crowder," which he had written in 1838 or 1839. Shortly thereafter he became a blackface performer and banjo player with the circus. From there he went with a friend to try the stage in New York.[4] When stage shows fell on hard times in 1842, many of the minstrels were out of work. At a minstrels' practice session in Emmett's room in 1843, four men joined together to form the Virginia Minstrels. Their first performance was in February 1843, and they were immediately successful. Emmett introduced the song "Old Dan Tucker," which soon became a well-known melody; both abolitionists and antirent farmers used the music for their own purposes, as did soldiers during the Mexican War. Other of Emmett's songs were used for war songs, and his blackface routines inspired songwriters during the Mexican War. His name is, however, more intimately connected with the Civil War.

After several tours with various minstrel companies, Emmett joined Bryant's Minstrels, one of the finest troupes in the country. Emmett wrote "Dixie" in 1859, when he was with Bryant's band.[5] Emmett claimed that the music of "Dixie" came to him from the depths of memory; in his childhood his grandmother sometimes sang him to sleep with a song entitled "Come, Philander" that opened with the lines "Come Philander, let's be marchin'/ Every one his true love sarchin.' "[6]

Several other composers have claimed "Dixie," but Emmett's most recent and most thorough biographer, Hans Nathan, has examined the technical features of the song, such as handwriting style and the type of paper used, and he confirms the tune to be, without doubt, Emmett's.[7] Of the many claims made for the origin of "Dixie," the most popular in the South was that "Dixie" was an old slave song or that it was an old English melody sung primarily by black laborers. It was, some southerners remarked, mere accident that patriotic words became appended to a traditional folk tune.[8]

The word "Dixie" has a mysterious origin, and, like the song, it too has been the subject of a number of colorful stories told in both the North and South. A New York publisher declared that a man named Dixie lived in Manhattan in earlier days and kept his slaves there. As he acquired more slaves than his land could support, he sent them South—but they never ceased to believe that Dixie's land was their true home. A second publisher avowed, logically enough, that Dixie's land was all the territory below the Mason-Dixon line. A third story, similar in some ways to the first, declares that Dixie was a southern planter who died, leaving his bereaved slaves to believe that he went to Heaven, which was thereafter Dixie's land. Yet another tale relates that Dixie is connected with French bank notes once used in Louisiana. These notes ostensibly had the word "Dix" (for ten) printed on them, and thus Americans called them Dixies. A final version of the origin of "Dixie" describes a minstrel character named Dixie who became an archetypal Negro; since most blacks at this time lived in the South, it became Dixie's land.[9]

Because Emmett waited for more than a year to obtain a copyright on "Dixie," several publishers pirated the song. After some legal conflicts, Emmett's publishers, Firth, Pond, and Company, generously gave Emmett the total sum of $300 for the rights to the already-famous song. Since this settlement took place in February 1861, some southern publishers ignored the legal (but northern) ownership of the tune.[10]

It is possible that "Dixie" first became well known in the South when it was played in a performance of the drama "Pocahontas," probably in 1860. In any case, once it arrived in the Confederate states, its popularity skyrocketed.[11] "Dixie" was played at the inauguration of Jefferson Davis in 1861; after that, it rose to the prominent place it has held for many decades in the South.

When the seceded South chose "Dixie" as a national war song, southerners adopted a well-recognized minstrel song popular in the North. When he heard that the South had appropriated his melody for use as a patriotic song, Emmett said, "If I had known to what use they were going to put my song, I will be damned if I'd have written it." Union soldiers, too, sang "Dixie" but only until 1863. For the rebels it was "the musical symbol of a new nationality."[12] Indeed, it might well have been this sentiment that helped Confederate soldiers to gird themselves for battle when they heard the song. General George Pickett evidently believed this to be the case, for he ordered the tune played before the historic charge at Gettysburg into the muzzles of the Union guns.[13]

The first change southern composers made in "Dixie" was to discard its comical dialect lyrics. Confederate General Albert Pike made a pleasing and popular war song of "Dixie" with his verses. His version urges rebel soldiers to undertake fearsome battle and to drive the Union dogs back "to their kennels."[14] The southern cause, he avers, is "the Lord's work." Without a doubt, the young Confederacy's future is a bright one since "victory shall soon bring them gladness."

One variation of "Dixie" is somewhat more literary than most. For example, the northern forces are called "myrmidons"[15] after the Greek warriors of antiquity. Another portion of the song reads, when referring to the opening of hostilities and alluding to the ethnic backgrounds of some Union soldiers, "Abe's proclamation in a twinkle,/Stirred up the blood of Rip Van Winkle." The song also mentions northern and southern leadership, calling the president of the United States and his government "kangaroos." In contrast, Confederate chiefs are spoken of as "great Jeff Davis" and "gallant Bragg and Beauregard."

Another notable version of the song uses some Mother-Goose-like verses in attacking Union leadership, especially Ambrose Burnside, John Pope, Irvin McDowell, and Nathaniel Banks. This rendition concludes with the biblical-sounding prediction that Confederate armies will drive Union forces away from the South "like sheep on the plains."[16]

The North also used "Dixie" as a war song, sometimes to insult southerners. Since it was originally composed by a northerner and a Union man, it is likely that the Confederacy's arbitrary piracy of the piece caused additional resentment in the North. In "Union Dixie," slighting references to the South as "the land of traitors,/rattlesnakes, and alligators"[17] indicate a distasteful view of the enemy. The jibe "cotton's king and men are chattels" is clearly intended to demean the southern way of life. A Confederate is portrayed as a "boy" who "must mind his Uncle Sam" or be shamefully punished as a recalcitrant child would be.

The Democrats picked up "Dixie" in 1864 for use in the presidential campaign of that year, but McClellan went down in defeat as surely as the Confederarcy soon would.[18] With the surrender of Lee, Lincoln believed that "Dixie," a melody that he had always favored, had been surrendered to the Union too. Lincoln so declared on 10 April 1865.[19]

Emmett continued to play his roles in minstrel shows, but his writing talent seems to have disappeared with the war's end. He lasted a few years as a performer, but finally he retired at age seventy-three to his home in Ohio. At the age of eighty he reclaimed his most famous tune during a tour with Al Field's minstrels, and his finale of "Dixie" brought him once again the acclaim of days past. He died nine years later.[20]

Second in popularity to "Dixie" in the Confederacy was Harry McCarthy's celebrated "Bonnie Blue Flag." McCarthy, an English actor who had come to America and become a popular theater player in the South, set his lyrics to the tune "The Irish Jaunting Car." Richard Harwell, the premier scholar of southern war music, has said that the "Bonnie Blue Flag" was artistically "inferior, [but] . . . it was the right song at a particular moment."[21] The song's one memorable line, a euphemistic one, says that southerners were "fighting for the property we gained by honest toil."[22] Slaves are obviously the property signified; later editions of the song change the word "property" to "liberty."[23] The text, composed in 1861, was probably inspired by the first Confederate flag, which matches the one described in the lyrics.[24] The song's influence in the South is best seen through General Benjamin Butler's reaction to it. As commander of the captured city of New Orleans, he made the singing or playing of the tune punishable by a twenty-five dollar fine.[25] The song inspired a number of imitations in both the North and South. The most interesting is a savage parody directed at McCarthy by John Hill Hewitt, the South's most prolific composer and often called the "Bard of the Confederacy."[26] The occasion for this song arose when McCarthy went to Philadelphia during the war, possibly to escape the draft; this action did not set well with the strongly pro-southern Hewitt.[27] Hewitt put his parody in McCarthy's voice, having him proudly claim of his flight North, "I've dodged the shells of war."[28] Further, Hewitt has McCarthy delightedly assert greed as his motive for composing the southern war song. Hewitt's McCarthy says, "My object was to fill my purse,/By tickling them with praise." The accused turncoat feels no qualms about deserting the southern cause and mocks his former friends with the thought that "May Lincoln be your king."

Southerners were also familiar with Hewitt's popular pre-war melody from "The Minstrel's 'Return," written in 1825, and they used it for the inspirational "Southern Song of Freedom."[29] This piece epitomizes the Confederate patriotic song with its mentions of "liberty"[30] twice in the first stanza. The Union army is depicted in terms that most southerners assuredly believed,

> The invaders rush down from the North,
> Our borders are black with their hordes,
> Like wolves for their victims they froth,
> While whetting their knives and their swords.

The watchword of these villains is " 'Booty and Beauty,'/[and] they aim to steal as they go." Like their enemies, militant southerners thought that they had God on their side. As the writer declares, "The God of our fathers looks down/and blesses the cause of the just." Southern songs, even the most fervent in support of southern rights, do not have the religious, crusading tone that pervades some northern tunes, particularly those of the abolitionists. The song does employ the word "southron," an archaic term for Englishmen. Strong believers in the Confederate cause used it to identify themselves. The word also served to link them with a romantic British past, one that existed only in the imaginations of men like Sir Walter Scott.[31]

Songs like "The Cavalier's Song," subtitled "A Song of the Olden Time," were printed in southern newspapers and helped to reinforce the chivalric ideal many southerners believed the Confederacy represented. "The Soldier Minstrel's Last Lay," with its debt to Scott's novel *The Lay of the Last Minstrel* in the title, looks at death from an unrealistic, cloyingly romantic view. As might be expected from these pieces, they contain little of substance. Many northerners did not believe in the Confederate cavaliers' image, and an anonymous composer in *The Liberator* offers an example of a New Englander's impression of a southern cavalier:

> My sword is gold-hilted, my charger is fleet,
> I am bullion and spangles from helmet to feet;
> I am fierce in my cups and most savagely bent
> On slaying the Yankees when safe in my tent;
> In short if I'm timid, I know how to blow,
> With my feet to the field and my back to the foe.[32]

Not all southerners thought of themselves as cavaliers or southrons. William G. Brownlow, editor of *Brownlow's Knoxville Whig*, came out vigorously against secession in one of several patriotic songs printed in his paper. The title of the song, "Union, Constitution, and the Laws," summarizes the attitude of the composer. If Brownlow did not author the piece, set to "Dixie," he wholeheartedly agreed with the sentiments "by the Stars and Stripes I take my stand."[33] The author declares, "Jeff Davis will have to die," presumably because his crime of sanctioning the breakup of the Union is unforgivably treasonous. Furthermore, the author writes, "the friends of the Union stand opposed,/to Northern and to Southern foes." While Brownlow and his supporters railed against the Copperheads and southern sympathizers in the North, the vast majority in the Confederacy thought of Brownlow and his followers as enemies of the South. Despite his bitter feelings against the rebels, the composer pleads for a consideration of the Union when he asks, "Secession brothers cease to stand,/So opposed to our fatherland." In a later song set to the Old German tune "O, Tannenbaum," titled "East Tennessee," Clara von Moschzisker salutes the eastern Tennessee region for its devotion to the Union cause. She says of the area that it is "still faithful 'mid the faithless found."[34] Her remark alludes to one of the sections of the South that still firmly considered itself part of the United States. She offers comforting words to those who support the Union when she encouragingly states "Bear on brave hearts, the dawn is near."

The Union's favorite derivative liberty and war songs were undoubtedly the pieces known first as "The John Brown Song" and later as "The Battle Hymn of the Republic." The melody is an old one and has true folk origins. It was the basis of drinking and sailors' songs until Charles Wesley, a well-known clergyman and brother of John Wesley, founder of the Methodist church, rescued the music from its baser uses and turned it into the foundation of a religious song supporting Methodist sentiments, with which the melody came to America.[35]

One Sergeant John Brown, a Boston soldier in the Twelfth Massachusetts Volunteer Infantry, was the first notable Civil War subject of a song using the old melody; the lyrics were fashioned to tease the young soldier about his name by identifying and purposely confusing him with the executed abolitionist John Brown. As Boyd Stutler notes, two of this song's lines have particular significance. "John Brown's body lies mouldering in the grave" is a jocular reference to Sergeant Brown's living presence as contrasted with that of the deceased abolitionist. "Gone to be a soldier in the army of the Lord" was the usual phrase that Union chaplains employed to describe Federal soldiers' enlistments. The song thus notably retains a religious reference.[36] The meanings in the song's lyrics that later came to be associated with abolitionist Brown might well have started when the Twelfth Massachusetts Regiment, in July 1861, reached the scene of Brown's failed rebellion at Harper's Ferry. The Union regiment sang the song as they traveled through the area, as did other northern units after them.[37]

Julia Ward Howe's lyrics to the old melody served to increase its popularity, especially among abolitionists. Like many creations, her song came to her, according to Howe's recollection, completely by chance. The process of composition began when she heard some soldiers singing the "John Brown Song" as they passed her carriage outside of Washington in the afternoon of 17 November 1861. In the early morning of the eighteenth she was awakened by "certain lines which though not entirely suited to the John Brown music, were yet capable of being sung to it."[38] Her lyrics, "The Battle Hymn of the Republic" (see appendix), and those of the "John Brown" version of the song, were sung during the remainder of the war. These two songs also provided inspiration for the Union cause and served as marching tunes for Union soldiers. One of the most noteworthy performances of the "Battle Hymn" was given at the House of Representatives on 3 February 1864 by the well-known abolitionist singer, chaplain Charles McCabe. Lincoln reportedly said of the song and McCabe's performance, "Take it all in all, the song and the singing, that was the best I ever heard."[39] The song was also sung on such notable occasions as 10 April 1865, the day after Lee's surrender,[40] and at a memorial service for Lincoln on 24 April 1865.[41]

The lyrics of "Battle Hymn" retain the old campsong flavor, in this case making a secular cause, the abolition of slavery, into a religious and sacred one; the cause not only has God's sanction, but indeed He commands that battle be pursued. This is abundantly clear in the line "Let the hero born of woman crush the serpent with his heel."[42] The second intended meaning in this line is the thought that secession, like slavery, is evil. Equating the Union cause with Christ's mission, "As he died to make men holy, let us die to make men free," would undoubtedly appeal to abolitionists. Not surprisingly, the South did not incorporate the John Brown melody into any of its patriotic or liberty songs.

The war leaders in both North and South were popular subjects for songs. The two chief executives, Abraham Lincoln and Jefferson Davis, received as much criticism as praise from Civil War composers. Lincoln was derided in the North for his looks and in the South for his lack of courage. Several northern writers also criticized his political views and decisions. Davis was the victim of several songs in the North about his capture by Union forces. Unlike Lincoln, he was not the subject of many songs approving his performance in office. Lincoln was also given many laudatory tributes after his untimely death. Some generals in both South and North were important figures in Civil War songs; several southern commanders were featured in song but in the North only McClellan and Grant became important figures in Union compositions. McClellan, especially during his 1864 campaign for the presidency, was the subject of musical criticism; some northern writers opposed his political views and noted his military failures.

As Abraham Lincoln rapidly learned, the preservation of the Republic would be made under a burden of criticism from those who did not completely support him. While Lincoln received much musical praise for his work, he was continually the target of abusive and lampooning songs that mocked him personally as well as politically. Songs critical of Lincoln were composed in both the North and South. In the 1860 election Lincoln's Democratic opponents poked fun at his physical features. For example, in a song titled "Old Abe and His Fights," Lincoln's opponents declared that it was permissible to compare Lincoln with Henry Clay, Daniel Webster, or Andrew Jackson, but they begged "Don't for God's sake—show his picture."[43]

Newspapers in the South, especially during the first year after Lincoln's election, published a number of scathing musical diatribes about Lincoln's character and his efforts to subdue the rebellious states. The most prolific southern musical critic was the Atlanta paper aptly named *The Southern Confederacy*. In a song published two days after Lincoln's inauguration, titled "Lincoln Doodle" and set to "Yankee Doodle," the physical danger to Lincoln is explained. Rumors of plots against the president-elect's life were widely circulated both before and during his trip from Springfield, Illinois, to the inauguration in Washington, and the general atmosphere in the North during the few days preceding the ceremony was one of concern for Lincoln's safety.[44] The song apparently confirming the danger to Lincoln was placed in the mouth of "a trav'lin' prophet"[45] speaking to the president; it left no doubt where the purported scheme to harm Lincoln originated. As the mysterious figure declares, "Jeff Davis . . . has set a trap." The conspiracy includes "a bombshell and torpedo,/Likewise assassins eight or ten." The song tells that Lincoln was on "a special train/At midnight's solemn hour." This statement is true in part, for Lincoln had been on a special train but changed trains from the special to a standard passenger train before midnight. The composer also accepted an incorrect newspaper report that Lincoln was disguised in a "cloak and Scotch plaid shawl." That "Abe dodged into Washington" was a fact that embarrassed Lincoln's friends and invoked jests from his enemies.[46] The writer finds Lincoln's dress "becoming to his station," and asks if Lincoln will "come upon a special train,/And whip the Southern nation."

In "Yankee Doodle," a southern parody of the original, Lincoln "scorns to be mere President—/He makes himself Dictator."[47] The writer unexplainably lapses into dialect in the third stanza when he presents "Uncle Tom," a curious reference to the character in Harriet Beecher Stowe's seminal antislavery novel *Uncle Tom's Cabin*. Suddenly and inexplicably the aged slave takes the rebel side, averring, "Master, we/can whip dem saitful debils." The song also alludes to a removal of the slaves "off to Cuba" as one of the Union's colonization attempts.

"Abraham Lincoln," set to the tune of "Old Dan Tucker," is, like its predecessors, a savage dig at the man so truly hated throughout much of the

South. Of Lincoln's presidential victory the song says, "Abraham Lincoln got elected!/Bigger fool than we expected!"[48] In an allusion to Lincoln's log splitting days, the writer states,

> Lincoln made a pledge,
> To save the Union with a *wedge*!
> Drove it in! but the more he hit it
> the worse the glorious Union split.

Lincoln is compared with a French tyrant who is "mighty mean with his Bastile." This statement probably refers to the large number of civilians arrested and confined without trials in the North during the war.[49] One of the last verses reads,

> There's a pile of pickaninny
> Lying 'round in old Virginny,
> Waiting 'till he came along
> To greet him with a cannon song.

It is clear from this verse that slave owners were confident that their slaves would completely support them.

But Lincoln had songs praising him, the most famous of which is the campaign song "Lincoln and Liberty." Set to the old Irish melody "Rosin the Beau," the song labels the candidate "brave and true"[50] and one who will effect a "great reformation" in America. The piece was originally printed in the *Hutchinson's Republican Songster for 1860* with words by Jesse Hutchinson, a member of the famous singing abolitionist family.[51] An untitled tune from the same music book, put to "Dixie," relates that "Honest Abe"[52] was "a true man."

"We Are Coming, Father Abr'am" is a song staunchly supporting Lincoln and his war policies. Although he was a Quaker, James Sloan Gibbons, the lyricist, agreed with Lincoln's request for additional troops for the Union army.[53] Large numbers of volunteers did not quickly answer the president's call of 2 July 1862, despite the strong musical support he received from "We Are Coming."[54] Well-known figures put Gibbon's inspirational words to their music, as did lesser-known melodists. Stephen Foster, by this time past his writing prime, contributed one of the melodies, while Patrick Sarsfield Gilmore, a Union bandleader, added another. One version used the "John Brown" melody. In spite of its popularity, the song had relatively undistinguished lyrics, aside from its rousing chorus of "We are coming, Father Ab'ram,/three hundred thousand more."[55] The song democratically includes men from all walks of life going to fight for the Union, among them those leaving their "plows and workshops." The tune numbers "those who have gone before" as "six hundred thousand loyal men." In the North the piece was savagely parodied in "How Are You, Green-Backs?" The opening lines give away the song's theme:

> We're coming, Father Abram,
> One hundred thousand more,
> Five hundred presses printing us,
> From morn 'til night is o'er.[56]

The Confederacy was not musically concerned with inflation in the North (theirs was much worse), but they did sing their fears about the subjects of emancipation and the potential use of black soldiers by the Union. The sentiments in "We're Coming, Fodder Abraham" mirror the considerable worry and anger in the South toward the abolitionist position in the North. Southerners believed that ultimately blacks might be used as Federal troops "to make de army bigger."[57] Just as mortifying to southerners was the thought that "de Nigger [will be] just as good as any odder man."

The beliefs of many of the soldiers who supported Lincoln are contained in the title of the song "We'll fight for Uncle Abe." The song was obviously written early in the war as a line in the third stanza indicates: "General McClellan, he's the man,/The Union for to save."[58] This thought was in total accord with George McClellan's own view of his mission. The lyricist declared that the South would have no chance of foreign "recognition" because "Johnny Bull and Mister France/are 'fraid of Uncle Abe." The author was ultimately right about diplomatic recognition of the Confederacy, not necessarily because the English and French governments feared Lincoln, but for a variety of reasons; not the least of these was the Rebels' failure to win a significant, devastating victory over Federal forces.

Lincoln's death evoked a wide variety of musical mourning songs, including dirges and songs of tribute and loss. The best of the genre is "Farewell Father, Friend and Guardian" with a melody by George Root. The writer's sentiments are the usual ones, and the tribute is customary but moving. The author declares that the "land is draped in mourning"[59] for "our loved, noble leader,/[who] sleeps his last, dreamless sleep." Although Lincoln had "fallen by a traitor's hand," the peerless war leader had "preserved his dearest treasure,/our redeem'd beloved land." The last verse projects Lincoln's greatness and his tragedy into the future: "Hearts unborn shall sigh for thee."

Jefferson Davis fared much worse than Lincoln in song. While he was the subject of several complimentary southern marches during the war, his notoriety in song began after his capture in 1865. The composer of "Jeff in Petticoats," a song mocking Davis' disguise at the time of his capture, asserts that Davis fled with "a mine of golden coin"[60] stolen from "banks and other places." He is called a common "thief" who, in a cowardly fashion, "dropped his pantaloons" for a woman's "crinoline" dress. Many northern songs documented Davis' supposed attempt to escape capture by cloaking his identity with his wife's garments; "Jeff Davis in Crinoline" has the fleeing Confederate president caught in a dress and carelessly forgetting to abandon his man's "boots and spurs."[61] His well-known "whiskers," which he somehow forgets to shave, finally give him away to his captors. Davis in disguise is pictured on the cover of a song titled "The Sour Apple Tree." The artist of this songsheet makes Davis look like a comic figure in a shawl with his beard prominently protruding from his disguise. The phrase "They will hang Jeff Davis on a sour apple tree,"[62] sums up much northern sentiment about Davis' deserved fate.

Many of the jibes about Davis' capture are based on misinformation. When Federal troops surprised Davis during his escape, he picked up his wife's raincoat by mistake as he attempted to flee. His wife, in the confusion, threw her shawl over his head. These events led to the erroneous notion that Davis had disguised himself as a woman. He was not captured with a fortune in gold; the almost empty trunk that Davis and his wife carried contained only a skirt.[63]

The major military leaders on both sides were the subjects of numerous songs, few of them of high quality. Several of the songs, however, are worth a closer look. The first hero of the war was the Confederate general P. G. T. Beauregard, who, probably because of his leadership positions at Manassas and then Fort Sumter, was heavily favored in southern song. Typical of these efforts was "Beauregard, A Song," written for the soldier of French ancestry. The chorus plays enthusiastically over his name and heritage. He is called in the most vigorous lines

> Beau-fusil, Beauregard!
> Beau-cannon, Beauregard!
> Beau-Sabreur, et beau-soldat, Beauregard!.[64]

Robert E. Lee, "Stonewall" Jackson, and the colorful cavalry leaders J. E. B. Stuart and John H. Morgan were the other major Confederate generals saluted in song. "The Sword of Robert E. Lee" equates Lee's sword with his character, as the weapon from "stain is free,"[65] and it served in "guarding the right." The Confederacy "still hoped on,/while gleamed the blade of noble Robert Lee." Lee, the great hero of the Confederacy, bore his defeats "proudly and peacefully."

"Stonewall Jackson's Way" was written during or shortly after Jackson's 1862 campaign in the Shenandoah Valley, for the "burly Blue Ridge" is mentioned. So is "Banks," Union General N. P. Banks, who was defeated by the brilliant rebel leader in the Valley campaign. In a detailed portrait, Jackson's description is given:

> The queer slouched hat
> Cocked o'er his eye askew;

The shrewd, dry smile; the speech so pat,
So calm, so blunt, so true!.[66]

This picture tallies with that Frank Vandiver paints in *Mighty Stonewall.*[67]
A steadfast Presbyterian, he was sometimes called "old Blue Light" by his
men because of his devout and frequent prayers.[68] His death shortly after
Chancellorsville was the subject of numerous poems and funeral songs
throughout the South, none of which had any special merit.

The song "Riding a Raid," subtitled "A Tribute to J. E. B. Stuart" is set
to the traditional Scots melody "The Bonnie Dundee." The essence of the
piece is in the chorus, which details the careful preparations that cavalrymen
must make before beginning a mission. The author says,

Come tighten your girth and slacken your rein;
Come buckle your blanket and holster again;
Try the click of your trigger and balance your blade
For he must ride sure that goes Riding a Raid.[69]

The lyrics say little of Stuart, but do praise the cavalry's work.

"How Are You, John Morgan" is essentially the story of an unsuccessful
raid by Morgan and his men into the North; much of the song describes
Morgan's escape from a Federal prison after his capture by Union forces.
The text is accurate in some details, but amiss in several others. For example,
Morgan was indeed captured in Ohio and given a "shaven crest,"[70] the mark
of a criminal. Not only was Morgan's hair shorn close to his skull, but his
beard was also shaved. He did not, however, procure the "greenbacks" used
to purchase railroad tickets after his escape. Although the song gives Morgan
credit for digging the tunnel that allowed the general and some of his officers
to escape, he actually had no part in the excavation. He did not ride away
"upon his mule," but traveled back to the South by train and canoe.[71]

The Union commander most frequently mentioned in song was George
B. McClellan, a popular general and political figure of note. His opposition
to Lincoln and the Republican party reached its height in 1864. In the
presidential election that year, McClellan ran against Lincoln, with whom
he disagreed on military and political issues. Often styled "Little Mac" in
campaign songs, he won this affectionate appellation from his troops for his
small stature. A song set to a Foster melody by Foster's sister Henrietta
shows not only her support for McClellan but also the virulent dislike some
Democrats felt for Lincoln. "Little Mac! Little Mac! You're the Man" does
not so much praise McClellan as villify Lincoln. He is called "Abraham the
Joker,"[72] and a reference is made to his inauguration trip to Washington in
his "Scotch Caps," a mistaken description discussed earlier. Lincoln's emancipation efforts are called rudely "nigger proclamations." Another less violent
McClellan campaign song, titled simply "McClellan for President," says that

the general "has proved himself a man,/who will stand by the Laws and Constitution."[73] Furthermore, the composer asserts "Union folks do know that Abe Lincoln don't want peace." McClellan will "bring back the South to the Union . . . with the OLIVE BRANCH."

The *Albany Evening Journal* did not agree that "Little Mac" could handle the office of president. An untitled campaign song put to "Rosin the Beau" remarks that McClellan is a "used up quack";[74] he is additionally called "little failure Mac," probably because he did not take Richmond during the Peninsula Campaign when he commanded the Union forces. He might possibly have ended the war earlier with prompt and carefully planned action. The author concludes' that "War Democrats are coming 'round/For Honest Old Abe and Johnson." Andrew Johnson was a War Democrat who supported the Union. The Tennessean made an ideal running mate for Lincoln because he came from a southern state and because he completely disavowed secession.

After McClellan, Grant was the most popular figure in Union songs.[75] Strangely, the best song about Grant was not strictly a war song. Daniel Emmett composed the premature campaign song called "U. S. G." in 1864; the song was one of the most interesting about a major military figure. The music, which is not extant, may well have been one of Emmett's earlier melodies, but the composer might have used an older melody not of his own creation as Hans Nathan does not list the song among Emmett's numerous works. Sparing no praise, Emmett called Grant "second to none but Alexander."[76] The chorus cleverly states Emmett's views and probably those of many other northerners in late 1864, shortly before the election. The composer boasts for his candidate that

> he dug a trench at Vicksburg, and sure as you're alive;
> He'll dig one more 'round the White House door in eighteen sixty-five.

Grant, however, waited four years to complete his trench in Washington.

For the first time in the American war song, composers recorded their shock at the sight of battlefields covered with dead and wounded. The optimism of the early war was replaced with anguish over monumental casualty lists. Another significant change in Civil War combat is chronicled in naval songs. Before the Civil War all ship-to-ship combat had been between wooden vessels. The magnitude of the first American use of ironclad ships is evident in naval songs; one of them even lists in detail the advantages of the ironclad ship over its wooden counterpart, while Southern raiders like the *Alabama* became the subjects of folksongs. Soldiers' songs also made a point not previously found in American war songs because combatants voiced complaints about army food (and its absence) and the privileged officer corps.

In the South many battle songs were written early in the war before weariness and defeat had set in. The young Confederacy was optimistic about the outcome of the war when the first shots were fired; this optimism was confirmed for many southerners with the Confederate victory at Manassas on 21 July 1861. The Union forces under Irvin McDowell, after initial success, fell back to Washington in a hurried and disorganized retreat. The Confederate triumph belonged to troops under Generals Joseph E. Johnston and P. G. T. Beauregard. As the writer of "Yankee Doodle's Ride to Richmond" confirms, southerners had no doubts about their ability to duplicate their first victory; they regarded themselves as superior to an army of "filthy Dutch and Irish from the Bogs."[77] The myth that the Union army was made up primarily of foreigners and immigrants continued into the twentieth century, but it does not bear up under careful scrutiny.[78] The Union army did have more foreigners than the Confederate army. It is possible that this fact increased southerners' fears that they were being "invaded" by a foreign power whose army consisted of detestable mercenaries. The last lines of the song read, in a confident and ominous warning to the North, "when next he doth come to fight, we'll run him back/again." This long piece is filled primarily with general boasts about southerners' military and cultural superiority over northerners. In "Flight of the Doodles," the narrator makes light of the ease with which southern forces defeated their enemies at Manassas, claiming that the fight was "a pocket full of fun."[79] His own exploits clearly symbolize those of the ordinary Confederate soldier. While not bashful about his experiences, the narrator surely realizes his own exaggeration when he asserts, "I killed forty Yankees with a single barrelled gun." This remark reinforced the widely held Confederate belief that man for man the southerners were better fighters than their Union counterparts.

A change from the light-hearted tone of the first battle songs to a more somber one is present in the songs about Shiloh. The battle of Shiloh indicated the kind of carnage that was to mark the major battles of the war. Although the North had won the battle, Grant's troops were bone weary and bloodied; the Confederates were in much the same condition, and they suffered the additional loss of their commander, Albert Sidney Johnston. The shock of seeing so many Americans dead and wounded is registered in a Texan's song about the fighting that occurred on 6 and 7 April 1862. In the first verse of "The Battle of Shiloh Hill," the composer declares, "The feeling of that hour/I do remember still."[80] In the next verse he describes that feeling which has continued to haunt him: "The horrors of the field/did my heart with anguish fill." In the fifth verse the author reports the scene on the field after the first day's combat:

The wounded men were crying
for help from everywhere,
While others, who were dying
Were offering God their prayer.

The soldier/composer wishes vainly that this might be the last such bloody encounter: "I hope the sight by mortal men may ne'er be seen again." Before Shiloh no battle fought in America had been so devastating; each side lost approximately 10,000 men. According to eyewitness accounts, the dead and wounded were stacked in piles, yet Shiloh was to rank only seventh among Civil War battles in the number of casualties totalled. As a result of later similarly large-scale battles, the Civil War was to result in more American casualties than any other war in which Americans have fought.[81]

Naval combat in the Civil War was also to take on a new dimension. For the first time in American naval history, large numbers of ironclad warships would be used. The Confederacy put its first one into action in March 1862; the ship was a former Union steam frigate that had been scuttled when Federal forces fled from Norfolk, Virginia. The rebels also changed its name from the *Merrimac* to the *Virginia* and added iron plates and an extended frontal ram. In its first conflict with Union blockaders, the *Virginia* destroyed the wooden ships *Cumberland* and *Congress*. Some in the South believed that this victory was the first step toward the end of the blockade and would ultimately lead to Confederate naval supremacy.[82]

That this battle signaled the demise of the wooden war vessel is evident in a remark made by the composer of "The *Cumberland* and the *Merrimac*." When the *Cumberland* fired on her opponent "no break in her iron [was] made, [and] no damage"[83] done. As the song relates, the *Merrimac*'s ram "went crashing through" the *Cumberland*'s side, causing the possibility that the *Merrimac* might well have been dragged to the bottom by the sinking *Cumberland*. Fortunately for the ironclad, her ram broke away. The song correctly reports some of the action after the ramming incident; the *Cumberland*'s crew valiantly "poured broadside after broadside" into the *Merrimac* without effect. The Union boat continued to fire away until water filled her guns. One hundred twenty-one of the crew went down with their ship.[84] "Iron Clad Jack: A Sea Song of the Future" clearly explains why wooden ships would give way to ironclad vessels. Printed originally in the British periodical *Punch* and afterwards in America in a New Orleans newspaper, the song tells that ironclad steam boats "were proof against steel, iron, and lead."[85] Furthermore, there was "no woodwork to riddle, alow or aloft,/[and] no canvas to shift or to tack."

Britain's involvement with the naval war between North and South went much farther than the composition of songs about ironclad boats. The well-known folksong "Roll, *Alabama*, Roll" tells in succinct fashion the story of the *Alabama*, one of the most famous English-built Confederate warships. The song accurately gives the site of its construction as "Birkenhead"[86] in the "yard of Jonathan Laird." The piece incorrectly includes the remark that "Liverpool fitted her with men and guns." The boat did carry an English crew, and no doubt many of the men were from the Liverpool area near the Laird shipyards, but the *Alabama* was armed and provisioned in the Azores.[87] The song erroneously gives the date of the *Alabama*'s last action as "sixty-five," although the Union vessel *Kearsarge* actually sank the Confederate raider on 19 June 1864. Thus with sixty-four captures to her credit the commerce raider "*Alabama* went to her grave."[88]

Naval actions were of scant immediate concern to ordinary soldiers in the field, who often faced death or injury in battle. They also had mundane needs, the most pressing of which were their daily rations. "Hard Crackers Come Again No More," a humorous piece set to Foster's "Hard Times Come Again No More," describes army food as "mummies of hard crackers."[89] When cornmeal mush was served to the soldiers as a replacement for hard bread, the soldiers said of the quantity and quality of their new rations, "we are starving now on horse-feed."[90] They begged for "hard crackers [to] come once again." Bread and cracker diets were especially prevalent when rations were short, as they were from time to time in both armies, but more often among Confederate forces.[91] The rebel song, "Short Rations," written by two men styling themselves "Ye Tragic and Ye Comic" to maintain their anonymity, expressed the southern soldiers' thoughts when "the army was all put on a diet/and the Board had diminished our rations."[92] The song certainly was written after the spring of 1862 when the Confederate government (the Board) ordered reduced rations for the first but not the last time. In combat or on campaigns, food was scarcer than during the lulls, especially in the eastern theater. As the writer declares, "We had one meal a day, [and] it was small." The composer, like many other soldiers, is fearful that one meal will soon become "none," as it sometimes did. Blaming the quartermasters, the author asks them to "put a curb on your maddening passions," presumably those of greed and self-indulgence. For a time the men were able to gather rations without authorization, for as the author humorously states, the "fowls and pigs were ferocious" and therefore had to be dispatched; fortunately, they served as food. While the soldiers were ordered not to provision themselves in this fashion, they were forced to subsist on grains. The "parched corn was tougher" than the meat had been, and many of the soldiers found it inedible because of the pain it caused them when they attempted to chew it. Songs like the widely sung southern piece "Goober Peas" originated because peanuts were sometimes issued in place of more substantial rations.[93] To the hungry rebels they were undoubtedly "delicious."[94]

One of the frequent complaints of enlisted men, besides their rations, concerned the actions and abilities of their officers. In the North an anonymous soldier composed a lengthy song titled "The Brass-Mounted Army" in which he indicts officers for their blatant abuse of rank. The officers "drink ... when there's danger."[95] When a plantation home is captured

> the general puts a guard;
> The sentry's then instructed to let no private pass—
> The rich man's house and table are fixed to suit the "brass."

Although the complaining writer is forced to eat "beef and corn bread," he vows that he will continue to "fight for Liberty." The composer looks forward to the time when he can "leave the army, the brass-mounted army,/The high-faluting army, where eagle buttons rule." A song printed in the Wilmington, North Carolina, daily paper, which was supposedly found in the pocket of a dead Union soldier, shows a Federal officer to be a coward. The piece may well have been composed in the South, as southern newspapers mentioned the battlefield discovery of Union songs on several occasions. "Song for the 9th Regiment New York State Militia" tells the tale of an "Adjutant who sneaked out of the way"[96] during a battle and then "skedaddled in 240 time." In a pile of "knapsacks stowed under a tree, [he] ensconced him[self] away from the fight." His countenance betrays his cowardice because "his face was so white you might fancy aright,/His liver through it you could see." "The Officers of Dixie," put to the melody "Dixie," has lyrics by a composer who aptly called himself "a growler"; certainly he represented many of his fellow soldiers. The writer states bitterly that the officers "the honors share, the honors wear."[97] The commanders also hold a higher social position, as he calls them the "brass button gentry." The officers win all the girls, as the women have said, "They'll have an officer or none." An officer killed becomes a "martyr," while "a private is not so honored." The song closes with a threadbare but revealing comment from the writer who bitterly remarks, "all that glitters is not gold." Although certainly not all soldiers disliked or disdained the officer corps, as in all wars, some combatants clearly resented the men who commanded them.

The songs composed and sung by slaves, black soldiers, and abolitionists represent the views of a large group of dissatisfied people. Slaves' songs, heard for the first time in many parts of the North, brought an understanding to white listeners of the unhappiness of the slave population. Black soldiers' songs declared that blacks would show doubters in the North as well as the South that they were brave, able fighters. The abolitionists' songs indicate a strong desire for black equality in addition to black freedom. They also demonstrate that abolitionists were conscious of the powerful opposition to their cause among some northerners. Songs about freedom and equal rights for blacks are a unique part of Civil War music.

One group of southerners brought an entirely new form of song to the North. Many of the blacks who escaped from the South to the Union lines brought with them freedom songs that had been sung in the cotton fields as religious songs, some of which were probably sung by black soldiers during the war. Northern commentator Lewis Lockwood's report on first hearing Negro songs in 1862 offers sentiments music critics and folklorists have acknowledged about black music. Lockwood writes, "the themes are generally devotional; but they have a prime deliverance melody."[98] The longing for freedom is especially evident in a song like "Go Down, Moses," which, as the title hints, is about Moses' efforts to free the Jews from Egyptian tyranny. Its chorus "Let my people go"[99] might well have been the reason that slaveholders forbade its recitation.[100] A song like "Steal Away" was probably in the same category because of lines such as "I ain't got long to stay here"[101] and "Steal away to Jesus." According to traditional folklore, one song that was definitely used as a freedom piece was "Follow the Drinking Gourd." Legend describes a peg-legged sailor who travelled from plantation to plantation throughout the lower South working as a painter or carpenter. He passed the song along to the slaves who sang it with a full knowledge of its secret message, which had been decoded for them by the mysterious seaman. The "drinking gourd"[102] is the big dipper with its handle always set toward the North Star, the slaves' infallible guide to free soil. Verse two gives directions to escaping slaves: "This riva' bank am a very good road." This line is a possible reference to the Tombigbee River, since "Peg Leg Joe" was most often seen in the area near Mobile, Alabama. The "dead trees/and lef' foot, peg foot goin' on" toward the North are additional guiding symbols. Finally, moving from that location northward, the slaves would come to the spot "wha the little riva'/meet the grea' big un." This reference would indicate that the journey would proceed up the Tennessee to the Ohio River, which was then crossed to free territory.[103]

One of the best of black soldiers' war songs was written by a white officer in a black regiment. Captain Lindley Miller's abolitionist opinions are evident in the choice of the "John Brown" melody for use with his "Marching Song of the First Arkansas Regiment." Miller wrote his song from a black soldier's point of view. The composer declares that black troops "mean to show Jeff Davis how the Africans can fight."[104] The song was clearly written after or during 1863, for that date and "the Proclamation" are mentioned. The "sable army" marches into battle to the melody "Yankee Doodle," as the last verse pointedly asserts.

The anonymously authored "Give Us a Flag" offers a brief description of the movement that finally led to the use of black soldiers in the Union army. The writer asserts that "Frémont . . . told them [the government] . . . /how to save the Union and the way it should be done."[105] Lincoln removed Frémont from his command for freeing slaves in Missouri without presidential authorization; Frémont was thereafter a hero to those who opposed slavery. The line "Kentucky swore so hard and old Abe he had his fears" refers to Lincoln's unwillingness to free the slaves lest he alienate the border states, especially Missouri and Kentucky. McClellan, who did not favor the use of black troops, is made to say, "Keep back the niggers." The author relates the warning that "Old Jeff says he'll hang us if we dare to meet him armed." Indeed, in *The Sable Arm*, a history of black troops in the Civil War, Dudley Cornish cites instances of alleged murders of some captured black soldiers and the selling of others into slavery.[106] The composer shows confidence in the black soldier when he states, "the Union must be saved by the colored volunteer." The song's last verse salutes the Fifty-Fourth Massachusetts Reg-

iment, probably the most famous of all black combat groups in the Civil War.
Fredrick Douglass helped to raise troops for the regiment through his encouragement of black volunteers. Robert Shaw, a white soldier who expressed
confidence in the fighting qualities of black troops, commanded the unit. At
Fort Wagner, South Carolina, where Shaw was killed, the regiment fought
valiantly,[107] leaving no doubt "about the courage of the colored volunteer."

Another white officer, Charles G. Halpine, who served with black troops
in South Carolina, wrote an ironic song about the enlistment of black soldiers
titled "Sambo's Right to be Killed." Halpine intended for his comic song to
bluntly demonstrate to whites the two uses to which Negro troops might be
put.[108] First, the author declares,

> I shouldn't at all object,
> If Sambo's body should stop a ball
> That's comin' for me direct.[109]

Undoubtedly many whites took Halpine's lyrics seriously. Halpine not only
offers a second reason for enlisting blacks, but he also condemns those northerners who decried the use of black troops when he writes,

> The men who object to Sambo
> Should take his place and fight
> Its better to have a nayger's hue
> Than a liver that's wake and white.
> Though Sambo's black as the ace of spades,
> His fingers a trigger can pull.

The abolitionists who fought so hard for black freedom and rights had
their songs, too, the majority of them with strongly religious overtones. One
of the most famous and controversial pieces was written by the well-known
poet John Greenleaf Whittier. The writer set his powerfully emotional lines
to Martin Luther's stirring hymn melody "Ein Feste Burg Ist Unser Gott"
(A Mighty Fortress is Our God). Whittier says of combat in the first stanza
"not painlessly doth God recast/and mold anew the nation."[110] With stark
imagery the poet sets forth the cause of the country's suffering,

> What whets the knife
> For the Union's life?—
> Hark to the answer:—/SLAVERY.

The author later implores Union supporters,

> Give prayer and purse
> To stay the Curse,
> Whose wrong we share,

Whose blame we bear,
Whose end shall gladden heaven!

This strongly religious statement condemns slavery while placing part of the responsibility for the country's dilemma with northerners for allowing the peculiar institution to endure so long. The song would not seem complete without a remark on the necessity of suffering before forgiveness is obtained. Whittier states, "Before the joy of peace must come/The pains of purifying." The first performance of the tune by the Hutchinson family before General Philip Kearney's troops caused the general to forbid the family to sing further for his brigade. Kearney protested that not all his troops shared the Hutchinson's sentiments. Lincoln later allowed the group to perform before the Union army if any of its commanders so requested.[111]

Not all abolitionist songs are so towering in their righteousness, although they certainly all share that quality. A piece called "Yankee Land" to the tune of "Dixie" by "Justitia" skillfully attacks those northerners who think that they are much superior to blacks. The phrase "Yankees' love for man is rotten"[112] is an example of the point the author intends with her song. Everywhere are these "vain men and women stalking." The arrogant, supercilious northerners also "turn their nose[s] up at a nigger,/ . . . [and] feel that they're a good deal bigger." The outraged author concludes her song with the thought that "They'll never be true men and women/Till they leave off this wholesale sinning." Their conceit violates the principle that all men are brothers; these sinners should do penance by "Looking 'round to give the suffering slave their hands." Sympathy with the slaves' condition is important, but it is not enough. Active participation in eliminating the slaves' plight is a necessary part of maintaining freedom for everyone because without it all people will "just as truly wear the fetter." The song also contains an allusion to the "higher law," a phrase Senator William Seward used in his famous speech of March 1850, when he declared that "there is a higher law than the Constitution." Seward was speaking eloquently for the right to freedom for all men. The South castigated Seward's speech and declared his idea dangerous and unacceptable.[113]

Never were William Lloyd Garrison and his followers so misled as to believe that all northern sentiment was with the cause of abolition. Garrison proved this point by printing a piece entitled "Farewell to Beecher," a violent diatribe against the abolitionist minister Henry Ward Beecher and his famous daughter Harriet Beecher Stowe. The author was an anonymous New Yorker who clearly believed in slavery. He asserts that Beecher's

eloquence is lost
On New York's arid soil;
We recognize the niggers' usefulness
When in cotton fields they toil.[114]

Beecher is called sarcastically "a spotless, stainless man" who "escaped the draft." His daughter's character fares no better in the song, for she is labelled a "nigger worshipper" and "rabid Republican" by the unabashedly Democratic author. Additionally, her literary accomplishments are commented upon by inference in the insulting query "are her stockings blue?" referring to the traditional female intellectual whom the writer finds obnoxious. This song is one of the truly violent musical protests against the abolition of slavery.

On the other hand, the antislavery forces musically supported a war to preserve the nation, as is shown in "A Yankee Soldier's Song." A strong protest against the rebels who "tore our flag"[115] precedes a complaint against the Fugitive Slave Law of 1850 in the lines,

> whip in hand a master came,
> and drove that man away, sir:
> We felt it was a burning shame,
> But could not have our way.

The composer alludes to the law's provision that made failure to aid in the pursuit of a runaway slave a crime; abolitionists especially abhorred this portion of the law. Many abolitionists desired "to make the *whole* land free" and were unwilling to let the South become an independent nation permitting slavery. The author declares that for the Union cause "Yankee boys will fight it out."

In both sections of the country women offered their services to aid the soldiers in the field. The best-known song about this subject is "The Southern Girl with the Home Spun Dress." At the heart of the song is the praise for virtuous women who do without "Northern goods."[116] One might assume that the piece originated in South Carolina because of the mention of the "Palmetto" hat; South Carolina is known as the Palmetto state because palmetto trees thrive there. The song reminds southern men of the sacrifice that their women are making when they "scorn to wear a bit of silk,/or a bit of Northern lace." "A Southern Woman's Song" confirms the notion that more than sacrifices to appearance were made by southern women. Women in the Confederacy worked to make uniforms and other garments for their fighting men. The composer declares that women's work was "to cloth the soldier . . ./while he wields the sabre."[117] The chorus "Stitch, stitch, stitch" reveals the urgency of the task. The women's hope was "substantial comforts" for the soldiers who would wear their work. The women were careful to "set the buttons close and tight." They worried little about the color of the clothing or its decoration; the usefulness of the garment was their reward and their concern.

In working to make their soldiers more efficient and comfortable, northern women refused to be outdone by their southern counterparts. By the time that "The Knitting Song" had been written, northern women had realized the need for warm winter clothing "on Southern hills."[118] That they clearly saw the dangers of soldiers being poorly clothed in winter is shown through their concentration on the making of "socks and mittens and gloves." Like southern women, they took special care with their work, being diligent to "narrow, widen and seam." Women undoubtedly recognized that well-made clothing might provide an ever-so-slight edge over the enemy on the balance sheet of the war. Concerned Union women might well have consulted with army suppliers, who at first provided Federal soldiers with uniforms made of shoddy, a cheap material that disintegrated in the elements.[119] As with most goods, northern equipment improved in quality during the war while southern goods gradually became less well made, when available at all.

One of the commodities that was available to all soldiers was a large quantity of sentimental songs. One of the major trends in mid-nineteenth-century song was the sentimental ballad; the most cursory examination of American music will leave any researcher with that conclusion. When the Civil War began, the magnitude of the tragedy increased the already strong popularity of the sentimental song. Not only were large numbers of tear-provoking tunes composed during the conflict, but also the sentimental vogue increased the immense popularity of older sentimental pieces, most notably "Home, Sweet Home" and "Lorena." "Home, Sweet Home" was composed in 1823 when an English melodist, Henry R. Bishop, teamed with American actor John Howard Payne to write it for a light opera. Its debut was in London, but it was soon transported to the United States, where it was widely sung throughout the remainder of the century.[120] Bell I. Wiley states that it was the soldiers' favorite among pre-war tunes sung during the war.[121] Although the lyrics are not particularly distinguished, the song's last line doubtless took many men back to the quiet familiarity and peacefulness of everyday life. Countless times each soldier must have thought to himself "there's no place like home."[122]

The men on the lines also thought of the girls at home, and when they did, especially in the South, one of their favorite tunes was "Lorena."[123] Mary Chesnut, the renowned southern diarist, quoted a guest visiting her home, Doctor Rufus, who offered a view of "Lorena" probably shared by many southerners: "it is supreme as to melody and also for beauty of versification."[124] The song was composed by two unrelated men named Webster, one of them a traveling minister. The two friends met while separately touring the country and published their musical effort in 1857. The Reverend H. D. Webster, the lyricist, wrote autobiographical words about a lost love; his sweetheart's name, Ella, would not fit the melody, but with Edgar Allan Poe's "Lenore" from the poem "The Raven" in mind, he fused the two names into "Lorena."[125] Perhaps the most appealing lines to soldiers, and those most appropriate to men away from home, were these:

Thy heart was always true to me:
A duty, stern and pressing, broke
The tie which linked my soul with thee.[126]

The last verse offers a hope of meeting again for the parted lovers, but it is in the next world where, "up there, 'tis heart to heart."

Many sentimental songs were incidental joint compositions; two composers collaborated to produce one or two hit songs. Though these original compositions were generally of better quality than their derivative counterparts, they lack the artistic quality of the best Civil War songs.

Of the sentimental songs written during the war, the best share several common and related themes: the death of a soldier is the first and most obvious; the second is the ever-present sense of loss that loved ones of the deceased will carry with them when a relative or lover has been lost; and, finally, a melancholy peace issues from the final lines of these songs. The first of this genre is a song usually titled "All Quiet Along the Potomac," but originally published as a poem titled "The Picket Guard." For a time authorship was debated between northerners and southerners, each claiming that the song originated on its side. Almost all current music scholars agree that the poem was written by Mrs. E. L. Beers, a Massachusetts native. The song was set to several scores; John Hill Hewitt, the noted southern composer, wrote the most memorable one.[127] The song includes a complaint about the War Department's apparently cavalier attitude toward the deaths of common soldiers. The "stray picket"[128] who is shot is "nothing" to commanders safely ensconced in Washington. Losses are just "a private or two now and then." Again the composer notes, "Not an officer lost, only one of the men/Moaning out all alone the death rattle." The guard's painful loneliness and his wandering thoughts form the major portion of the text of the song while the last line sums up the whole complex of feelings the author wishes to convey: "The picket's off duty forever."

Officers' deaths, too, were the subjects of a number of songs. George Root and Henry Washburn combined to write one of these, which shows the effect of the loss of a young officer on his family. The setting of "The Vacant Chair" is particularly noteworthy because the officer's death occurred just before Thanksgiving. The piece was written about the family of Lieutenant J. W. Grout of the Fifteenth Massachusetts Regiment, who died in action shortly before he was to receive a scheduled Thanksgiving leave.[129] Despite its sadness, the family decides it "shall meet/[leaving] one vacant chair"[130] to commemorate its departed member. The sorrowful peacefulness of death is shown in the final four lines, which read,

> Sleep today, O early fallen,
> In thy green and narrow bed,
> Dirges from the pine and cypress
> Mingle with the tears we shed.

As has been noted earlier, nature seems to mourn for the brave.

"Weeping Sad and Lonely" (see appendix), by the popular sentimental writers Charles Sawyer and Henry Tucker, is a plaintive song placed in the mouth of a young woman who imagines the unhappy fate of her intended. Although the youthful speaker pictures the death scenes that are her "many cruel fancies,"[131] her beau survives into the last verse, where she speaks to him of duty and prays for his protection from harm. She proudly reminds him that "our country called you" and hopes that "Angels will cheer your way." The song produced a multitude of imitations of varying quality in the North and South.

"Somebody's Darling" does have a typical sentimental war song ending. The music was written by John Hill Hewitt, and his name, combined with the song's doleful subject matter and tone, almost guaranteed that it would be a hit. The description of the dying soldier at the center of the piece drips with adjectives designed to make his untimely death even more tragic. Phrases like "the lingering light of his boyhood's grace,"[132] "tresses of gold," and "purple vein'd brow" evoked intense emotions from Civil War audiences. The listener is asked in the final lines

> to drop on [the soldier's] grave a tear;
> [and] carve on the wooden slab over his head,
> Somebody's darling is slumbering here.

The song so impressed Margaret Mitchell that she used it to advantage in *Gone with the Wind*.[133]

Along with sentimental songs, patriotic tunes shared the honor of comprising the largest category of derivative and joint composition pieces. Two patriotic songs from the Civil War have become among the most well known of American songs. For many Americans, "Dixie" is as symbolic of the South as "The Battle Hymn of the Republic" is of the North. The contemporary variation and the derivative song had finally achieved a rare blend of quality and popularity. Certainly one of the largest clusters of Civil War songs centered around wartime leaders. The three most often mentioned figures, Lincoln, Davis, and McClellan, all share one characteristic: they are the recipients of as much musical criticism as praise. The most interesting collection of songs about an individual are those treating Abraham Lincoln; strangely enough not a single major artistic song was written for or about Lincoln during his lifetime. Nevertheless, his wartime actions had the musical approval of the great composers George F. Root and Henry Clay Work. Military songs offer some new thoughts. The battle song shows a consciousness of the new trend toward gigantic battles where thousands of men died in a few days while naval songs show composers' reactions to the ironclad as a remarkable achievement. Finally, for the first time soldiers' songs offer numerous complaints about army life, especially the food and the officers. Although a small group, black songs were beginning to filter into America's musical consciousness, and they added another dimension to American song. For the first time the demands for black freedom and equality were asserted in the war song. Additionally, slaves' work songs were finally carried into the North.

While American liberty and war songs had progressed from the origination of a few themes in the Revolutionary period to a process of high quality original war compositions written during the Civil War, British soldiers continued to sing almost exclusively such older songs as "The British Grenadiers" and "The Girl I Left Behind Me." British war song composers had not kept pace with their more prolific and innovative American counterparts.[134]

NOTES

1. Bell Irvin Wiley, *Life of Johnny Reb* (New York: The Bobbs-Merrill, 1943), p. 157.

2. Bell Irvin Wiley *Life of Billy Yank* (New York: The Bobbs-Merrill, 1951), p. 158.

3. David Ewen, *Great Men of American Popular Song* (Englewood Cliffs, N. J.: Prentice-Hall, 1970), p. 17. While he is generally reliable, portions of Ewen's work have been questioned.

4. Hans Nathan, *Dan Emmett and the Rise of Early Negro Minstrelsy* (Norman: University of Oklahoma Press, 1962), pp. 107–113.

5. Ewen, 18–19.

6. Richard B. Harwell, *Confederate Music* (Chapel Hill: University of North Carolina Press, 1950), p. 47.

7. Nathan, 251.

8. Harwell, 48–51.

9. Nathan, 262–266.

10. Ibid., 269–270.

11. Harwell, 42.

12. Nathan, 269–275.

13. Ewen, 20.

14. "Pike's Dixie," reprinted in Irwin Silber, ed., *Songs of the Civil War* (New York: Columbia University Press, 1960), p. 19. This song was reprinted in a number of different newspapers in the South in abbreviated versions such as one in the *Charleston Mercury*, 10 June 1861.

15. "Dixie," *Richmond Enquirer*, 4 June 1861. Peculiarly enough, the prestigious *Southern Literary Messenger* did not print a single version of this song, although it did print other war songs.

16. Wiley, *The Life of Johnny Reb*, 154.

17. "Union Dixie," reprinted in Silber, 64.

18. Kenneth A. Bernard, *Lincoln and the Music of the Civil War* (Caldwell, Idaho: Caxton Printers, 1966), p. 251.

19. Ibid., 300.

20. Ewen, 20–21.

21. Richard B. Harwell, "The Star of the Bonnie Blue Flag," *Civil War History* 4 (1958), 285–288.

22. "The Bonnie Blue Flag," reprinted from the original sheet music in Richard B. Harwell, *Songs of the Confederacy* (New York: Broadcast Music, 1951), pp. 11–13.

23. Silber, 53.

24. Wiley, *The Life of Johnny Reb*, 155.

25. Paul Glass and Louis Singer, eds., *Singing Soldiers: A History of the Civil War in Song* (New York: Da Capo Press, 1968), p. 16.

26. Richard Jackson, ed., *Popular Songs of Nineteenth-Century America* (New York: Dover Publications, 1976), p. 261.

27. Harwell, "Star of Bonnie Blue Flag," 289.

28. An untitled parody of "The Bonnie Blue Flag," reprinted in Harwell, *Confederate Music*, 58.

29. Harwell, *Confederate Music*, 26.

30. "Southern Song of Freedom," *Richmond Enquirer*, 14 May 1861.

31. *Oxford English Dictionary*, s. v. "southron."

32. "The Cavaliers' Song," *The Liberator*, 2 August 1861.

33. "Union, Constitution, and the Laws," *Brownlow's Knoxville Whig and Rebel Ventilator*, 6 July 1861.

34. "East Tennessee," *Brownlow's Knoxville Whig and Rebel Ventilator*, 2 April 1864.

35. Boyd B. Stutler, "John Brown's Body," *Civil War History* 4 (1958): 260.

36. Ibid., 256.

37. Bernard, 102.

38. Julia Ward Howe, "Note on the 'Battle Hymn of the Republic,' " *Century Magazine* 34 (1887): 629–630.

39. Quoted in Bernard, 220.

40. Ibid., 299.

41. Ibid., 308.

42. "The Battle Hymn of the Republic," reprinted in Silber, 21–23.

43. "Old Abe and His Fights," reprinted in Vera Brodsky Lawrence, *Music for Patriots, Politicians, and Presidents: Harmonies and Discords of the First Hundred Years* (New York: Macmillan, 1975), p. 343.

44. James G. Randall, *Lincoln the President: Springfield to Bull Run*, vol. 1 (New York: Dodd, Mead and Co., 1956), p. 275.

45. "Lincoln Doodle," *Southern Confederacy*, 6 March 1861.

46. Randall, 1:289–291.

47. "Yankee Doodle," *Southern Confederacy*, 30 August 1861.

48. "Abraham Lincoln," *Southern Confederacy*, 12 October 1861.

49. James M. McPherson, *Ordeal by Fire: The Civil War and Reconstruction* (New York: Alfred A. Knopf, 1982), p. 294.

50. "Lincoln and Liberty," reprinted in Silber, 96.

51. Bernard, 56–57.

52. Untitled campaign song reprinted in Lawrence, 344.

53. Glass and Singer, 120.

54. McPherson, 251.

55. "We're Coming Father Abraham," reprinted from the original sheet music in Richard Jackson, ed., *Stephen Foster Song Book* (New York: Dover Publications, 1974), pp. 153–155.

56. "How Are You, Green-Backs," reprinted in Fletcher Hodges, Jr., *Stephen Foster, Democrat* (Pittsburgh: University of Pittsburgh, 1946), pp. 28–29. This pam-

phlet was originally published as an article in the *Lincoln Herald*, (Harrogate, Tenn.) June 1945.

57. "We're Coming Fodder Abraham," reprinted in Lawrence, 365.

58. "We'll Fight for Uncle Abe," reprinted in Silber, 108–111.

59. "Farewell Father, Friend and Guardian," reprinted in Lawrence, 429.

60. "Jeff in Petticoats," reprinted in Willard A. Heaps and Porter W. Heaps, *The Singing Sixties: The Spirit of the Civil War Days Drawn from the Music of the Times* (Norman: University of Oklahoma Press, 1960), p. 358.

61. "Jeff Davis in Crinoline," reprinted in Heaps, 358–359.

62. "John Brown's Body," reprinted in Frank Moore, *The Civil War in Song and Story, 1860–1865* (New York: F. P. Collier, 1889), p. 509.

63. Shelby Foote, *The Civil War: A Narrative*, vol. 3, *Red River to Appomattox* (New York: Random House, 1974), pp. 1010–1011.

64. "Beauregard Song," *Southern Literary Messenger* 34 (1862): 102.

65. "The Sword of Robert E. Lee," reprinted from the original sheet music in Harwell, *Songs of the Confederacy*, 110–112.

66. "Stonewall Jackson's Way," reprinted in Heaps, 318.

67. Frank E. Vandiver, *Mighty Stonewall* (Westport, Conn.: Greenwood Press, 1957), p. 253.

68. Ibid., 202–203.

69. "Riding a Raid," reprinted from the original sheet music in Harwell, *Songs of the Confederacy*, 86–87.

70. "How Are You, John Morgan," reprinted in Silber, 224.

71. Samuel C. Reid, *The Capture and Wonderful Escape of General John H. Morgan*, ed. J. J. Mathews (Atlanta: Emory University Press, 1947), pp. 13–18.

72. "Little Mac! Little Mac! You're the Man," reprinted in Hodges, 20.

73. "McClellan for President," reprinted in Lawrence, 417.

74. Untitled campaign song, *Albany Evening Journal*, 13 October 1846.

75. Sherman's exploits are rousingly recorded in one excellent song, Henry Clay Work's "Marching Through Georgia," which is treated in the next chapter. Most songs about Civil War leaders, like those about battles, were much like those of earlier wars. Those lines with some artistic merit dealing with leaders and their victories are also discussed in the next chapter.

76. "U. S. G.," reprinted in Lawrence, 418.

77. "Yankee Doodle's Ride to Richmond," *Wilmington* (North Carolina) *Daily Journal*, 15 February 1862.

78. McPherson, 358.

79. "Flight of the Doodles," reprinted in Silber, 240–242.

80. "The Battle of Shiloh Hill," reprinted in Silber, 246–247.

81. McPherson, 226–229. See also Wiley's two works cited earlier for confirmation of soldiers' thoughts about Civil War carnage.

82. J. G. Randall and David Donald, *The Civil War and Reconstruction*, 2d ed. (Boston: D. C. Heath, 1965), p. 442.

83. "The Cumberland and the Merrimac," reprinted in Silber, 256–257.

84. Bern Anderson, *By Sea and By River: The Naval History of the Civil War* (New York: Alfred A. Knopf, 1962), pp. 82–83.

85. "Iron-Clad Jack," *New Orleans Times-Picayune*, 27 May 1862.

86. "Roll, Alabama, Roll" reprinted in Silber, 251–252.

87. Randall and Donald, 450–451.

88. Anderson, 208.

89. "Hard Crackers Come Again No More," reprinted in Glass and Singer, 146–147.

90. Variation of "Hard Crackers Come No More," reprinted in Edward A. Dolph, ed., *"Sound Off!": Soldiers Songs from the Revolution to World War II* (New York: Farrar and Rinehart, 1942), p. 322.

91. Wiley, *Billy Yank*, 224–227.

92. "Short Rations," reprinted from the original sheet music in Harwell, *Songs of the Confederacy*, 82–84.

93. Wiley, *Johnny Reb*, 89–96.

94. "Goober Peas," reprinted in Manly Wade and Francis Wellman, *The Rebel Songster* (Charlotte, N. C.: Heritage House, 1959), pp. 42–43.

95. "Brass-Mounted Army," reprinted in Silber, 198–200.

96. "Song for the 9th Regiment New York State Militia," *Wilmington* (North Carolina) *Daily Journal*, 30 April 1863.

97. "The Officers of Dixie," reprinted in Silber, 63–64.

98. Quoted in Dena J. Epstein, *Sinful Times and Spirituals: Black Folk Music to the Civil War* (Chicago: University of Illinois Press, 1977), p. 244.

99. "Go Down Moses," reprinted in Langston Hughes and Anna Bontemps, *The Book of Negro Folklore* (New York: Dodd, Mead and Co., 1958), p. 292.

100. Ibid., 286.

101. "Steal Away" reprinted in Hughes and Bontemps, 296.

102. "Follow the Drinking Gourd," reprinted in Silber, 278–280.

103. H. B. Parks, "Follow the Drinking Gourd," *Publications of the Texas Folk-Lore Society*, ed. J. Frank Dobie (Austin: University of Texas Press, 1928), pp. 82–84.

104. "Marching Song of the First Arkansas Regiment," reprinted in Silber, p. 26.

105. "Give Us a Flag," reprinted in Silber, 295.

106. Dudley Cornish, *The Sable Arm: Negro Troops in the Union Army, 1861–1865* (New York: Longmans, Green, 1956), pp. 162–167.

107. Ibid., 108–111.

108. Silber, 308.

109. "Sambo's Right to Be Kilt," reprinted in Silber, 328–330.

110. "Ein Feste Burg Ist Unser Gott," *The Liberator*, 28 June 1861.

111. Phillip D. Jordan, *Singin' Yankees* (Minneapolis: University of Minnesota Press, 1946), pp. 233–235.

112. "Yankee Land," *The Liberator*, 2 August 1861.

113. McPherson, 66–67.

114. "Farewell to Beecher," *The Liberator*, 2 October 1863.

115. "A Yankee Soldier's Song," *The Liberator*, 11 October 1862.

116. "The Southern Girl with the Home Spun Dress," *Southern Confederacy*, 9 May 1863.

117. "A Southern Woman's Song" *New Orleans Times Picayune*, 27 October 1861.

118. "The Knitting Song," reprinted in Lawrence, 389.

119. McPherson, 167.

120. Jackson, *Popular Songs*, 270.

121. Wiley, *Billy Yank*, 161.

122. "Home! Sweet Home!" reprinted from the original sheet music in Jackson, *Popular Songs*, 80–82.

123. Wiley, *Johnny Reb*, 152.

124. Mary Chesnut, *Mary Chesnut's Civil War*, ed. C. Vann Woodward (New Haven, Conn.: Yale University Press, 1981), p. 451.

125. Jackson, *Popular Songs*, 274–275.

126. "Lorena," reprinted from the original sheet music in Harwell, *Songs of the Confederacy*, 52–54.

127. Harwell, *Confederate Music*, 80–81.

128. "All Quiet Along the Potomac," reprinted from the original sheet music in Harwell, *Songs of the Confederacy*, 88–89. Even the *Southern Literary Messenger* 35 (1863) disclaimed southerner Lamar Fontain's claim to authorship of the song.

129. Ewen, 38.

130. "The Vacant Chair," reprinted in National Committee for the Preservation of Existing Records of the National Society of the Colonial Dames of America, *American War Songs* (Philadelphia: privately printed, 1925), p. 83.

131. "Weeping Sad and Lonely," reprinted in Silber, 124–126.

132. "Somebody's Darling," reprinted from the original sheet music in Harwell, *Songs of the Confederacy*, 44–45.

133. Ibid., 44.

134. Lewis Winstock, *Songs and Music of the Redcoats: A History of the War Music of the British Army, 1642–1902* (Harrisburg, Pa.: Stackpole Books, 1970), p. 268.

7

Original Sounds

The Civil War marks a watershed in American musical history because from that conflict emerged a form of liberty and war music that was distinctly American in character. Not only was war and patriotic music being written by American-born composers, but American war and popular nonwar music had taken a form unlike any music found elsewhere in the world. American music had become an artistic endeavor with one man composing the lyrics and music of numbers of songs that bore his individual musical signature. From the Civil War emerged a large group of well-known liberty and war-song composers, most notably George F. Root and Henry Clay Work, whose compositions reached high levels of artistry.

Of the numerous composers of original war songs, one group holds a minor but not completely insignificant place. These were the songwriters, most of them from northern states, who wrote one or more well-received war songs. A few of the minor wartime composers, like Septimus Winner, also wrote popular nonwar pieces that were more widely sold and performed than their war songs. Some others, like Patrick S. Gilmore, the Union bandmaster, were more famous for their incidental musical accomplishments than for their songs. The minor composers are examined first.

The unique figure among these minor writers, in terms of his war loyalties, was memorably named William Shakespeare Hays. As a Kentuckian, he felt caught in the middle of the conflict, clearly supporting neither secession nor abolition, but merely hoping for the war to end quickly. His outlook on life was, however, similar to that of many rural southerners in that he looked back to the peaceful country life and its many simple pleasures. Much of Hays' work has lapsed into obscurity since his time, but works like his best war song, "The Drummer Boy of Shiloh," are the reason he is remembered.[1] He is also a footnote in music history because he declared that he had written "Dixie."[2] The owner of the music store in which Hays worked endorsed his employee's authorship of the song. He was simply one of many writers who made this same claim; as has been earlier noted, and as Richard Harwell, Confederate music authority declares, this assertion has been generally rejected.[3]

The success of "The Drummer Boy of Shiloh" undoubtedly belongs to Hays. While the lyrics lack profundity or eloquence, the song's sentiments appealed to an audience watching and participating in a war involving monumental loss and suffering. The courage of a young man facing death calmly and with complete presence of mind added another bit of sadness. The boy's prayerful last moments complete the poignant lyrics. The final lines read, "He smiled, shook hands—death seized the boy/Who prayed before he died."[4]

Many of the minor war-song composers wrote in the sentimental vein. Perhaps the most saccharine of Civil War songwriters was Charles Carroll Sawyer, whose most important songs center on one of the war's most popular topics, soldiers' mothers. The Connecticut-born composer was so careful in keeping politics and regional peculiarities from his songs that he drew a wide following in both the North and South.[5] Sawyer appended a note to two of his most popular songs, explaining how a soldier who was dying came to think of his mother just before he expired. "Who Will Care for Mother Now?" purportedly repeats the last words of a youthful combatant who was informed by a battlefield surgeon that he was dying. In the most sorrowful lines of the tune, the soldier exclaims,

> Even now I think I see her
> Kneeling, praying for me!
> How can I leave her in anguish?
> Who will care for mother now?[6]

Another Sawyer favorite, "Mother Would Comfort Me," features the final words of a hospitalized New York veteran.[7] The fatally wounded man asserts that "No one but Mother can cheer me today."[8] In a complete lapse into mother worship, Carroll has his speaker say, "One kiss from her lips, or one look from her eye,/Would make me contented or willing to die." The author closes the song with a thought that might well be expected: "In clouds or in sunshine, pleasures or pain,/Mother's affection is ever the same." Sawyer's "I Dreamed My Boy Was Home Again" changes the persona from son to mother. In this song the son has not died but is simply grieved for in his absence. The writer has the mother declare, "My heart is sad, my tears will flow/Until my boy is here again."[9]

The mother-song craze spawned dozens of songs, both serious and humorous. Of the large number of spoofs on the subject, two were especially well done. "Who Will Care for Micky Now" was a denigration of Irish immigrants ironically put into the mouth of an Irish soldier who has left home for the first time to fight for the Union; the song represents a lament to his mother. The piece features an intentionally comic and purposely stilted brogue. For example, the helpless Irishman cries, "Och, millia mother! I am drafted."[10] In the closing lines the speaker remarks to his mother on his physical inability to desert:

> One of my legs is stiff, dear,
> Since I was kicked by Murphy's cow,
> I'm afeared I niver can skedaddle,
> Who will care for Micky now?

This may well be a lightly disguised musical criticism of Irish Catholics and their general support of the Democrats. Many New Englanders and other staunch Republicans believed the majority of Irish to be active copperheads and thus less than avid about joining the battle against the rebels.[11]

"Mother on the Brain" is a more direct and telling parody on the mother-song genre. As the writer remarks, "I've arranged a list of mother songs, together in a string."[12] The author of this compendium has taken a line or title from a number of songs and added his own parenthetical and irreverent comments. For instance, one intentionally comic line reads, "I'm lonely since my mother died (from drinking lager beer)."

Walter Kittridge saw little humor in the war and chose the sentimental vein to indicate his thoughts and feelings about the conflict. Kittridge, a New Hampshire ballad singer, was a close friend of the Hutchinson family, whose beliefs about abolition he shared. After receiving a draft notice, Kittridge composed "Tenting on the Old Camp Ground."[13] He was, however, judged unacceptable for service because of a childhood bout with rheumatic fever.[14] The first publisher to look at the song refused to print it, but with Asa Hutchinson's influence, the large Boston firm of Oliver Ditson published it in 1864. Kittridge and Hutchinson divided the royalties on the song, making the princely sum, for the time, of one thousand dollars each within two years.[15] The song ultimately produced more profit for Asa Hutchinson than any of the family's tunes. It became a post-war favorite with the Grand Army of the Republic at its reunions[16] and was used as recently as the 1960s as a war protest song, sung by Pete Seeger among others.[17]

The song "Tenting on the Old Camp Ground" is a mournful one about the anguish and loss caused by war. It is clearly a hope for peace as evidenced in the lines,

> Many are the hearts that are weary tonight,
> wishing for the war to cease;
> Many are the hearts, looking for the right,
> To see the dawn of peace.[18]

The last chorus poignantly describes the battlefield:

> We've been fighting today on the old campground,
> Many are lying near;
> Some are dead and some are dying,
> Many are in tears.

This song undoubtedly had an effect on the minds of concerned northerners during the first year of its publication, when Grant's losses in the eastern campaign were devastatingly high; for example, in his army about twelve thousand men were killed and wounded, many at the outset of the action at Cold Harbor on 3 June 1864.[19]

Among those concerned about the Union forces was Patrick S. Gilmore, who wrote a musical assurance that Union soldiers would return home. Gilmore, who enlisted with his entire band in 1861, was also anxious to see the end of the war and pictured the home folks' reaction to its conclusion in the much discussed tune "When Johnny Comes Marching Home."[20] The melody of the song has been the subject of debate; some music historians, including Willard Heaps, believe it to be an old Irish tune.[21] Other specialists (for example, Irwin Silber) find no direct evidence for this belief, arguing that no record exists of the song's performance before the Civil War. Silber believes that Gilmore, who was born and raised in Ireland, may have "reached back into his own portion of Irish folk memory to recall—and reconstruct— a tune." He declares that until otherwise proven, "Gilmore's claim should be acknowledged."[22]

The melody is the distinguishing feature of the song; also important, however, is the thought that peace will be at hand "when Johnny comes marching home."[23] Each family will realize at that time that the war is over because their sons will stand in front of them. The tune caught the fancy of composers, who borrowed it for use in parodies soon after its publication. One of the most notable songs using Gilmore's melody was "Abe Lincoln went to Washington," which tells the history of Lincoln's presidency in five short verses covering the time period from 1861 to 1865 and ending when "John Wilkes Booth took Lincoln's life."[24] "For Bales," the most prominent southern song using the melody, describes in brief, general statements the Red River Campaign of 1864, in which Confederate generals Richard Taylor and Edmund Kirby-Smith "burned up the cotton and whipped "Old Banks."[25] Banks was the commander of the Federal forces who failed to seize the Confederate "bales" of cotton in Louisiana and Texas.

Unlike Gilmore, Septimus Winner, a Philadelphia music-shop owner and author of musical instruction books, had several hit songs during the war; his most famous song, "Listen to the Mockingbird," was written before the war, however.[26] The South used the melody in a march titled "The Mockingbird Quickstep."[27] The composer's other hits (not related to the war) include "Oh Where Has My Little Dog Gone?" and "Whispering Hope." Although he was completely pro-Union in sentiment, Winner was detained by government authorities when his song "Give Us Back Our Commander: Little Mac, the People's Pride" began to sell widely. The song clearly shows Winner's support for McClellan, removed by Lincoln from his position of commander of Union forces because of his inability to make efficient use of his army. The song's title summarizes its theme and explains why it was banned. Winner was released when he consented to stop the sale of his offensive song,[28] but he remained a firmly committed Democrat and unwavering McClellan partisan.[29]

Early in the war Winner showed his respect for Lincoln in "Abraham's Daughter." "Columbia," who represents the love of liberty in America, is the "child of Abraham, or Uncle Sam."[30] Clearly Winner approves of Lincoln, equating him with a patriotic symbol of the United States. McClellan is also praised as the leader who will "show the foe no quarter." His feeling for the fallen president is apparent in the tribute to Lincoln, "A Nation Mourns Her Martyred Son." Winner expresses his belief in Lincoln's generosity but does not assign responsibility for the assassination to anyone in particular in the lines," [Lincoln] acted well a manly part/To those who planned the fatal blow."[31] His reply to "Weeping Sad and Lonely" was nearly as well received as the original. Winner's strong support for the Union is obvious in the first stanza of "Yes, I would the Cruel War Were Over," in which he declares, "the war cannot be ended/until the Union is restored."[32] He acknowledges the tragedy of the "cruel struggle" but asserts, "we'll battle for our nation,/What soe'er it may cost."

Just as firm in his loyalty to his section was the important Confederate composer John Hill Hewitt. Hewitt attended West Point, and it was there that he first became involved in musical studies (he also wrote poetry). Hewitt was scheduled to graduate in 1822, but because of his part in a cadet riot in 1820, his graduation was postponed for a year. After refusing to spend another year at the academy, the young man went into the theatrical business with his father. Later he became a newspaper editor in Baltimore.[33] He also wrote for Henry Clay, whose ideas he supported in print.[34] After the publication of *Uncle Tom's Cabin*, Hewitt wrote a savage dialect song titled "Aunt Harriet Beecher Stowe," which presents a southerner's distaste for the book.[35] When the war began, Hewitt initially concentrated most of his attention on writing drama, turning out eighteen patriotic plays during the course of the war. Before the war began, however, he had begun to write music again, composing the melody for "Rock Me to Sleep Mother," with lyrics by Elizabeth Akers. The song was first published in 1860 and continued in publication until 1889. Hewitt also supplied the music for "Somebody's Darling," one of the most popular sentimental songs (discussed earlier). In addition, he wrote the words for "When Upon the Field of Glory," a Confederate response to "Weeping Sad and Lonely," as well as "The Soldier's Farewell, or the South Shall Yet Be Free."[36]

Hewitt composed lyrics and music for two of the South's popular tunes of 1863, "You Are Going to the Wars, Willie Boy!" and "The Young Volunteer." Both pieces are portraits of a youthful soldier, and both are in the sentimental genre. "You Are Going to the Wars, Willie Boy!" is told from the point of view of the soldier's sweetheart. She cheers him on with the thought that he is protecting southern "rights and laws."[37] She adds proudly, "With your uniform all new, and your shining buttons, too/You'll win the hearts of pretty girls, but none like me so true." The piece ends, as might be guessed, with the faithful young woman exclaiming to her true love that if he should die, she will "pine away my life/[and] never wear a smile again." "The Young Volunteer" presents the same sentiments from the soldier's viewpoint. Like his lover, the young man sees his responsibility clearly, as is evident in his vision of the stars and bars. In his eyes is the Confederate "flag that woos the wind,"[38] and that same "flag shall kiss the wind." Approaching the possibility of his not returning from combat, the speaker tells his sweetheart to "remember the Young Volunteer." These companion pieces, while presenting patriotic sentiments, are hardly profound or exceptional; the answering voices of two songs written in the same year probably reflect Hewitt's wartime play writing, which was his finest work. Even at his best, the South's singular Civil War composer falls far short of his northern counterparts in artistic song writing; his songs merely serve as carefully constructed musical propaganda. As Harwell asserts, Hewitt might have taken on too much work in too many areas. Indeed, his talents might have been better suited to another subject than music. In any case, like many other war song composers, his fame is essentially assured because of his war work. He became a teacher and magazine writer in the post-war period, but he never again became a public figure with a large following.[39]

On the Union side were three important composers, the first of whom was the great artist Stephen Collins Foster. Foster, a Pennsylvania native, was born in 1826. By 1841 he had written his first piece of music. His first commercial success was "Oh! Susanna," published in 1848, the same year that saw the publication of "Old Uncle Ned," his first major dialect song. Although he wrote classic sentimental songs like "Jeanie with the Light Brown Hair" and "Beautiful Dreamer," he is also considered a significant writer of minstrel show tunes. In 1850 Foster began to write for E. P. Christy's famous minstrel group. Before the composer had ever visited a slave state, he had written several of what were called his "Ethiopian" tunes, songs like "De Camptown Races" and "Massa's in de Cold, Cold Ground." The year after he visited Kentucky, Foster wrote "Old Folks at Home."[40] As was the case with most of his other songs, he received little direct renumeration and little from royalties for the "Old Folks at Home"; for example, Christy usually paid Foster ten dollars for allowing him to place his name on a composition as its performer. In the case of "Old Folks at Home," Christy gave Foster an extra five dollars to allow Christy the full credit for authoring the piece.[41]

The Civil War created additional financial problems for Foster because his sentimental songs, reminiscent of a peaceful South, were not in demand after the commencement of hostilities.[42] He consequently turned his talents toward war songs. Music critics like John Tasker Howard believe that Foster's musical talent was greatly diminished after 1860. Howard, however, does declare that Foster was always a "careful workman" where his lyrics were concerned; his war songs' lyrics show that his attention to his craft remained undiminished.[43] While his melodic talents might have stagnated somewhat, he had not lost his abilities completely, as "Beautiful Dreamer," his last composition, indicates.

Foster's first major war song was "Better Times Are Coming," published in April 1862. To show why his optimism is justified, the writer praises numerous Union leaders, including Lincoln, Secretary of State William Seward, Secretary of War Edwin Stanton, and Generals McClellan and Ambrose Burnside. Foster also commends naval celebrities John Ericsson, the *Monitor's* designer, and "Captain Foote."[44] Andrew H. Foote was later to become an admiral.[45] The song is noteworthy in two respects. First, it offers a salute to the sometimes maligned Irish soldiers in the phrase, "From the land of Shamrock there's stuff that never yields." The author also praises "brave Colonel Corcoran." Michael Corcoran came to the United States in 1849; in the war he attained the rank of general.[46] "Gallant General Shields" was Irish immigrant James Shields who later became a United States senator.[47] Second, it indicates that Foster kept up with the naval war because he alludes to the *Monitor's* battle with the Confederate ship *Merrimac* when he mentions that "Worden with the *Monitor* came into Hampton Roads." Lieutenant John Worden, skipper of the ironclad *Monitor*, received a wound that cost him one of his eyes in the first iron-ship battle in America. The *Monitor* withdrew from the combat, although neither boat severely damaged its opponent. The first ironclad battle thus ended inconclusively.

"That's What's the Matter" is one of the few Foster war songs music critics mention by name. Their remarks usually center on the opening line "We live in hard and stirring times, too sad for mirth, too rough for rhymes."[48] Some music scholars, David Ewen for instance, claim that these lines are autobiographical, reflecting the composer's frustration at the loss of his creative abilities.[49] Although this may be true, what is certain is that the song discusses northern unity and determination to win the war. The unmistakable autobiographical lines read, "The Rebels thought we would divide,/And Democrats would take their side." Foster was a Democrat, as were all of the members of his immediate family.[50] But unlike many members of his family, Foster was a war Democrat, and the composer's war songs indicate an unwavering loyalty to the Union cause. Foster's sister Henrietta, however, did not share her brother's opinion on the Union, and to prove it she wrote "Sound the Rally," a campaign song for Clement Vallandigham, a copperhead exiled in Canada running for governor of Ohio on the Democratic ticket.[51] Foster's brother Morrison and sister Ann Eliza were also opposed to his melodic contributions in support of the North.[52] Foster sometimes appears politically inconsistent. In "That's What's the Matter" he says "all party feeling was gone." But he emphatically adds that the "Secession dodge is *all* played out."

Foster's concern with finding a commander who would be able to defeat the secessionists is expressed in "I'm Nothing but a Plain Old Soldier." The song is unusual because it is told from the point of view of a Revolutionary War veteran who offers his long-past experiences as a comment upon the present war. He pointedly remarks that George Washington was the sole commander of American forces during the War of Independence. In a question implying a contrast between the two wars, the old veteran asks, "who'll bring the trouble to an end?"[53] At some point Foster might well have supported McClellan, and this song might be a disguised complaint at McClellan's removal from command of the Army of the Potomac. It might also serve as a chiding reminder of the number of commanders that Lincoln appointed in the first years of the war. As the writer bluntly states, the Union has "had many Generals from over the land" who could not effectively marshall the northern armies. Grant would not become Lincoln's Washington until 1864, and in the meantime, the command of the Army of the Potomac would continue to shift unsatisfactorily.

Foster is unique in one respect among all major Civil War composers. Unlike many who collaborated with several other writers in wartime compositions, Foster chose to work extensively with only one lyricist, George Cooper. The two men jointly wrote twenty-three tunes, fourteen of them published in 1863; only five were printed after that date. They made little money from their work, and Cooper, who served for a time with the Twenty-second New York Regiment, declared that some of their songs were quickly sold to Wood's minstrels for twenty-five dollars.[54] Among their more notable compositions were "When This Dreadful War Has Ended" and "Willie Has Gone for a Soldier," sentimental ballads much along the order of Hewitt's war work. "For the Dear Old Flag" is a saccharine attempt to seize on two trends of the day, the death of a drummer boy and his last words to his mother. "A Soldier in de Colored Brigade" expresses Cooper's view that the Union is "Worth more than twenty millions ob de Colored Brigade."[55] Just how much Foster agreed with Cooper's sentiments is not known, but he did write the music for the song.[56] As a Democrat and McClellan partisan, Foster might have shared Cooper's opinion.

Musicologist William Austin finds the cooperative efforts at songwriting between Foster and Cooper to be relatively "spontaneous" and "craftsman-like" and indicates that at least one recent music scholar has come to see the merits of the two composers' often maligned works.[57] Their works did not leave an enduring legacy of the highest merit, but they do show that two men could work together to produce good music. The two men have become the only notable team of American liberty and war-song composers.

Although most of Foster's greatest work was behind him when the war began, his war songs have interest if for no other reason than that they are works of a major American composer. His neglected war works, while not great music, are competent productions and consequently worthy of study. Foster's untimely and unexpected death at thirty-seven in 1864 ended any possibility that the composer might find greatness in the realm of the war song. Fittingly, it was Foster's friend Cooper who notified his family of the great composer's death.[58]

With the advent of the conflict, the talents of George F. Root were made manifest. Root was the first of the two most exceptionally gifted and prolific individual songwriters of the period here discussed. The Chicago music firm, Root and Cady, established by his brother and Chauncy M. Cady, published twenty-eight of Root's songs that were written to encourage the northern war effort.[59] Root, born in 1820 and raised in Massachusetts, had become a fine organist and singer by 1850, although he had yet to attempt a significant composition. His first effort at songwriting produced a ballad of the sad, melodious type common in 1851. Between that time and the outbreak of the Civil War, Root was to write ballads and to attempt, with some success, to write hymns. During the war he wrote sentimental songs, battle hymns, and one imitative dialect song. It was primarily in the first two of these forms that Root's best songs were composed, and in these areas Root became an acknowledged master of the war song. He helped to raise the composition of liberty and war music to an art.

When the war erupted in 1861, Root was working as a printer at his brother's publishing house. Before the end of April 1861, Root had written and imprinted "The First Gun is Fired." Soon after this encouragement to Union forces to press the attack, he wrote another tune to stir Federal troops, "Forward, boys, Forward."[60] Root was certain that through his music he could serve his homeland, remarking that "If I could not shoulder a musket in defense of my country I might serve her this way."[61]

With this thought in mind, he poured out his beliefs in one of the finest Civil War songs, "The Battle Cry of Freedom" (see appendix). The song grew out of Lincoln's call in July 1862 for additional troops. With a true propagandist's fervor, Root asserted in "Battle Cry" that "We are springing to the call of our brothers gone before. . . . And we'll fill the vacant ranks with a million freemen more."[62] With Miltonic grandeur, he declares, "we'll hurl the Rebel crew from the land we love the best." In a variation of the song, Root authored a battle hymn depicting the northern troops as possessing "fearless heart[s] and true."[63] The soldiers are "Loyal men" and "our comrades brave" who fight for the glorious cause of "Liberty and Union."

"The Battle Cry of Freedom" is such a rousing song that it was used by the South with a slight variation in words and melody. Southerners construed the word "freedom" to mean the right to possess slaves and the inviolable right of state self-determination on the secession question.[64]

Many recorded instances of the inspirational nature of "Battle Cry" exist. One soldier recalls, "It was often ordered to be sung as the men marched into action. More than once its strains arose on the battlefield and made obedience more easy to the lyric command to rally 'round the flag."[65] At Vicksburg the song was sung by the Lumbard brothers, a Union singing group, to cheer the spirits of the wounded.[66] Root tells a story of an Iowa regiment that lost four hundred men at Vicksburg but nonetheless emerged from battle singing "The Battle Cry of Freedom."[67] It has been recorded that Clara Barton sang the song, albeit somewhat off-key, as she worked with the wounded at Vicksburg.[68] A singing group freshly arrived at Murfreesboro, Tennessee, from Chicago so inspired the troops with "Battle Cry" that they behaved as if they had just won a battle.[69]

In June 1864 Lincoln attended a performance of the play "The Seven Sisters" that featured a last act titled "Rally 'Round the Flag." When the last song of the play was finished, the entire cast came out onto the stage to conclude the performance. Among the performers was Tad Lincoln, dressed in an army uniform and waving a flag. He sang, with other members of the cast, "The Battle Cry of Freedom." At the conclusion of the song, the crowd applauded Lincoln.[70]

Two episodes describe southern reaction to "The Battle Cry of Freedom." In 1865 an encounter took place at Five Forks, Virginia, between an outnumbered and demoralized Confederate force and a large body of Federal troops. In a letter to his wife about the battle, Confederate general George Pickett wrote that when he raised a blood-stained banner and urged his men into battle, they charged, singing a version of the song.[71] A Confederate major, recalling "The Battle Cry of Freedom," paid an undeniable tribute to its inspirational power:

I shall never forget the first time I heard "Rally 'Round the Flag." 'Twas a night during the "Seven Days" fight, and if I remember just rightly it was raining. I was on a picket, when, just before "taps," some fellow on the other side struck that song and others joined in the chorus until it seemed to me the whole Yankee army was singing. Tom B. who was with me, sung out, "Good Heavens, Cap, what are those fellows made of anyway? Here we've licked 'em six days running, and now on the eve of the seventh day they're singing "Rally 'Round the Flag." I am not naturally superstitious, but I tell you that song sounded like the "knell of doom," and my heart went down to my boots; and though I've tried to do my duty, it has been an up-hill fight with me ever since that night.[72]

"The Battle Cry of Freedom" obviously exercised a powerful effect on the emotions of its listeners, as did many of Root's songs. Its appealing lyrics and spirited melody have spread its popularity across America and Europe.

Many people agreed with Louis Gottschalk, one of America's finest nineteenth-century composers, that Root's hymn should have become our national anthem.[73]

Root was not content, however, to write a great patriotic liberty hymn, and consequently he turned his attention to one of the major problems of the conflict, the prisoner-of-war question. Besides Root's "Tramp! Tramp! Tramp!," a number of tunes dealt with the prisoner-of-war problem. Both folksongs and formal compositions touch on various facets of this sensitive issue, but none had the impact of Root's work.[74] The title of this song is onomatopoeic, capturing the weariness and boredom that the prisoners faced each day. Despite the overly sentimental line "Thinking, Mother, dear, of you,"[75] the song accurately reflects the thoughts of heartweary, homesick men deprived of all that is most meaningful in their lives. Its optimism is slightly overstated in Root's assurance that the captured soldiers had "heard the cry of victory" as the enemy left the field. While the prisoners are hopeful of rescue, it is unlikely that they are in the mood to reflect on the "starry flag." The "hollow eye" mentioned in the piece is undoubtedly accurate. That image captures the fatigue, hunger, and danger that were part of the daily ordeal of the imprisoned soldier. In this image also is the spectre of the "dead line"—marks that captives could not cross under penalty of immediate execution. Even when immediate danger and the threat of sudden death were not present, lack of proper clothing and shelter were serious concerns of the hollow-eyed prisoner.[76]

Root's concern for Union prisoners and his success with "Tramp! Tramp! Tramp!" caused him to write two other songs about the plight of the captive combatant, but his success with them was slight compared with that of his hit tune. "Tramp!" became popular with the worried northern citizens who had sons and husbands in the war, and the soldiers favored it as a marching tune. The South, once again, took up a Root song with a variation in the lyrics. It has retained its popularity so well that it has been discovered in the songs of labor movements and was used in Ireland in the early twentieth century as a liberty song.[77]

In another vein, that of the sentimental ballad, Root writes one of the most popular songs of the war: "Just Before the Battle, Mother" (see appendix). The song purports to describe the thoughts and feelings of a soldier about to charge into battle. The major themes of the song are soldiers' bravery and mothers' sacrifices. The emotional call of a soldier to his mother was so effective that reportedly over one million copies of the tune were sold.[78] The phrases "some will sleep beneath the sod"[79] and "we'll perish nobly there" sound stilted and foolishly romantic to the modern ear, but apparently they exercised a profound effect on both northerners and southerners, who also knew the composition. Root included two unusual references in this song. First, in "Just Before the Battle," Root mentions his earlier hit, "The Battle Cry of Freedom," capitalizing on its enormous popularity and doubtless correctly believing that soldiers sang it for inspiration while marching into battle. Root's second reference is a thinly veiled criticism of the copperheads he found so pernicious. Root calls them "traitors"

> who kill with cruel words
> . . . our soldiers,
> by the help they give the foe.

"Just Before the Battle, Mother" had genuine currency among the troops, for it was even sung among prisoners of war at Danville, Virginia.[80] It had an equally powerful effect on a Union colonel who had heard the song just before the Battle of Franklin. The colonel came near to death, but during a fourteen-month period of recuperation, he claimed to have heard the tune in his mind many times each day.[81]

The song inspired a number of parodies, two of them especially interesting. The Republicans used the piece in the election campaign in 1864 as an attempt to discredit the Democrats. The parody was designed to appeal to soldiers as well as civilians; it is titled "A Voice from the Army." It associates the Democratic party with southern sympathies when it refers to Democrats as "the enemy in view."[82] More than a subtle threat of vengeance is apparent when the Republicans declare, "We'll not forget those traitors/When this bloody war is through." The second parody is a sharp Confederate piece titled "Farewell, Mother" that mocks the courage of the northern soldiers. Lines like "When I saw the Rebels marching/To the rear I quickly flew"[83] and "If I can only skedaddle/Dear mother I'll come home again" clearly indicate the anonymous author's sectional bias.

Root's sentimental musical pictures of family did not end with his "mother" tunes. "Never Forget the Dear Ones: A Home Song" continues his family theme and capitalizes on the soldiers' yearning for home. The composer not only mentions mother and father but "sister dear and brother/[who] long for thee to come."[84] Akin to the theme of family is the brotherhood of all soldiers that Root celebrates in "Foes and Friends." For his subjects he has chosen two combatants, a Georgian veteran and a New Hampshire veteran, who speak to each other of their families at home as they lie dying on the battlefield. The last verse touches on the quintessential tragedy of war. Root says of his two symbolic soldiers,

> The dying lips of pardon breathe,
> The dying hands entwine;
> The last ray dies and over all
> The stars of heaven shine.[85]

But like some other authors, Root is not satisfied with a bittersweet, other-worldly ending. His last line pragmatically tells of the two men's daughters who "were fatherless that night."

Trying his hand at a different form, Root attempted to take advantage of Henry Clay Work's success with the dialect song. "De Day ob Liberty's Coming" is almost a shadow of Work's superb "Kingdom's Coming," but it has a couple of extra touches. The song is flavored with Daniel Emmett's ideas and music as well as those from "Go Down, Moses."[86] This song is noteworthy only because it shows the composer's willingness to experiment with new forms; Root's dialect work does not rank with his sentimental songs or battle hymns.

Root's creative zenith was the Civil War period. His music was likely sparked by his intense patriotism and his strong sense of the tragedy of war; perhaps he reached his peak when he ostensibly received this compliment from Lincoln: "You have done more than a hundred generals and a thousand orators." Although after 1865 Root, who became a noted music teacher, was no longer capable of the brilliant work he had published earlier, his contributions to the Union cause and American music had won him a well-deserved place in American musical history.[87]

The firm of Root and Cady also benefited handsomely from the talents of another exceptional songwriter, Henry Clay Work. Like Root, Work was a Chicago resident and the second of the war's great composers. An incident from his youth in Illinois must have impressed itself on the young Work and undoubtedly shaped much of his Civil War music. Work's father was imprisoned in Illinois for helping fugitive slaves escape to freedom. While his father's imprisonment may have saddened and shocked the young man, it did not impair his lively sense of humor, as is clearly evident in some of his war music, but it probably did increase his abolitionist feelings.

The intensity of antislavery sentiments and the popularity of the minstrel show combined to give Work the inspiration for his songs. With these themes in mind, Work wrote his first song in 1850, a piece titled "We Are Coming, Sister Mary," sung by the Christy Minstrels. The same group also sang a rendition of Work's first Civil War song, written in dialect and titled "Kingdom Coming (Year of Jublio)" (see appendix). The widely publicized "Kingdom Coming" was an instant success.[88] Many of the dialect songs and blackface routines were not at that time regarded (by whites) as degrading to blacks and were used by abolitionists to advertise their views.[89]

With abundant good humor, Work puts his quasi-hymn "Kingdom Coming" in the mouth of a slave who describes the events on his former plantation as northern gunboats are approaching. The master, a robust six-foot-tall gentleman so portly that he cannot afford to pay for the quantity of material required for a coat and who "drills so much dey call him captain,"[90] his taken to his heels in fear of the certain arrival of the Union army. Fortunately for his late owner, the slave remarks that the master is "so dreful tanned" he may be able to escape as "contraband," a word used by northerners to describe escaped or captured slaves as former Confederate property. The slaves have decided to care for their master's house in his absence, especially his parlor, while additionally sampling his "wine an' cider in de kitchen." They are quick to seize the opportunity, for they too will indulge themselves. To make completely sure of their freedom, the slaves have locked the overseer in the cellar. They have realized, "It must no be de kingdom comin'/An de year ob Jublio."

The song's popularity is undisputable since it was performed on a number of significant occasions. Northern troops in Louisiana sang the song on a captured plantation.[91] It was also sung in Washington at many of the rallies during Lincoln's campaign for reelection.[92] Union soldiers held their lines at a battle near Resaca, Georgia, when a military band played "Yankee Doodle" and "Kingdom Coming" to inspire them.[93] While marching into Richmond and Petersburg in 1865, the conquering Union forces and especially the black units sang the song; ironically, the Confederate troops sang a version of the song as they withdrew from Petersburg.[94] Numbers of freed slaves stood on the ground of the Lee mansion, two nights after the surrender at Appomattox, singing Work's famous freedom song.[95]

Work followed this success with a similar abolition song, also in dialect, "Babylon is Fallen." Work's song was inspired by a government announcement that Negro troops would be recruited. The piece was not so universally performed as Work's earlier composition, but it was, nonetheless, exceptionally popular.[96] The Republicans' militantly patriotic election rallies often featured "Babylon is Fallen," and a large group of Lincoln's supporters in Philadelphia sang it as they awaited news of the outcome of the 1864 election.[97] The song was also a favorite of Negro soldiers, who liked to sing it in camp.[98]

The song has a prophetic, hymnlike tone, with a touch of humor in the final stanza. The black fighters in the piece are so brave and resourceful, Work declares, that if cannonballs become scarce, they will use pumpkins. The Confederate soldiers, like the slaves' masters, are called "cowards."[99] The slaves see the end of an evil empire and their own benefit from it when they declare, "Babylon is fallen/And we're agwine to occupy the land." At the end of the song, in an unusual conclusion, the slaves and their masters exchange places, as the slaves happily sing, "We will be de massa,/[And] he will be de servant." It is unlikely that even many northerners, however, would have been willing to go as far as to see the roles of master and slave reversed.

In "Wake Nicodemus" Work uses the mythic notion of rebirth to symbolize freedom. The tune tells the story of an aged, highly respected slave whose last request was "Wake me up for the great Jubilee,"[100] clearly a reference to the freeing of the slaves. The "storm which seemingly banished the dawn" is allegorically the Civil War. (This phrase may also refer to early Confederate victories.) This 1864 song predicts certain Union success, because of Union victories such as Gettysburg and Grant's successes; the composer calls prematurely "Wake Nicodemus today," perhaps indicating that the slaves should celebrate their freedom. Peculiarly, this song, unlike Work's other freedom songs, is not in dialect.

Work's concern for minorities extended beyond the winning of freedom for slaves. In defense of the German-Americans, Work composed his sometimes humorous "Colonel Schnapps." Of his patriotism, Work's hero asserts, "I fights der pattles of te flag to set mine countries free."[101] Work is much less adept at handling German dialect than at representing black speech, and consequently the song is sometimes difficult to understand. Unlike the faithful lovers in many war songs, Schnapps' sweetheart "coes mit another man" when he leaves for war. He tells of the standard hardships of battle but finally manages to improve his lot when his unit captures a southern town. Of his captured rations he says, "I kits me sour kraut, much as I can eat,/ And plenty local pier." He fares no better with a southern lady than he did with his former beloved. When he meets an attractive woman, he "makes to her von ferry callant pow." Her scorn for him is unmistakable as he sadly and with surprise declares, "she schpits on me." In spite of the comic and stereotypical aspects of the song, it is clear that Work sympathizes with his character as he tries to show that German loyalties were to the Union. He is probably trying to refute the notion that because many Germans were Democrats, they were dissatisfied with a Republican war and therefore were sometimes slackers.[102] The piece may also be an attempt to improve the image of the German as a fighting man, for poor performances by German-American units at Chancellorsville and Gettysburg had given them a bad reputation.[103] A derivative song entitled "I Goes to Fight Mit Sigel" repeats Work's sentiments, avowing German-American loyalty to the Union and declaring German military prowess in the lines, "Dem Deutschmens mit Sigel's band/At fighting have no rival."[104]

In 1862 Work also turned his attention to the role of women in the war. Before they were officially taken into the military, Work granted them combat status. His angry persona in "We'll Go Down Ourselves" states that women are ready to "go down . . ./And teach the rebels something new."[105] Females are ready to take the military offensive "If as of yore,/The army's marches end beside . . . Potomac's waters." A Frank Moore story confirms Work's belief that women were ready to defend their country and their property. Moore, the well-known song and story collector, tells of a Kentucky Unionist who killed one rebel and captured ten others when they invaded her home. She personally delivered her prisoners to Federal forces.[106] As in previous wars, women acted as spies and for the first time served officially as nurses.

Work's next song dealt with a common and much discussed problem, the recruitment of soldiers for the army. "Grafted into the Army" attacked the manpower problems of the North in a humorous fashion, yet it is clear that the 1863 "graft" seriously disturbed Work. He was no doubt bothered by the $300 payment required to avoid service and, indeed, by the entire concept of such substitution. The standard complaint of the times condemned the conflict as "a rich man's war and a poor man's fight."[107] The language of the song indicates "Jimmy's"[108] social status and adds touches of humor and pathos through the use of occasional malapropisms. For example, Jimmy's uniform is called a "unicorn" and his mother's vision is a "provision." She is a "lone widder" who has lost at least two sons in "Alabarmy," but still her youngest is not spared the draft. The song closes with the pitiful question, "What if the ducky should up and die/Now they've grafted him into the army?" Work's song gave occasion to a number of parodies and imitations, but none of them became as significant as his song. One little-known composer, however, authored a reply to the famous songwriter that praised Jimmy's service.[109]

Work's "Marching Through Georgia" (see appendix) was one of the North's favorite late war tunes, and its popularity rapidly spread beyond America and the Civil War. It is one of the finest Civil War campaign songs and the only one written by a major war-song composer. The song was Work's celebration and vindication of Sherman's monumental march to the port of Savannah and beyond. Since it is one of the rare songs covering an entire campaign, a bit of background will show the omission of important details in the song and will describe the belief northerners held in their cause.

In 1864 Sherman took command of the Union armies he was to lead through Atlanta and ultimately to the sea. The purposes of the march were to destroy the will of the South to fight and at the same time eliminate communications and supply lines between the lower Confederate states and Lee's forces. Sherman's army of sixty-two thousand was to proceed through Georgia from Atlanta to Savannah, foraging for supplies and destroying anything of military value that could not be carried or used. The railroads were a prime target of destruction, and Sherman's soldiers rendered them inoperable. Sherman's army cut a sixty-mile-wide path from Atlanta to the coast. When Savannah was captured at Christmas in 1865, Sherman presented the city as a gift to Lincoln. Sherman's march continued, and it was a signal that the end was near for the dying Confederacy.[110]

Work's "Marching Through Georgia," like most battle songs, telescopes the action of the campaign. The song contains some putative facts, some oblique references, and at least one important omission. Neither does the piece specifically mention any of the battles of the campaign nor does it discuss any of Sherman's strategies or tactics. None of the participants, except Sherman, is mentioned by name.

While it is true that the "darkeys shouted"[111] and were joyful when they saw the liberating armies, it is distinctly contrary to fact that the army the freed slaves followed was "fifty thousand strong." Sherman's army numbered approximately twelve thousand more men than the song claims for it. It is barely probable that "there were Union men who wept with joyful tears" when they saw the determined invaders. If, indeed, there were Union men there at the time, it is likely that they were few and quiet. The "turkeys" and "sweet potatoes" Work mentions might have existed, but not in unlimited quantities. Sherman's foragers, however, did keep his army supplied with food.

The assertion that "Treason fled" implies that more than the Confederate army retreated before the powerful Union forces. Perhaps here Work intends "Treason" to stand for the idea of secession. Also implicit in these words is the downfall of an evil cause, defeated by a just and righteous one. There is a missionary zeal in this phrase and in the line "resistance was in vain." The powers of right, at least in Work's mind and in the minds of kindred souls in the North, had assumed unquestionable supremacy.

The line "Sherman's dashing Yankee boys will never reach the coast" flings in the face of the Confederacy the failed strategy of Hood to either defeat the Union force or turn Sherman from his goal. This "handsome boast" must surely have been on the lips and in the hopes of many southerners, both soldiers and civilians. Grant called Jefferson Davis' strong remarks regarding the fate of any Union force attempting the conquest of the South a "boasted threat."[112]

Work's most blatant omission, and one that any Union supporter might overlook, is the possibility that Sherman's soldiers stole private property and committed acts of depredation beyond the call of duty. Southern observations on the conduct of Sherman's troops are plentiful and, if exaggerated on occasion, without doubt true to some extent.[113] Whether Work knew or approved of these actions is uncertain; if he did, he—wisely from a propaganda standpoint—omitted the least mention of them from his song.

Of Work's melodic effort to promote the cause of the Union in his name, Sherman remarked in 1890, in an angry reference to the influence of "Marching Through Georgia," "If I had thought when I made that march that it would have inspired anyone to compose such a piece, I would have marched around the state."[114] Sherman's businesslike approach to war made him disdainful of any accolades for his work. Work's publisher and friend, George Root, probably would have been dismayed by such a detour since he believed that "Marching Through Georgia" was a fine song, fit for soldiers and similar groups.[115] The effect of "Marching Through Georgia" on the South was one of lasting enmity. As late as 1916, when it was struck up at the Democratic National Convention, it caused a stir among the southerners. Not surprisingly, many southerners were inclined to leave the assembly. Its melodic power carried over into World War I and II, however, where it was used as a marching song.

Work closed his wartime career with two tributes to the Union. In "Washington and Lincoln" the composer provided his audience with the first major musical tribute to the two figures in a liberty song. At the time he wrote the song, Work believed that "History's pages can never excel the story of Washington and Lincoln."[116] Certainly today many would agree with the author. One of the most important contributions that both men have made to their country is "Peace, only peace"; no doubt Work purposely understates its value for ironic reasons. The simple absence of conflict is important to a nation, but more significant are the individual contributions of Washington "who gave us independence on continent and sea" and Lincoln "who saved the glorious Union and set a people free." In comparing the two leaders' merits, Work finds them equally great.

In "Tis Finished or Sing Hallelujah" Work concluded his wartime song-writing with a hymn of celebration at the end of hostilities. This piece does not condemn southerners as traitors or jeer their cause but is quietly thankful that "the dread and awful task is done."[117] Like a liberty song, it calls upon its singers as "patriots" and "free men" to "sing the vict'ry won." An optimistic Work sees a "message that is gladness to waiting souls" and a future that holds "the brightest era ever known." As is proper for a hymn, the author offers praise "to God on high." He closes the song with a line that indicates his appreciation for Union and peace: "For the old flag with the white flag is hanging in the azure sky."

Work's music shows him to be a compassionate, patriotic man devoted to the Union cause and freedom for all men. Work's career was to outlast the Civil War; his greatest financial rewards came after this period. In 1875 he finally published "Grandfather's Clock," a song that he had agonized over for several years until he was satisfied with it. It brought him tremendous success. His publishers printed and sold more than 800,000 copies of the tune which earned him the handsome sum of four thousand dollars.[118] Work was not to enjoy happiness in his life, however, for he fell into poverty and died after the loss of his wife.[119]

George F. Root, Henry Clay Work, and to a much lesser degree Stephen Foster and the minor composers left a legacy of musical excellence in the liberty and war song whose power is undeniable; Root's and Work's songs reached an artistic plateau seldom attained by war and liberty song composers. The wide distribution and performance of their music is irrefutable proof of the popularity of the songs of the two great wartime composers. The numerous testaments in letters, newspapers, and memoirs to the effects of the great war songs on the minds and hearts of soldiers and citizens is a tribute to the inspirational value of their war music.[120] Each of the two great songwriters had at least one song that sold many thousand copies. For example, *The Song Messenger*, a musical trade magazine published by Root and Cady in 1867, lists figures for a few of Root's and Work's best-selling songs. "Kingdom Coming" is shown as having sold 75,000 copies, "The Battle Cry of Freedom" is given credit for 350,000 copies sold, "Just Before the Battle, Mother" logged 100,000 copies sold, and "Tramp! Tramp! Tramp!" is cited as having sold 150,000 sheets. Each of these figures is a one-year sales total. Even if these figures are slightly inflated (as they may very well be), the sales totals are nonetheless impressive and certainly indicate the wide appeal of quality work.[121]

The influence of the Civil War song carried on directly into the twentieth century. The sentimental ballad became standard fare both in the theaters of American and the music halls of Britain. Civil War songs were the prototypes of tunes like "Keep the Home Fires Burning" and "There's a Long, Long Trail." Root and Work had at least two successors of note in George M. Cohan and John Philip Sousa. A rousing patriotic tune like "The Battle Cry of Freedom" found a World War I companion in Cohan's "Over There," which garnered for Cohan a congressional medal for special service to his country.[122] Sousa, who was born in 1854, remembered hearing Union bands in Washington during his childhood play some of the great war songs like "The Battle Cry of Freedom" and Tramp! Tramp! Tramp!" His stirring "Stars and Stripes Forever," for which he also composed a set of lyrics, is probably the only American patriotic composition more stirring than "The Battle Cry of Freedom."[123]

The dialect and minstrel songs by Work and others were also influential. Authentic black music came to the North by way of former slaves, ballad collectors, and folklorists. Black songs and dialect pieces as well as minstrel music helped to pave the way for ragtime. The informal quality of these forms of music might well have contributed to the improvisational nature of modern jazz. Thus from the Civil War came a thriving popular music that enriched American culture and gave it a distinct flavor.

NOTES

1. Irwin Silber, ed., *Songs of the Civil War* (New York: Columbia University Press, 1960), p. 120.

2. *Dictionary of American Biography*, s. v. "Hays, William Shakespeare."

3. Richard B. Harwell, *Confederate Music* (Chapel Hill: University of North Carolina Press, 1950).

4. "The Drummer Boy of Shiloh," reprinted in Paul Glass and Louis Singer, eds., *Singing Soldiers: A History of the Civil War in Song* (New York: Da Capo Press, 1968), p. 83.

5. Willard A. Heaps and Porter W. Heaps, *The Singing Sixties: The Spirit of the Civil War Days Drawn from the Music of the Times* (Norman: University of Oklahoma Press, 1960), p. 185.

6. "Who Will Care for Mother Now?" an original broadside reprinted in Heaps, 187.

7. Ibid., 197.

8. "Mother Would Comfort Me," reprinted in Glass and Singer, 256–258.

9. "I Dreamed My Boy Was Home Again," reprinted in Heaps, 232.

10. "Who Will Care for Micky Now?" reprinted in Silber, 160.

11. Robert Kelley, *The Cultural Pattern in American Politics: The First Century* (New York: Alfred A. Knopf, 1979), pp. 236–237.

12. "Mother on the Brain," reprinted in Vera Brodsky Lawrence, *Music for Patriots, Politicians, and Presidents: Harmonies and Discords of the First Hundred Years* (New York: Macmillan, 1975), p. 373.

13. Richard Jackson, ed., *Popular Songs of Nineteenth Century America* (New York: Dover Publications, 1976), p. 28.

14. Silber, 167.

15. Jackson, 239.

16. Silber, 167.

17. Jackson, *Popular Songs*, 282.

18. "Tenting on the Old Camp Ground," reprinted in National Committee for the Preservation of Existing Records of the National Society of the Colonial Dames of America, *American War Songs* (Philadelphia: privately printed, 1925), pp. 107–108.

19. J. G. Randall and David Donald, *The Civil War and Reconstruction*, 2d ed. (Boston: D. C. Heath, 1965), p. 420.

20. *The New Grove Dictionary of Music and Musicians*, s. v. "Gilmore, Patrick Sarsfield."

21. Heaps, 348.

22. Silber, 174–175.

23. "When Johnny Comes Marching Home," reprinted in *Colonial Dames*, 119–120.

24. "Abe Lincoln Went to Washington," reprinted in Silber, 213.

25. "For Bales," reprinted in Glass and Singer, 192–193.

26. *The New Grove Dictionary of Music and Musicians*, s. v. "Winner, Septimus."

27. Harwell, *Confederate Music*, 88.

28. Kenneth A. Bernard, *Lincoln and the Music of the Civil War* (Caldwell, Idaho: Caxton Printers, 1966), p. 80.

29. Silber, 91.

30. "Abraham's Daughter of the Raw Recruit," reprinted in Glass and Singer, 102–103.

31. "A Nation Mourns Her Martyred Son," reprinted in Heaps, 363.

32. "Yes, I Would the Cruel War Were Over," reprinted in Lawrence, 403.

33. Harwell, *Confederate Music*, 28–31.

34. *Dictionary of American Biography*, s. v. "Hewitt, John Hill."

35. Lawrence, 326.

36. Harwell, *Confederate Music*, 34–36.

37. "You Are Going to the Wars, Willie Boy," reprinted from the original sheet music in Richard B. Harwell, *Songs of the Confederacy* (New York: Broadcast Music, 1951), pp. 68–69.

38. "The Young Volunteer," reprinted from the original sheet music in Harwell, *Songs of the Confederacy*, 76–77.

39. Harwell, *Confederate Music*, 40. For another point of view on Hewitt's music see Charles Hamm, *Yesterdays: Popular Song in America* (New York: W. W. Norton and Co., 1979), p. 108.

40. David Ewen, *Great Men of American Popular Song* (Englewood Cliffs, N. J.: Prentice-Hall, 1970), pp. 24–29.

41. John Tasker Howard, *Stephen Foster, America's Troubadour* (New York: Thomas Y. Crowell, 1934), p. 198.

42. Ewen, 30.

43. Howard, 188.

44. "Better Times are Coming," reprinted from the original sheet music in Rich-

ard Jackson, ed., *Stephen Foster Songbook* (New York: Dover Publications, 1974), pp. 10–13.

45. *Civil War Dictionary*, s. v. "Foote, Andrew H."

46. Ibid., s. v. "Corcoran, Michael."

47. Ibid., s. v. "Shields, James."

48. "That's What's the Matter," reprinted from the original sheet music in Jackson, *Stephen Foster Songbook*, 123–125.

49. Ewen, 30.

50. "How Are You, Green-Backs?" reprinted in Fletcher Hodges, Jr., *Stephen Foster, Democrat* (Pittsburgh: University of Pittsburgh Press, 1946), p. 6.

51. Ibid., 17–19.

52. William W. Austin, *"Susanna," "Jeannie,"* and *"The Old Folks at Home": The Songs of Stephen C. Foster From His Time to Ours* (New York: Macmillan, 1975), p. 99.

53. "I'm Nothing But a Plain Old Soldier," reprinted from the original sheet music in Jackson, *The Stephen Foster Songbook*, 84–87.

54. Howard, 317–318.

55. "A Soldier in De Colored Brigade," reprinted in Austin, 189.

56. Hodges, 9. Hodges believes that Cooper and Foster shared the same views about black soldiers.

57. Austin, 189.

58. Howard, 341.

59. Dena J. Epstein, "The Battle Cry of Freedom," *Civil War History* 4 (1958): 313.

60. Ewen, 37–38.

61. George F. Root, *The Story of a Musical Life: An Autobiography by George F. Root* (Cincinnati: John Church, 1891), p. 133. Root's age, forty-one in 1861, might have been the reason for his not having been called into service.

62. "The Battle Cry of Freedom," reprinted in Silber, 19.

63. "The Battle Cry of Freedom, II (Battle Song)," reprinted in Silber, 19.

64. Ibid., 10.

65. Brander Matthews, "The Songs of the War," *Century Magazine* 34 (1887): 625.

66. Bernard, 251.

67. Root, 133.

68. Epstein, 314.

69. C. A. Browne, *The Story of Our National Ballads* (New York: Thomas Y. Crowell, 1919), pp. 323–324.

70. Bernard, 83–84.

71. Epstein, 316.

72. Richard Wentworth Browne, "Union War Songs and Confederate Officers," *Century Magazine* 34 (1887): 478. This remark was made during a period when Confederate and Union soldiers praised each other's performance in the war. In addition, it must be noted that "Rally 'Round the Flag" had not been written at the time of the Seven Days' battles.

73. Bernard, 76. For a European musician's view of the war, see Louis Gottschalk, *Notes of a Pianist*, ed. Clara Gottschalk, trans. Robert E. Peterson (Philadelphia: J. B. Lippincott, 1881).

74. Silber, 13–14.

75. "Tramp! Tramp! Tramp!" reprinted in Colonial Dames, *American War Songs*, 86.

76. Heaps, 206–214.

77. Silber, 14.

78. Ibid., 116.

79. "Just Before the Battle, Mother," reprinted in Colonial Dames, *American War Songs*, 81–82.

80. Bernard, 284.

81. Root, 136.

82. "A Voice From the Army," reprinted in Bernard, 287.

83. "Farewell, Mother," reprinted in Silber, 153.

84. "Never Forget the Dear Ones," reprinted in Glass and Singer, 238–240.

85. "Foes and Friends," reprinted in Glass and Singer, 264–266.

86. Silber, 307.

87. Ewen, 39–40. This quotation is not included in any of the major biographies of Lincoln or in Lincoln's writings.

88. Ibid., 41–42.

89. Silber, 306.

90. "Kingdom Coming," from the original sheet music reprinted in Henry Clay Work, *Songs*, ed. H. Wiley Hitchcock (New York: Da Capo Press, 1974), pp. 162–164.

91. Bernard, 138.

92. Ibid., 235.

93. Ibid., 247.

94. Ibid., 294–295.

95. Ibid., 300.

96. Silber, 307.

97. Bernard, 246–247.

98. Bell Irwin Wiley, *The Life of Billy Yank* (New York: Bobbs-Merrill, 1951), p. 169.

99. "Babylon is Fallen," reprinted from the original sheet music in Work, 32–34.

100. "Wake, Nicodemus," reprinted from the original sheet music in Work, 10–12.

101. "Corporal Schnapps," reprinted from the original sheet music in Work, 124–126.

102. Kelley, 236.

103. James M. McPherson, *Ordeal by Fire: The Civil War and Reconstruction* (New York: Alfred A. Knopf, 1982), pp. 321–326.

104. "I Goes to Fight with Sigel," reprinted in Silber, 326.

105. "We'll Go Down Ourselves," reprinted in Lawrence, 389.

106. Frank Moore, *The Civil War in Song and Story, 1860–1865* (New York: F. P. Collier, 1889), p. 708.

107. Silber, 304.

108. "Grafted into the Army," reprinted in Silber, 311–312.

109. Ibid., 305.

110. C. A. Browne, 185–192.

111. "Marching Through Georgia," reprinted from the original sheet music in Work, 18–20.

112. Randall and Donald, 430.

113. Ibid., 431–432.

114. Ewen, 43–44.

115. Root, 138.

116. "Washington and Lincoln," reprinted from the original sheet music in Work, 84–86.

117. "Tis Finished," reprinted from the original sheet music in Work, 96–98.

118. Work, 6.

119. Ewen, 43–44.

120. James Stone's article "War Music and War Psychology in the Civil War," *Journal of Abnormal and Social Psychology* 36 (1941): 543–560, discounts the importance of patriotic music among soldiers. As has been shown in this chapter, soldiers remembered many songs. Contrary to Stone's conclusion, the "music of war" is not necessarily "the music of peace" (558).

121. Dena J. Epstein, *Music Publishing in Chicago Before 1871: The Firm of Root and Cady* (Detroit: Information Coordinators, Inc., 1969), p. 48. The best general guide to nineteenth century American music publishers is Harry Dichter and Elliott Shapiro, *Early American Music: Its Lure and Lore, 1768–1889* (New York: R. R. Bowker, 1941).

122. Ward Morehouse, *George M. Cohan: Prince of the American Theatre* (New York: J. B. Lippincott, 1943).

123. John Phillip Sousa, *Marching Along: Recollections of Men, Women, and Music* (St. Clair Shores, Mich.: Scholarly Press, 1977; originally published in 1928), pp. 14–17.

8

Conclusions and Observations

The development of American liberty and war songs in the period from 1765 to 1865 parallels the growth of American culture, and thus the emergence of an important American musical form is a major topic of interest to scholars of history and music. The American liberty and war song was born from a few protest songs of British derivation before the Revolutionary War. By the end of the Civil War, American composers of note like George F. Root and Henry Clay Work were creating an authentic American song style that had developed into a significant form of popular music.

The first major crisis to present an opportunity for the composition of American liberty songs was the passage of the Stamp Act in 1765. During the next ten years, American liberty music demonstrated Americans' concern for their rights; it also documented British oppression and corruption. With the coming of the American Revolution, the American war song was born. The most famous war song, using a melody often found in American martial music, is "Yankee Doodle," liberated from the British at Bunker Hill early in the war. The Revolution also inspired songs from America's first important war-song composers. Francis Hopkinson, a writer of comic songs and a well-known patriot, and William Billings, a New England composer, produced inspirational patriotic music. The Revolution also saw the composition of the first naval songs, a trend that was continued and greatly expanded during the War of 1812.

Dialect war songs, like naval songs, were at first few in number but within a few years became much more numerous and widely popular. The first dialect war songs were composed during the War of 1812, and by the time of the Civil War, under the influence of the minstrel show, they became a major genre of the war song. Songs like Daniel Emmett's "Dixie" and many of Henry Clay Work's compositions such as "Kingdom Coming" attest to the widespread appeal of the dialect song.

Another important group of songs first appearing during the Revolution consists of songs by and about women. The first female figures in American song are standard women characters: patriotic sweethearts and wives waiting for their absent warriors to return. By the time of the Mexican War, women are ready to shoulder rifles and serve in combat with the men they love. Civil War songs show women not only as warriors but also as concerned producers of wartime products.

The voices of both male and female persona changed during the years between 1812 and 1846. The songs of the War of 1812 show the same anxiety for winning and preserving freedoms that characterized American war songs during the Revolution. The Mexican War inspired many cheerful war songs eagerly anticipating the territory to be won from a weak and ethnically inferior enemy. For the first time American liberty and war songs celebrated American offensive might and its capacity for making the United States an important power.

Not all Americans approved of the use of the U. S. Army as a tool for the conquest of new territories. Some New Englanders, led by William Lloyd Garrison, openly protested the war, both in editorials and in song. *The Liberator* was the first publication to carry American musical protests against the war. The angry tone of the songs and their obvious antiwar sentiments reflect the conflict between the opponents and proponents of the war; the antiwar protestors considered the supporters of the war barbaric and disdainful of God's commandments. One of the protestors' chief fears was that any newly acquired land would serve to nurture slavery, something Garrison and his followers had long fought. The ground was thus prepared for the heated disputes between North and South that would culminate in the Civil War.

During the Civil War, several important developments in liberty and war songs occurred. First, printing methods had improved and consequently music publishers were able to print large numbers of the most popular war tunes. Fewer songs were printed in broadsides and newspapers. Second, many war-song composers had written at least one popular antebellum song. Third, for the first time in the history of American popular music, two men, Stephen Foster and George Cooper, worked over an extended period of time to produce a large number of war songs. Finally, and most important, two native American composers, George Root and Henry Clay Work, gave liberty and war music a well-defined and recognizable American voice. Between them, the two men composed many popular and well-crafted works in all genres of American song. As with American literature in the 1850s, the American liberty and war song had finally become truly American; by contrast, British war music was to retain its traditional character for the remainder of the nineteenth century.

This new American music left a rich legacy to modern music. First, Root's and Work's liberty and war songs bequeathed their optimistic tone and patriotic messages to the music of George M. Cohan, John Philip Sousa, and Irving Berlin, as well as to the numerous lesser composers of the modern era. Second, from the dialect war song, minstrel show songs, and slave and black soldier songs came a form of music that was to influence the blues and jazz, the most clearly original American musical contributions to world culture.

Much work remains to be done in the study of liberty and war songs written after the Civil War. Little examination has been made of the music of the Spanish-American War. Some World War I songs have been collected, mostly by the well-known musician and collector John Jacob Niles, but no comprehensive analysis has been made of those pieces as historical documents or of their relation to popular culture. Much the same may be said of World War II and Korean War songs, although two fine collections of war songs include works from those wars. The conflict in Viet Nam offers much available material for the collection and analysis of antiwar songs. A detailed survey of liberty and war songs of the period from the Spanish-American War through the conflict in Viet Nam would undoubtedly also reveal much about the development of American culture since the Civil War.

Appendix:
Selected Song Lyrics

THE LIBERTY SONG

Come join hand in hand, brave Americans all,
And rouse your bold hearts at fair Liberty's call;
No tyrannous acts, shall suppress your just claim,
Or stain with dishonor America's name.

In freedom we're born, and in freedom we'll live;
Our purses are ready,
Steady, Friends, steady,
Not as slaves, but as freeman our money we'll give.

Our worthy forefathers—let's give them a cheer—
To climates unknown did courageously steer;
Thro' oceans to deserts, for freedom they came,
And, dying, bequeath'd us their freedom and fame.

The Tree, their own hands had to Liberty rear'd,
They lived to behold growing strong and rever'd;
With transport then cried—"Now our wishes we gain,
For our children shall gather the fruits of our pain."

How sweet are the labors that freemen endure,
That they shall enjoy all the profit, secure,—
No more such sweet labors Americans know,
If Britons shall reap what Americans sow.

Swarms of placemen and pensioners' soon will appear,
Like locusts deforming the charms of the year:
Suns vainly will rise, showers vainly descend,
If we are to drudge for what others shall spend.

Then join hand in hand brave Americans all,
By uniting we stand, by dividing we fall;
In so righteous a cause let us hope to succeed,
For Heaven approves of each generous deed.

This bumper I crown for our sovereign's health,
And this for Britannia's glory and wealth;
That wealth, and that glory immortal may be,
If she is but just, and we are but free.[1]

CHESTER

Let tyrants shake their iron rod,
    And slav'ry clank her galling chains;
We fear them not, we trust in God,
    New-England's God forever reigns.

Howe and Burgoyne and Clinton too,
    With Prescott and Cornwallis join'd,
Together plot our overthrow,
    In one Infernal league combin'd.

When God inspir'd us for the fight,
    Their ranks were broke, their lines were forc'd,
Their ships were shatter'd in our sight,
    Or swiftly driven from our coast.

The Foe comes on with haughty stride,
    Our troops advance with martial noise,
Their Vet'rans flee before our youth,
    And Gen'rals yield to beardless boys.

What grateful off'ring shall we bring
    What shall we render to the Lord?
Loud Hallelujahs let us sing,
    And praise His name on ev'ry chord.[2]

A NEW WAR SONG

My lords, with your leave,
    An account I will give,
That deserves to be written in metre:
    For the rebels and I,
    Have been pretty nigh,
Faith almost too nigh for Sir Peter.

    With much labor and toil,
    Unto Sullivan's Isle,
I came firm as Falstaff or Pistol,
    But the Yankees, 'od rot'em,

I could not get at'em,
Most terribly maul'd my poor *Bristol*.

Bold Clinton by land,
 Did quietly stand,
While I made a thundering clatter;
 But the channel was deep,
 so he only could peep,
And not venture over the water.

Now bold as a Turk,
 I proceed to New York,
Where with Clinton and Howe you may find me.
 I've the wind in my tail,
 And am hoisting my sail,
To leave Sullivan's Island behind me.

But my Lords, do not fear,
 For before the next year,
Although a small island could fret us,
 The Continent whole,
 We shall take, by my soul,
If the cowardly Yankees will let us.[3]

THE DANCE

A Ballad, to the tune of "Yankey Doodle."

Corwallis led a country dance,
 The like was never seen, sir,
Much retrograde, and much advance,
 And all with general Greene, sir.

Greene, in the fourth, then danc'd a set,
 And got a mighty name, sir,
Cornwallis jigg'd with young Fayette,
 But suffered in his fame, sir.

Though men so gallant ne'er were seen,
 While saunt'ring on parade, sir,
Or wriggling o'er the park's smooth green,
 Or at a masquerade, sir.

Yet are red heels, and long sat'd skirts,
 For stumps and briars meet, sir,
Or stand they chance with hunting shirts,
 Or hardy veteran feet, sir.

Now hous'd in York he challeng'd all,
 At minuet or all'mande,
And legions for a courtly ball,
 His guards by day and night conn'd.

This challenge known, full soon there came,
   A set who had the bon ton,
DeGrasse and Rochambeau, whose fame,
   Fut brilliant pour un long tems.

And Washington, Columbia's son,
   Whom easy nature taught, sir,
That grace, which can't by pains be won,
   Or Plutus' gold be bought, sir.

Now tories all what can ye say?
   Come—Is not this a griper?
That while your hopes are danc'd away,
   'Tis you must pay the piper.[4]

THE STAR-SPANGLED BANNER

O! say can you see by the dawn's early light,
   What so proudly we hailed at the twilight's last gleaming,
Whose broad stripes and bright stars through the perilous night,
   O'er the ramparts we watch'd, were so gallantly streaming?
And the Rockets' red glare, the Bombs bursting in air,
Gave proof through the night, that our Flag was still there;
   O' say does that star-spangled Banner yet wave,
   O'er the Land of the free, and the home of the brave?

O' thus be it ever when freemen shall stand!
   Between their lov'd homes, and the war's desolation,
Blest with vict'ry and peace, may the Heav'n rescued land,
   Praise the Power that hath made and preserv'd us a nation!
Then conquer we must, when our cause it is just,
And this be our motto—In God is our Trust
   And the star-spangled Banner in triumph shall wave,
   O'er the Land of the Free, and the Home of the Brave.[5]

BATTLE HYMN

Over, over the Mexican border!
   Onward, on to the Mexican land!
'Tis by Polk's particular order,
   'Tis by the War Department's command.
Plenty of shot, and plenty of powder,
   This is the soldier's principal pay;
Publish the faster and brag the louder,
   Mexicans always run away!

   This is the way,
   Our rulers say,
   That the rule of the free,

From sea to sea,
Shall ever increase,
In kindness and peace!

On to the halls of the Montezumas!
  There, if too many do not lag,—
There, if the fever don't consume us,—
  There will we plant our peaceful flag!
Plenty of churches, plenty of idols,
  Melt very well into solid gold;
Golden stirrups, and bits for our bridles,
  Such as the bandits had of old,

What care we for Mexican bushes!
  Are not the volunteers flocking in?
What if we do have the hardest brushes,
  While the officers get the glory and 'tin'
Won't we figure in 'killed and wounded,'
  Washington Union, column 3d?
Isn't the soldier's fame unbounded?
  Isn't our eagle a noble bird?

By and by, when the fight is ended,
  We, who are left, will straggle back:—
See how the soldier will be befriended,
  When health and fortune are both a wreck
Plenty of shot, and plenty of powder,
  This is the soldier's principal pay;
Publish the faster and brag the louder,
  Mexicans always run away![6]

THE BATTLE HYMN OF THE REPUBLIC

Mine eyes have seen the glory
  of the coming of the Lord;
He is trampling out the vintage
  where the grapes of wrath are stored,
He hath loosed the fateful lightning
  of His terrible swift sword;
  His truth is marching on.

> *Glory! Glory! Hallelujah!*
> *Glory! Glory! Hallelujah!*
> *Glory! Glory! Hallelujah!*
> *His truth goes marching on.*

I have seen him in the watch-fires
  of a hundred circling camps;
They have builded Him an altar
  in the evening dews and damps,

I have read His righteous sentence
  by the dim and flaring lamps;
  His day is marching on.

He has sounded forth the trumpet
  that shall never call retreat;
He is sifting out the hearts of men
  before His judgment seat;
Oh be swift, my soul, to answer Him—
  be jubilant my feet!
  Our God is marching on.

In the beauty of the lilies
  Christ was born across the sea,
With a glory in his bosom that
  transfigures you and me,
As He died to make men holy,
  let us die to make men free,
  While God is marching on.[7]

WEEPING SAD AND LONELY

Dearest love, do you remember
When we last did meet?
How you told me that you loved me,
Kneeling at my feet?
Oh, how proud you stood before me
In your suit of blue (gray)
When you vowed to me and country
Ever to be true. (ne'er to go astray)

> *Weeping, sad and lonely,*
> *Hopes and fears how vain!*
> *When this cruel war is over,*
> *Praying that we meet again!*

If amid the din of battle,
Nobly you should fall,
Far away from those who love you,
None to hear you call.
Who would whisper words of comfort,
Who would soothe your pain?
Ah! and many cruel fancies
Ever in my brain.

When the summer breeze is sighing
Mournfully along;
Or when autumn leaves are falling,
Sadly breathes the song.
Oft in dreams I see thee lying

On the battle-plain,
Lonely, wounded, even dying,
Call, but in vain.

But our country called you, darling,
Angels cheers your way;
While our nation's sons are fighting,
We can only pray.
Nobly strike for God and liberty,
Let all nations see
How we love the starry banner,
Emblem of the free.[8]

THE BATTLE CRY OF FREEDOM

Yes, we'll rally round the flag, boys,
   We'll rally once again
Shouting the Battle Cry of Freedom.
We will rally from the hillside,
   We'll gather from the plain
Shouting the battle cry of freedom.

The Union forever, hurrah, boys, hurrah,
Down with the traitor and up with the stars
While we rally round the flag, boys,
Rally once again,
Shouting the Battle Cry of Freedom.

We are springing to the call
   Of our brothers gone before,
Shouting the Battle Cry of Freedom;
And we'll fill the vacant ranks
   With a million freemen more,
Shouting the Battle Cry of Freedom.

We will welcome to our numbers
   The loyal, true and brave,
Shouting the Battle Cry of Freedom;
And altho' they may be poor,
   Not a man shall be a slave
Shouting the Battle Cry of Freedom.

So we're springing to the call
   From the East and from the West,
Shouting the Battle Cry of Freedom;
And we'll hurl the rebel crew
   From the land we love the best,
Shouting the Battle Cry of Freedom.[9]

JUST BEFORE THE BATTLE, MOTHER

Just before the battle, Mother
  I am thinking most of you
While upon the field we're watching
  With the enemy in view.
Comrades brave are round me lying
  Filled with thoughts of home and God,
For well they know that on the morrow
  Some will sleep beneath the sod.

    Farewell, Mother, you may never
      Press me to your heart again,
    But O you'll not forget me, Mother,
      If I'm numbered with the slain.

O, I long to see you, Mother,
  And the loving ones at home.
But I'll never leave our banner
  Till in honor I can come.
Tell the traitors all round you
  That their cruel words we know
In every battle kill our soldiers
  By the help they give the foe.

Hark, I hear the bugles sounding,
  'Tis the signal for the fight.
Now may God protect you, Mother,
  As He ever does the right.
Hear the "Battle Cry of Freedom"
  How it swells upon the air.
O yes we'll rally round the standard
  Or we'll perish nobly there.[10]

KINGDOM COMING

Say, darkeys, hab you seen de massa,
  Wid de muffstash on his face,
Go 'long de road some time dis mornin',
  Like he gwine to leab de place?
He seen a smoke way up de ribber,
  Whar de Linkum gumboats lay;
He took his hat, an' lef' berry sudden,
  An' I spec' he's run away!

    De massa run? ha, ha!
    De darkey stay? ho, ho!
    It mus' be now de kingdom' comin',
    An' de year ob Jublio!

He six foot one way, two foot tudder,
   An' he weigh t'ree hundred pound,
His coat so big, he couldn't pay de tailor,
   An' it won't go half way round.
He drill so much, dey call him Cap'an,
   An' he get so drefful tanned,
I spec' he try an' fool dem Yankees,
   For to t'ink he's contraband.

De darkeys feel so lonesome libing
   In de log-house on de lawn,
Dey move dar t'ings to massa's parlor,
   For to keep it while he's gone.
Dar's wine an' cider in de kitchen,
   An' de darkeys dey'll hab some;
I s'pose dey'll all be cornfiscated,
   When de Linkum sojers come.

De oberseer he make us trouble,
   An' he dribe us round a spell:
We lock him up in de smoke-house cellar,
   Wid de key t'rown in de well.
De whip is lost, de han'-cuff broken,
   But de massa'll hab his pay;
He's ole enough, big enough, ought to know better,
   Dan to went, an' run away.[11]

MARCHING THROUGH GEORGIA

Bring the good old bugle, boys! we'll sing another song—
Sing it with a spirit that will start the world along—
Sing it as we used to sing it, fifty thousand strong.
   While we were marching through Georgia.

*   Hurrah, hurrah! we bring the jubilee!*
*   Hurrah, hurrah! the flag that makes you free!*
*   So we sang the chorus from Atlanta to the sea,*
*   While we were marching through Georgia.*

How the darkies shouted when they heard the joyful sound!
How the turkeys gobbled which our commissary found!
How the sweet potatoes even started from the ground,
   While we were marching through Georgia.

Yes, and there were Union men who wept with joyful tears
When they saw the honored flag they had not seen for years;
Hardly could they be restrained from breaking forth in cheers
   While we were marching through Georgia.

So we made a thoroughfare for Freedom and her train.

Sixty miles in latitude, three hundred to the main:
Treason fled before us, for resistance was in vain,
  While we were marching through Georgia.[12]

NOTES

1. "The Liberty Song," edited from a version reprinted in Frank Moore, *Songs and Ballads of the American Revolution* (Port Washington, N. Y.: Kennikat Press, 1964; originally published in 1855), pp. 37–39.

2. "Chester," reprinted in Vera Brodsky Lawrence, *Music for Patriots, Politicians, and Presidents: Harmonies and Discords of the First Hundred Years* (New York: Macmillan, 1975), p. 81.

3. "A New War Song," reprinted in Moore, 135–137.

4. "The Dance," edited from a version printed in the *Pennsylvania Packet*, 27 November 1781.

5. "The Star-Spangled Banner," edited from a version in the *Baltimore American and Daily Adviser*, 21 September 1814.

6. "Battle Hymn," printed in *The Liberator*, 10 July 1846.

7. "The Battle Hymn of the Republic," edited from a version reprinted in Irwin Silber, ed., *Songs of the Civil War* (New York: Columbia University Press, 1960), pp. 21–23.

8. "Weeping Sad and Lonely," reprinted in Silber, 124–126.

9. "The Battle Hymn of Freedom," reprinted in National Committee for the Preservation of Existing Records of the National Society of the Colonial Dames of America, *American War Songs* (Philadelphia: privately printed, 1925), pp. 78–79.

10. "Just Before the Battle, Mother," reprinted in Colonial Dames, 81–82.

11. "Kingdom Coming," reprinted in Henry Clay Work, *Songs*, ed. H. Wiley Hitchcock (New York: Da Capo Press, 1974), pp. 162–164.

12. "Marching Through Georgia," reprinted in Work, 18–20.

Bibliography

PRIMARY SOURCES

Song Collections

Contemporary

Moore, Frank. *The Civil War in Song and Story, 1860–1865*. New York: F. P. Collier, 1889.
———. *Songs and Ballads of the American Revolution*. Port Washington, New York: Kennikat Press, 1964. Originally published in 1855.
An Officer in General Taylor's Army. *Rough and Ready Songster*. New York: Nafis and Cornish, n.d.

Noncontemporary

Anderson, Gillian B. *Freedom's Voice in Poetry and Song*. Wilmington, Del.: Scholarly Research, 1977.
Carey, George A., ed. *A Sailor's Songbag: An American Rebel in an English Prison*. Amherst: University of Massachusetts Press, 1976.
Dolph, Edward A., ed. *"Sound Off!": Soldier Songs from the Revolution to World War II*. New York: Farrar and Rinehart, 1942.
Glass, Paul, and Louis Singer, eds. *Singing Soldiers: A History of the Civil War in Song*. New York: Da Capo Press, 1968.
Harwell, Richard B. *Songs of the Confederacy*. New York: Broadcast Music, 1951.
Heaps, Willard A., and Porter W. Heaps. *The Singing Sixties: The Spirit of the Civil War Days Drawn from the Music of the Times*. Norman: University of Oklahoma Press, 1960.
Hughes, Langston, and Anna Bontemps. *The Book of Negro Folklore*. New York: Dodd, Mead, and Co., 1958.
Jackson, Richard, ed. *Popular Songs of Nineteenth-Century America*. New York: Dover Publications, 1976.

―――. *Stephen Foster Song Book*. New York: Dover Publications, 1974.

Lambert, Barbara, ed. *Music in Colonial Massachusetts, 1630–1820*. Vol. 1, *Music in Public Places*. Charlottesville: University Press of Virginia, 1980.

Lawrence, Vera Brodsky. *Music for Patriots, Politicians, and Presidents: Harmonies and Discords of the First Hundred Years*. New York: Macmillan Co., 1975.

Lomax, John A. *Cowboy Songs and Other Frontier Ballads*. New York: Macmillan, 1925.

National Committee for the Preservation of Existing Records of the National Society of the Colonial Dames of America. *American War Songs*. Philadelphia: privately printed, 1925.

Neeser, Robert, ed. *American Sea Songs and Ballads*. New Haven: Yale University Press, 1938.

Pound, Louise, ed. *American Songs and Ballads*. New York: Charles Scribner's Sons, 1972.

Rabson, Carolyn. *Songbook of the American Revolution*. Peaks Island, Maine: NEO Press, 1974.

Silber, Irwin, ed. *Songs of the Civil War*. New York: Columbia University Press, 1960.

Silber, Irwin, and Earl Robinson. *Songs of the Great American West*. New York: Macmillan Co., 1967.

Thompson, Harold W. *Body, Boots, and Britches: Folktales, Ballads, and Speech from Country New York*. Syracuse, N.Y.: Syracuse University Press, 1979.

Wade, Manly, and Francis Wellman. *The Rebel Songster*. Charlotte, N.C.: Heritage House, 1959.

Winslow, Ola Elizabeth, ed. *American Broadside Verse*. New Haven: Yale University Press, 1930.

Work, Henry Clay. *Songs*. Edited by H. Wiley Hitchcock. New York: Da Capo Press, 1974.

Memoirs and Diaries

Chesnut, Mary. *Mary Chesnut's Civil War*. Edited by C. Vann Woodward. New Haven: Yale University Press, 1981.

Davis, W. W. H. *El Gringo: New Mexico and Her People*. Lincoln: University of Nebraska Press, 1982. Originally published in 1857.

Gottschalk, Louis Moreau. *Notes of a Pianist*. Edited by Clara Gottschalk. Translated by Robert E. Peterson. Philadelphia: J. B. Lippincott and Co., 1881.

Reid, Samuel C. *The Capture and Wonderful Escape of General John H. Morgan*. Edited by J. J. Mathews. Atlanta: Emory University Press, 1947.

Root, George F. *The Story of a Musical Life: An Autobiography*. Cincinnati: John Church Co., 1891.

Smith, George Winston, and Charles Judah, eds. *Chronicles of the Gringos: The U.S. Army in the Mexican War, 1846–1848*. Albuquerque: The University of New Mexico Press, 1968.

Sousa, John Philip. *Marching Along: Recollections of Men, Women and Music*. St. Clair Shores, Mich.: Scholarly Press, 1967. Originally published in 1928.

Articles

Browne, Richard Wentworth. "Union War Songs and Confederate Officers." *Century Magazine* 34 (1887): 478.

Howe, Julia Ward. "Note on 'The Battle Hymn of the Republic.' " *Century Magazine* 34 (1887): 629–630.

Newspapers and Periodicals

Albany Evening Journal, 1985.
Baltimore American and Daily Advertiser, 1813–1848.
Boston Gazette, 1776–1781.
Boston Spectator, 1814.
Brownlow's Knoxville Whig and Rebel Ventilator, 1861–1865.
Charleston Mercury, 1812–1861.
Columbia Centinel, 1814.
Connecticut or New London Gazette, 1770–1783.
The Liberator, 1846–1865.
The London Times, 1845–1846.
London Standard, 1845–1846.
National Intelligencer, 1812–1848.
New Orleans Times-Picayune, 1846–1862.
Pennsylvania Packet, 1774–1781.
Punch, 1862.
Richmond Enquirer, 1814–1865.
The Rough and Ready, 1847.
Santa Fe Republican, 1846–1848.
Southern Confederacy, 1860–1864.
Southern Literary Messenger, 1860–1864.
Virginia Gazette, 1765–1781.
*Wilmington (*North Carolina*) Daily Journal*, 1861–1863.

SECONDARY SOURCES

Biographies

Dyer, Brainerd. *Zachary Taylor*. New York: Barnes and Noble, 1946.

Hamilton, Holman. *Zachary Taylor: Soldier of the Republic*. New York: The Bobbs-Merrill Co., 1941.

Howard, John Tasker. *Stephen Foster, America's Troubadour*. New York: Thomas Y. Crowell Co., 1934.

Jacobs, James Ripley. *Tarnished Warrior: Major-General James Wilkinson*. New York: Macmillan Co., 1938.

Morison, Samuel Eliot. *John Paul Jones: A Sailor's Biography*. Boston: Little, Brown and Co., 1959.

Nathan, Hans. *Dan Emmett and the Rise of Early Negro Minstrelsy.* Norman: University of Oklahoma Press, 1962.

Randall, James G. *Lincoln the President.* Vol. 1, *Springfield to Bull Run.* New York: Dodd, Mead, and Co., 1956.

Remini, Robert. *Andrew Jackson and the Course of American Empire, 1767–1821.* New York: Harper and Row, 1967.

Vandiver, Frank E. *Mighty Stonewall.* Westport, Conn.: Greenwood Press, 1957.

Ward, John William. *Andrew Jackson: Symbol for an Age.* New York: Oxford University Press, 1962.

Monographs and General Works

Anderson, Bern. *By Sea and By River: The Naval History of the Civil War.* New York: Alfred A. Knopf, 1962.

Austin, William W. *"Susanna," "Jeanie," and "The Old Folks at Home": The Songs of Stephen C. Foster From His Time to Ours.* New York: Macmillan, 1975.

Banner, James M. *To the Hartford Convention: The Federalists and the Origin of Party Politics in Massachusetts 1789–1815.* New York: Alfred A. Knopf, 1970.

Bauer, K. Jack. *The Mexican War, 1846–1848.* New York: Macmillan Co., 1974.

Bernard, Kenneth A. *Lincoln and the Music of the Civil War.* Caldwell, Idaho: Caxton Printers, 1966.

Brand, Oscar. *Songs of '76: A Folksinger's History of the Revolution.* New York: M. Evans and Co., 1972.

Browne, C. A. *The Story of Our National Ballads.* New York: Thomas Y. Crowell Co., 1919.

Camus, Raoul F. *Military Music of the American Revolution.* Chapel Hill: University of North Carolina Press, 1976.

Chase, Gilbert. *America's Music: From the Pilgrims to the Present.* New York: McGraw-Hill Book Co., 1955.

Christ-Janer, Albert, Charles W. Hughes, and Carlton Sprague. *American Hymns Old and New.* New York: Columbia University Press, 1980.

Coffin, Tristram Potter. *The British Traditional Ballad in North America.* Austin: University of Texas Press, 1977.

———. *Uncertain Glory: Folklore and the American Revolution.* Detroit: Folklore Association, 1971.

Coggins, Jack. *Ships and Seamen of the American Revolution.* New York: Stackpole Books, 1969.

Colbourn, H. Trevor. *The Lamp of Experience: Whig History and the Intellectual Origins of the American Revolution.* Chapel Hill: University of North Carolina Press, 1965.

Coles, Harry L. *The War of 1812.* Chicago: Chicago University Press, 1965.

Connor, Seymour V., and Odie B. Faulk. *North America Divided: The Mexican War, 1846–1848.* New York: Oxford University Press, 1971.

Cornish, Dudley. *The Sable Arm: Negro Troops in the Union Army, 1861–1865.* New York: Longmans, Green, 1956.

Davis, Ronald L. *A History of Music in American Life.* Vol. 1, *The Formative Years 1620–1865.* Malabar, Fla.: Robert Krieger Co., 1982.

Dichter, Harry, and Elliott Shapiro. *Early American Music: Its Lure and Lore, 1768–1887*. New York: R. R. Bowker, 1941.

Epstein, Dena J. *Music Publishing in Chicago Before 1871: The Firm of Root and Cady*. Detroit: Information Coordinators, Inc., 1969.

———. *Sinful Tunes and Spirituals: Black Folk Music to The Civil War*. Chicago: University of Illinois Press, 1977.

Ewen, David. *Great Men of American Popular Song*. Englewood Cliffs, N.J.: Prentice-Hall, 1970.

Foote, Shelby. *The Civil War: A Narrative*. Vol. 3, *Red River to Appomattox*. New York: Random House, 1974.

Forester, C. S. *The Age of Fighting Sail: The Naval War of 1812*. Garden City, N.Y.: Doubleday, 1956.

Fowler, William M., Jr. *Rebels Under Sail: The American Navy during the Revolution*. New York: Charles Scribner's Sons, 1976.

Gipson, Lawrence Henry. *The Coming of the Revolution, 1763–1775*. New York: Harper and Row, 1962.

Hamm, Charles. *Yesterdays: Popular Song in America*. New York: W. W. Norton, 1979.

Harwell, Richard B. *Confederate Music*. Chapel Hill: University of North Carolina Press, 1950.

Hodges, Fletcher, Jr. *Stephen Foster, Democrat*. Pittsburgh: University of Pittsburgh, 1946.

Horsman, Reginald. *The War of 1812*. New York: Alfred A. Knopf, 1969.

Howard, John Tasker, and George Kent Bellows. *A Short History of Music in America*. New York: Thomas Y. Crowell Co., 1957.

Jacobs, James Ripley, and Glenn Tucker. *The War of 1812: A Compact History*. New York: Hawthorn Books, 1969.

Johannsen, Robert W. *To the Halls of the Montezumas: The Mexican War in the American Imagination*. New York: Oxford University Press, 1985.

Jordan, Phillip D. *Singin' Yankees*. Minneapolis: University of Minnesota Press, 1946.

Kelley, Robert. *The Cultural Pattern in American Politics: The First Century*. New York: Alfred A. Knopf, 1979.

Lavender, David. *Climax at Buena Vista: The American Campaigns in Northern Mexico, 1846–1847*. New York: J. B. Lippincott Co., 1966.

McPherson, James M. *Ordeal by Fire: The Civil War and Reconstruction*. New York: Alfred A. Knopf, 1982.

Mahan, Alfred T. *Sea Power and Its Relation to the War of 1812*. 2 vols. New York: Charles Scribner's Sons, 1903. Reprint. Cambridge: The University Press, 1905.

Merk, Frederick. *Manifest Destiny and Mission in American History: A Reinterpretation*. New York: Alfred A. Knopf, 1963.

———. *Slavery and the Annexation of Texas*. New York: Alfred A. Knopf, 1972.

Morehouse, Ward. *George M. Cohan: Prince of the American Theatre*. New York: J. B. Lippincott Co., 1943.

Muller, Joseph, ed. *The Star-Spangled Banner: Words and Music Issued between 1814–1864*. New York: G. A. Baker and Co., 1935.

Niles, John Jacob. *Singing Soldiers*. Detroit: Singing Tree Press, 1968.

Parks, H. B. "Follow the Drinking Gourd." In *Publications of the Texas Folk-Lore Society*, edited by J. Frank Dobie. Austin: University of Texas Press, 1928.

Randall, David A., ed. *"Yankee Doodle" to the "Conquered Banner" with Emphasis on the "Star-Spangled Banner."* Bloomington: Indiana University Press, 1968.

Randall, J. G., and David Donald. *The Civil War and Reconstruction*, 2d ed. Boston: D. C. Heath and Co., 1965.

Scott, John Anthony, ed. *The Ballad of America: The History of the United States in Story and in Song*. New York: Bantam Books, 1966.

Silverman, Kenneth. *A Cultural History of the American Revolution*. New York: Thomas Y. Crowell Co., 1976.

Singletary, Otis A. *The Mexican War*. Chicago: University of Chicago Press, 1960.

Smelser, Marshall. *The Democratic Republic, 1801–1815*. New York: Harper and Row, 1968.

Smith, Justin H. *The War with Mexico*. 2 vols. Gloucester, Mass.: Peter Smith, 1963. Originally published in 1919.

Sonneck, Oscar George Theodore. *Report on "The Star-Spangled Banner," "Hail Columbia," "America," and "Yankee Doodle."* New York: Dover Publications, 1972. Originally published in 1909.

Van Doren, Carl. *Secret History of the American Revolution*. New York: Viking Press, 1968.

Wallace, Willard M. *Appeal to Arms: A Military History of the American Revolution*. Chicago: Quadrangle Books, 1964.

Ward, Christopher. *The War of the Revolution*. Edited by John Richard Alden. 2 vols. New York: Macmillan Co., 1952.

Wiley, Bell Irvin. *The Life of Billy Yank*. New York: The Bobbs-Merrill Co., 1951.
———. *The Life of Johnny Reb*. New York: The Bobbs-Merrill Co., 1943.

Winstock, Lewis. *Songs and Music of the Redcoats: A History of the War Music of the British Army, 1642–1902*. Harrisburg, Pa.: Stackpole Books, 1970.

Wright, Louis B. *The Cultural Life of the American Colonies, 1607–1763*. New York: Harper and Row, 1962.

Yall, Paul M., ed. *Comical Spirit of Seventy-Six: The Humor of Francis Hopkinson*. San Marino, Calif.: Huntington Library, 1976.

Articles

Epstein, Dena J. "The Battle Cry of Freedom." *Civil War History* 4 (1958): 307–318.

Greene, Jack P. "Political Mimesis: A Consideration of the Historical and Cultural Roots of Legislative Behavior in the Colonies in the Eighteenth Century." *American Historical Review* 75 (1969): 337–361.

Harwell, Richard B. "The Star of the Bonnie Blue Flag." *Civil War History* 4 (1958): 285–289.

Matthews, Brander. "The Songs of the War." *Century Magazine* 34 (1887): 619–629.

Stone, James. "War Music and War Psychology in the Civil War." *Journal of Abnormal Psychology* 36 (1941): 543–560.

Stutler, Boyd B. "John Brown's Body." *Civil War History* 4 (1958): 251–260.

Miscellaneous

Civil War Dictionary, s. v. "Corcoran, Michael," "Foote, Andrew H.," "Shields, James."

Dictionary of American Biography, s. v. "Hays, William Shakespeare," "Hewitt, John Hill."

A Dictionary of Slang and Unconventional English, s. v. "bullgine," "duff," "free and easy," "swell."

Encyclopedia of Black America, 1981, s. v. "Mexican War."

The New Grove Dictionary of Music and Musicians, s. v. "Gilmore, Patrick Sarsfield," "Printing and Publishing of Lyrics," "Winner, Septimus."

Oxford Companion to Classical Literature, s. v. "Anacreon."

Oxford Companion to English Literature, 3d edition, s. v. "Tyburn."

Oxford English Dictionary, s. v. "bantling," "bunter," "language," "lawn sleeves," "pelf," "perry," "rattan," "southron," "tompions," "welkin," "yaws."

Penguin Encyclopedia, s. v. "Jacobites."

Princeton Encycopedia of Poetry and Poetics, s. v. "fourteeners."

The Reader's Encyclopedia, s. v. "Roncesvalles."

Index

About the Author

KENT A. BOWMAN teaches American History and English in Denton, Texas, and has a special interest in the interrelationship of music, literature, art, and history.